West's Law School Advisory Board

Global Issues in Intellectual Property Law

By

John Cross
Grosscurth Professor of Law
University of Louisville School of Law

Amy Landers
Associate Professor of Law
University of the Pacific, McGeorge School of Law

Michael Mireles
Associate Professor of Law
University of the Pacific, McGeorge School of Law

Peter K. Yu
Kern Family Chair in Intellectual Property Law
Director, Intellectual Property Law Center
Drake University Law School

AMERICAN CASEBOOK SERIES®

WEST®
A Thomson Reuters business

Mat #40569872

American Casebook Series is a trademark registered in the U.S. Patent and Trademark Office.

© 2010 Thomson Reuters
  610 Opperman Drive
  St. Paul, MN 55123
  1-800-313-9378
Printed in the United States of America

ISBN: 978-0-314-17953-1

Dedication

_____

To B.

— John

To David, Elizabeth, Max and Andrew

— Amy

To my family

— Mike

To my parents

— Peter

Preface

Although courses on international intellectual property law were rarely offered a decade ago, many law schools now offer seminars or classes in the subject. Casebooks on international intellectual property law have also appeared on the market. In addition, a growing number of instructors and textbook authors have now incorporated some international and comparative materials into the domestic course. Intellectual property is therefore an ideal topic for a book in the *Global Issues Series*.

Intellectual property law, however, presents a special challenge to the approach taken in this Series. Unlike most other subject areas, there is a well-developed body of international and transnational intellectual property laws. It is both interesting and pedagogically useful to compare intellectual property laws and policies in the United States with those in other countries. Moreover, international law, multilateral treaties, and their resulting obligations have a tremendous influence on the development of domestic laws, such as the imposition of minimum—and, on rare occasions, maximum—standards. Such development also has a significant impact on the domestic economy, regulatory policies, and the local business environment. Accordingly, we consider comparative, international, and transnational questions in this *Global Issues* book.

While we have different interests, perspectives, and pedagogical approaches, this book represents our best effort to "harmonize" our views to provide a unified whole, which perceptive readers may find sometimes different from our individually authored works. Principal responsibility was divided as follows: John authored the sections on special cross-border considerations, the protection of product designs and utility models, and other forms of intellectual property. Amy and Mike authored the sections on patents and trademarks and similar indicia. Peter authored the section on copyrights.

This book does not seek to paint a comprehensive picture of the international intellectual property system. Instead, it focuses on materials that we believe will best stimulate classroom discussion. The first chapter provides a brief overview of the international intellectual property system, focusing on the Berne and Paris Conventions, the TRIPS Agreement of the World Trade Organization, and treaties developed through the World Intellectual Property Organization. The remaining chapters highlight the differences

v

between intellectual property laws and policies in the United States and those in other countries. Coverage includes copyrights, patents, trademarks, trade secrets, computer software, product designs, geographical indications, utility models, and rights of publicity.

Written with a domestic intellectual property survey course in mind, this book can be assigned as a companion text, optional reading, or even as a stand alone text for a short international intellectual property seminar that builds on a pre-existing domestic survey course. The introductory notes for each substantive area and the notes and questions sections were specially designed to facilitate understanding without consultation of outside sources. We do not anticipate readers to have prior training or background in international law.

In the excerpts, we tried hard to preserve not only the core of the discussion, but also some of the more interesting "side" issues. Nevertheless, we edited down the materials to enhance readability. Specifically, we deleted, without indication, virtually all footnotes and most of the citations in the excerpted texts. We also removed the paragraph and section numbers in cases, statutes, and secondary sources, even though we are conscious of the fact that some of these references may be useful in the international context.

Where edits have been made, we used ellipses to indicate deletion of text and bracketed texts to provide additional explanation or to improve the flow of the material. We took the liberty of fixing minor typographical and grammatical errors. However, we did not Americanize grammar, punctuation, style, or usage in the original materials. Footnotes retain the original numbering when they are kept, and citations are updated in full to enhance referential value.

We hope you will find the materials useful, interesting, and engaging. We welcome comments and suggestions for improvements in future editions.

JOHN CROSS

AMY LANDERS

MICHAEL MIRELES

PETER YU

December 2009

Acknowledgements

John would like to thank the students, both at the University of Louisville and elsewhere, who endured prior versions of his materials, all the while remaining positive and willing to provide their comments.

Amy would like to thank all of those who contributed to this book, including the administration, faculty and staff at the University of the Pacific, McGeorge School of Law. Additionally, she thanks the S.J. Quinney School of Law, University of Utah, where she undertook some of the work underlying her portion of the book.

Mike would like to thank his coauthors for their collegiality, expertise, helpful suggestions, and patience. He thanks Dean Elizabeth Parker, Associate Deans Phil Wile, Julie Davies and Thomas Main for their support; and Dragomir Cosanic, Monica Sharum, and Jack Shroeder for their excellent research assistance. He also thanks his partner, Shannon Sturgess, for her patience and support.

Peter would like to thank his deans, colleagues, and students at both Drake University Law School and Michigan State University College of Law for their support, and his colleagues and students at Benjamin N. Cardozo School of Law at Yeshiva University for getting him started on thinking seriously about international intellectual property issues. He is also grateful to Mike Mireles for initiating this project and bringing the team together and to Elizabeth Townsend–Gard and Tulane University Law School for providing the venue for an organizational workshop at an early stage of this book.

Finally, we gratefully acknowledge the permission to reprint materials from the following authors, organizations, and publishers:

Books, Reports and Articles

AMERICAN LAW INSTITUTE, INTELLECTUAL PROPERTY: PRINCIPLES GOVERNING JURISDICTION, CHOICE OF LAW, AND JUDGMENTS IN TRANSNATIONAL DISPUTES (Discussion Draft, 2006). © 2007 The American Law Institute. Reprinted by permission of the American Law Institute.

GRUBB, PHILLIP W., PATENTS FOR CHEMICALS, PHARMACEUTICALS AND BIOTECHNOLOGY: PRACTICE AND STRATEGY (Oxford University Press 2005). Reprinted by permission of the Oxford University Press.

INTERNATIONAL BAR ASSOCIATION, INTELLECTUAL PROPERTY & ENTERTAINMENT LAW COMMITTEE, INTERNATIONAL SURVEY OF SPECIALISED INTELLECTUAL PROPERTY COURTS AND TRIBUNALS (2007). Reprinted by permission of the International Bar Association, Valentina Zoghbi, Anurag Bana, and Clive Elliot.

Adler, Amy M., *Against Moral Rights*, 97 CAL. L. REV. 263 (2009). Reprinted courtesy of Amy Adler and the California Law Review.

Bagley, Margo A., *Patently Unconstitutional: The Geographical Limitation on Prior Art in a Small World*, 87 MINN. L. REV. 679 (2003). © 2003 Minnesota Law Review. Reprinted courtesy of Margo Bagley and by permission of the Minnesota Law Review.

Kerr, Ian R., Alana Maurushat & Christian S. Tacit, *Technical Protection Measures: Tilting at Copyright's Windmill*, 34 OTTAWA L. REV. 7 (2002). Reprinted courtesy of Ian Kerr and the Ottawa Law Review.

Kwall, Roberta Rosenthal, *Copyright and the Moral Right: Is an American Marriage Possible?*, 38 VAND. L. REV. 1 (1985). Reprinted courtesy of Roberta Kwall.

Li Xuan, *Novelty and Inventive Step: Obstacles to Traditional Knowledge Protection under Patent Regimes: A Case Study in China*, 29 EUR. INTELL. PROP. REV. 134 (2007). © 2007 Sweet & Maxwell. Reprinted by permission of Sweet & Maxwell.

Okediji, Ruth, *Toward an International Fair Use Doctrine*, 39 COLUM. J. TRANSNAT'L L. 75 (2000). Reprinted courtesy of Ruth Okediji.

Strahilevitz, Lior Jacob, *The Right to Destroy*, 114 YALE L.J. 781 (2005). Reprinted courtesy of Lior Strahilevitz and by permission of The Yale Law Journal Company, Inc.

Thompson, Bryan, *New Zealand Tackles the Maori Issue*, MANAGING INTELL. PROP., Feb. 2002, at 48. Reprinted by permission of Bryan Thompson, the law firm of A.J. Park, and Managing Intellectual Property.

Yu, Peter K., *Anticircumvention and Anti-anticircumvention*, 84 DENV. U. L. REV. 13 (2006). © 2006 Peter K. Yu. Reprinted courtesy of Peter Yu.

Zhang Yurong & Yu Xiang, *The Patent Protection for Business Method Inventions in China*, 30 EUR. INTELL. PROP. REV. 412 (2008). © 2007 Sweet & Maxwell. Reprinted by permission of Sweet & Maxwell.

Translated Cases

Matim Li Fashion Chain for Large Sizes Ltd v. Crazy Line Ltd, translated by Zohar Efroni in 38 INT'L REV. INTELL. PROP. & COMP. L. 238 (2007). Reprinted by permission of Zohar Efroni and the International Review of Intellectual Property and Competition Law.

Turner Entertainment Co. v. Huston, translated in ENT. L. REP., Mar. 1995, at 3. Reprinted courtesy of Turner Entertainment Co. and Lionel Sobel.

Global Issues Series

Series Editor, Franklin A. Gevurtz

Titles Available Now

Global Issues in Civil Procedure by Thomas Main, University of the Pacific, McGeorge School of Law
ISBN 978–0–314–15978–6

Global Issues in Constitutional Law by Brian K. Landsberg, University of the Pacific, McGeorge School of Law and Leslie Gielow Jacobs, University of the Pacific, McGeorge School of Law
ISBN 978–0–314–17608–0

Global Issues in Contract Law by John A. Spanogle, Jr., George Washington University, Michael P. Malloy, University of the Pacific, McGeorge School of Law, Louis F. Del Duca, Pennsylvania State University, Keith A. Rowley, University of Nevada, Las Vegas, and Andrea K. Bjorklund, University of California, Davis
ISBN 978–0–314–16755–2

Global Issues in Copyright Law by Mary LaFrance, University of Nevada
ISBN 978–0–314–19447–3

Global Issues in Corporate Law by Franklin A. Gevurtz, University of the Pacific, McGeorge School of Law
ISBN 978–0–314–15977–9

Global Issues in Criminal Law by Linda Carter, University of the Pacific, McGeorge School of Law, Christopher L. Blakesley, University of Nevada, Las Vegas and Peter Henning, Wayne State University
ISBN 978–0–314–15997–7

Global Issues in Employee Benefits Law by Paul M. Secunda, Marquette University Law School, Samuel Estreicher, New York University School of Law, Rosalind J. Connor, Jones Day, London
ISBN 978–0–314–19409–1

Global Issues in Employment Discrimination Law by Samuel Estreicher, New York University School of Law and Brian K. Landsberg, University of the Pacific, McGeorge School of Law

ISBN 978–0–314–17607–3

Global Issues in Employment Law by Samuel Estreicher, New York University School of Law and Miriam A. Cherry, University of the Pacific, McGeorge School of Law
ISBN 978–0–314–17952–4

Global Issues in Environmental Law by Stephen McCaffrey, University of the Pacific, McGeorge School of Law and Rachael Salcido, University of the Pacific, McGeorge School of Law
ISBN 978–0–314–18479–5

Global Issues in Family Law by Ann Laquer Estin, University of Iowa and Barbara Stark, Hofstra University
ISBN 978–0–314–17954–8

Global Issues in Freedom of Speech and Religion by Alan Brownstein, University of California, Davis School of Law and Leslie Gielow Jacobs, University of the Pacific, McGeorge School of Law
ISBN 978–0–314–18454–2

Global Issues in Income Taxation by Daniel Lathrope, University of California, Hastings College of Law
ISBN 978–0–314–18806–9

Global Issues in Intellectual Property Law by John Cross, University of Louisville School of Law, Amy Landers, University of the Pacific, McGeorge School of Law, Michael Mireles, University of the Pacific, McGeorge School of Law and Peter K. Yu, Drake University Law School
ISBN 978–0–314–17953–1

Global Issues in Labor Law by Samuel Estreicher, New York University School of Law
ISBN 978–0–314–17163–4

Global Issues in Legal Ethics by James E. Moliterno, College of William & Mary, Marshall–Wythe School of Law and George Harris, University of the Pacific, McGeorge School of Law
ISBN 978–0–314–16935–8

Global Issues in Property Law by John G. Sprankling, University of the Pacific, McGeorge School of Law, Raymond R. Coletta, University of the Pacific, McGeorge School of Law, and M.C. Mirow, Florida International University College of Law
ISBN 978–0–314–16729–3

Global Issues in Tort Law by Julie A. Davies, University of the Pacific, McGeorge School of Law and Paul T. Hayden, Loyola Law School, Los Angeles
ISBN 978–0–314–16759–0

Summary of Contents

Table of Contents

Table of Cases

The principal cases are in bold type. Cases cited or discussed in the text are in roman type. References are to pages. Cases cited in principal cases and within other quoted materials are not included.

Global Issues in
Intellectual
Property
Law

Chapter 1

SPECIAL CROSS–BORDER CONSIDERATIONS IN INTELLECTUAL PROPERTY LAW

A. THE PRINCIPLE OF TERRITORIALITY

Most casebooks for intellectual property survey courses focus exclusively on United States law, and infringements that occur within the boundaries of the United States. But with the steady growth in both international trade and activities on the Internet, it is increasingly common for parties outside the United States to copy a protected invention, work, mark, or trade secret. To what extent does United States intellectual property law—or, for that matter, the intellectual property law of any nation—protect a party against acts that occur in other nations?

SUBAFILMS, LTD. v. MGM–PATHE COMMUNICATIONS CO.

24 F.3d 1088 (9th Cir. 1994) (en banc)

D.W. NELSON, Circuit Judge.

In 1966, the musical group The Beatles, through Subafilms, Ltd., entered into a joint venture with the Hearst Corporation to produce the animated motion picture entitled "Yellow Submarine" (the "Picture"). Over the next year, Hearst, acting on behalf of the joint venture (the "Producer"), negotiated an agreement with United Artists Corporation ("UA") to distribute and finance the film. Separate distribution and financing agreements were entered into in May 1967. Pursuant to these agreements, UA distributed the Picture in theaters beginning in 1968 and later on television.

In the early 1980s, with the advent of the home video market, UA entered into several licensing agreements to distribute a num-

1

ber of its films on videocassette. Although one company expressed interest in the Picture, UA refused to license "Yellow Submarine" because of uncertainty over whether home video rights had been granted by the 1967 agreements. Subsequently, in 1987, UA's successor company, MGM/UA Communications Co. ("MGM/UA"), over the Producer's objections, authorized its subsidiary MGM/UA Home Video, Inc. to distribute the Picture for the domestic home video market, and, pursuant to an earlier licensing agreement, notified Warner Bros., Inc. ("Warner") that the Picture had been cleared for international videocassette distribution. Warner, through its wholly owned subsidiary, Warner Home Video, Inc., in turn entered into agreements with third parties for distribution of the Picture on videocassette around the world.

In 1988, Subafilms and Hearst ("Appellees") brought suit against MGM/UA, Warner, and their respective subsidiaries (collectively the "Distributors" or "Appellants"), contending that the videocassette distribution of the Picture, both foreign and domestic, constituted copyright infringement and a breach of the 1967 agreements. . . . Appellees were awarded $2,228,000.00 in compensatory damages, split evenly between the foreign and domestic home video distributions. In addition, Appellees received attorneys' fees and a permanent injunction that prohibited the Distributors from engaging in, or authorizing, any home video use of the Picture.

A panel of this circuit, in an unpublished disposition, affirmed the district court's judgment on the ground that both the domestic and foreign distribution of the Picture constituted infringement under the Copyright Act. With respect to the foreign distribution of the Picture, the panel concluded that it was bound by this court's prior decision in *Peter Starr Prod. Co. v. Twin Continental Films, Inc.*, 783 F.2d 1440 (9th Cir. 1986), which it held to stand for the proposition that, although " 'infringing actions that take place entirely outside the United States are not actionable' [under the Copyright Act, an] 'act of infringement within the United States' [properly is] alleged where the illegal authorization of international exhibitions t[akes] place in the United States". Because the Distributors had admitted that the initial authorization to distribute the Picture internationally occurred within the United States, the panel affirmed the district court's holding with respect to liability for extraterritorial home video distribution of the Picture.

We granted Appellants' petition for rehearing *en banc* to consider whether the panel's interpretation of *Peter Starr* conflicted with our subsequent decision in *Lewis Galoob Toys, Inc. v. Nintendo of Am., Inc.*, 964 F.2d 965 (9th Cir. 1992), which held that there could be no liability for authorizing a party to engage in an infringing act when the authorized "party's use of the work would not violate the Copyright Act". . . .

[Section 106 of the Copyright Act gives the copyright owner the exclusive right "to do or authorize" certain acts involving the copyrighted work, including the rights to reproduce, publicly display, and publish. The court first held that the copyright owner's exclusive right to "authorize" was not a separate and independent right. Instead, noting that the "authorize" language was meant to capture concepts of secondary liability, the court held that a party could be liable for authorizing an act only when the authorized act itself would infringe the copyright owner's rights under § 106. The court then turned to the issue of whether acts that occurred outside the United States could violate the copyright owner's rights under the United States Copyright Act.]

Appellees additionally contend that, if liability for "authorizing" acts of infringement depends on finding that the authorized acts themselves are cognizable under the Copyright Act, this court should find that the United States copyright laws do extend to extraterritorial acts of infringement when such acts "result in adverse effects within the United States." Appellees buttress this argument with the contention that failure to apply the copyright laws extraterritorially in this case will have a disastrous effect on the American film industry, and that other remedies, such as suits in foreign jurisdictions or the application of foreign copyright laws by American courts, are not realistic alternatives.

We are not persuaded by Appellees' parade of horribles. More fundamentally, however, we are unwilling to overturn over eighty years of consistent jurisprudence on the extraterritorial reach of the copyright laws without further guidance from Congress.

The Supreme Court recently reminded us that "[i]t is a long-standing principle of American law 'that legislation of Congress, unless a contrary intent appears, is meant to apply only within the territorial jurisdiction of the United States.'" Because courts must "assume that Congress legislates against the backdrop of the presumption against extraterritoriality," unless "there is 'the affirmative intention of the Congress clearly expressed'" congressional enactments must be presumed to be "'primarily concerned with domestic conditions.'"

The "undisputed axiom" that the United States' copyright laws have no application to extraterritorial infringement predates the 1909 [Copyright] Act, and ... the principle of territoriality consistently has been reaffirmed. There is no clear expression of congressional intent in either the 1976 Act or other relevant enactments to alter the preexisting extraterritoriality doctrine. Indeed, the *Peter Starr* court itself recognized the continuing application of the principle that "infringing actions that take place entirely outside the United States are not actionable in United States federal courts."

Furthermore, we note that Congress chose in 1976 to expand one specific "extraterritorial" application of the Act by declaring that the unauthorized importation of copyrighted works constitutes infringement even when the copies lawfully were made abroad. *See* 17 U.S.C.A. § 602(a). Had Congress been inclined to overturn the preexisting doctrine that infringing acts that take place wholly outside the United States are not actionable under the Copyright Act, it knew how to do so.

Appellees, however, rely on *dicta* in a recent decision of the District of Columbia Circuit for the proposition that the presumption against extraterritorial application of U.S. laws may be "overcome" when denying such application would "result in adverse effects within the United States." *Environmental Defense Fund, Inc. v. Massey*, 986 F.2d 528, 531 (D.C. Cir. 1993) (noting that the Sherman Act, Lanham Act, and securities laws have been applied to extraterritorial conduct). However, the *Massey* court did not state that extraterritoriality would be *demanded* in such circumstances, but that "the *presumption* is *generally not applied* where the failure to extend the scope of the statute to a foreign setting will result in adverse [domestic] effects." In each of the statutory schemes discussed by the *Massey* court, the ultimate touchstone of extraterritoriality consisted of an ascertainment of congressional intent; courts did not rest *solely* on the consequences of a failure to give a statutory scheme extraterritorial application. More importantly, as the *Massey* court conceded, application of the presumption is particularly appropriate when "[i]t serves to protect against unintended clashes between our laws and those of other nations which could result in international discord," *Aramco*, 499 U.S. at 248.

We believe this latter factor is decisive in the case of the Copyright Act, and fully justifies application of the *Aramco* presumption even assuming *arguendo* that "adverse effects" within the United States "generally" would require a plenary inquiry into congressional intent. At the time that the international distribution of the videocassettes in this case took place, the United States was a member of the Universal Copyright Convention ("UCC"), and, in 1988, the United States acceded to the Berne Convention for the Protection of Literary and Artistic Works ("Berne Conv."). The central thrust of these multilateral treaties is the principle of "national treatment." A work of an American national first generated in America will receive the same protection in a foreign nation as that country accords to the works of its own nationals. Although the treaties do not expressly discuss choice-of-law rules, it is commonly acknowledged that the national treatment principle implicates a rule of territoriality. 3 MELVILLE B. NIMMER & DAVID NIMMER,

NIMMER ON COPYRIGHT § 17.05, at 17–39 (1991) ("The applicable law is the copyright law of the state in which the infringement occurred, not that of the state of which the author is a national or in which the work was first published.").…

In light of the *Aramco* Court's concern with preventing international discord, we think it inappropriate for the courts to act in a manner that might disrupt Congress's efforts to secure a more stable international intellectual property regime unless Congress otherwise clearly has expressed its intent. The application of American copyright law to acts of infringement that occur entirely overseas clearly could have this effect. Extraterritorial application of American law would be contrary to the spirit of the Berne Convention, and might offend other member nations by effectively displacing their law in circumstances in which previously it was assumed to govern. Consequently, an extension of extraterritoriality might undermine Congress's objective of achieving " 'effective and harmonious' copyright laws among all nations." Indeed, it might well send the signal that the United States does not believe that the protection accorded by the laws of other member nations is adequate, which would undermine two other objectives of Congress in joining the convention: "strengthen[ing] the credibility of the U.S. position in trade negotiations with countries where piracy is not uncommon" and "rais[ing] the like[li]hood that other nations will enter the Convention." …

Accordingly, … we conclude that the *Aramco* presumption must be applied. Because the presumption has not been overcome, we reaffirm that the United States copyright laws do not reach acts of infringement that take place entirely abroad. It is for Congress, and not the courts, to take the initiative in this field.

Appellees raise a number of additional arguments for why the district court's judgment should be affirmed.… Appellees maintain that they may recover damages for international distribution of the Picture based on the theory that an act of direct infringement, in the form of a reproduction of the negatives for the Picture, took place in the United States. Appellees also suggest that they may recover, under United States law, damages stemming from the international distribution on the theory that the distribution was part of a larger conspiracy to violate their copyright that included actionable infringement within the United States. In addition, they maintain that Appellants are liable for the international distribution under foreign copyright laws. Finally, Appellees argue that the district court's damage award can be sustained under the breach of contract theory not reached by the panel.

We resolve none of these questions, but leave them for the panel, in its best judgment, to consider. A remand to the district court might well be necessary to permit further factual development in light of our decision to overrule aspects of *Peter Starr*. The panel, however, is free to take whatever action it views as appropriate that is consistent with our mandate.

Notes and Questions

1. *Subafilms* reflects the core principle of *territoriality* that sets the stage for international intellectual property law. The principle is quite simple: in most cases, a given intellectual property right exists only within the boundaries of the jurisdiction that grants the right. If a party with a copyright in one nation wants to obtain similar protection elsewhere, she must obtain a new copyright in the other nations.

Since the mid–1800s nations have entered into a number of multilateral treaties dealing with intellectual property. The Berne Convention discussed in *Subafilms* is one of these treaties. These treaties do not change the basic axiom of territoriality, but instead accept it as a given. The main goal of the treaties is to make it easier for a party with rights in one nation to obtain protection elsewhere.

2. Patents are also territorial. Therefore, a party acting outside the boundaries of the United States may freely make, use, or sell any invention protected by a United States patent. Unlike in copyright law, where the courts had to apply basic principles of statutory construction to determine that copyrights are territorially circumscribed, § 271 of the United States Patent Act explicitly deals with the issue:

> Except as otherwise provided in this title, whoever without authority makes, uses, offers to sell, or sells any patented invention, *within the United States* or imports into the United States any patented invention during the term of the patent therefor, infringes the patent.

17 U.S.C. § 271(a) (2006) (emphasis added).

3. *Importation.* The territoriality rule can pose a problem for United States rights holders. A crafty competitor could undermine a United States copyright or patent owner's position simply by setting up shop in some other nation, producing copies there, and importing the copies into the United States for distribution. Anticipating this possibility, both the Patent and Copyright Acts explicitly bar importation of copies, even if those copies were perfectly legal where made. The Copyright Act provision is mentioned in *Subafilms*. Do you see how this provision limits the remedies available to a copyright owner? The Patent Act provisions are set both in § 271(a) (quoted in the prior paragraph), and § 271(g), which bars importation of any good made outside the United States using a *process* patented under United States law.

4. *Producing components.* The Patent Act goes one step further. Under § 271(f), a party may be liable for supplying components of a

patented invention, if he intends those components to be combined overseas into a product that would infringe the United States patent if produced domestically. Unlike the importation provisions discussed in the previous note, this provision applies *even if the final product is not imported into the United States.* The provision applies if the party provides either "all or a substantial portion of the components" (§ 271(f)(1)) or "any component of a patented invention that is especially made or especially adapted for use in the invention and not . . . suitable for substantial noninfringing use" (§ 271(f)(2)).

The United States Supreme Court construed § 271(f) in *Microsoft v. AT&T*, 550 U.S. 437 (2007). This case dealt with a feature of the Microsoft Windows® operating system that records and compresses speech. This feature infringed a United States patent held by AT&T. However, Microsoft also sent copies of a master disk containing the operating system to facilities in other countries, where the software was installed on computers. Overturning the lower courts, the Supreme Court held that Microsoft did not violate § 271(f) when it exported the software and installed it on computers made and sold abroad. The basis for the Court's holding was that an operating system was not a "component" as that term is used in § 271(f). Does the Supreme Court's ruling accurately reflect the language of § 271(f)? The spirit of that provision?

5. As alluded to in *Subafilms*, the rule of territoriality that applies to trademarks is somewhat different. A party may recover under United States trademark law not only for acts of infringement that occur in the United States, but also for acts that are intended to have an "effect" on the United States market. *Steele v. Bulova Watch Co.*, 344 U.S. 280 (1952). However, although this "effect" rule sounds like a significant extension of the territoriality principle, in practice it is construed fairly narrowly. The analysis turns in part on whether the defendant is an American citizen, in which case United States law is more likely to apply. For a good review of the precedent, see *McBee v. Delica Co.*, 417 F.3d 107 (1st Cir. 2005).

6. Many states recognize a "right of publicity," which gives an individual, often a celebrity, considerable control over unauthorized use of his name, likeness, or other aspects of his persona. Does this right of publicity extend beyond the boundaries of a particular state? (Because the right of publicity is a state-law right, the territoriality principle, if applicable, would confine the right to a single state rather than the United States as a whole.) Unlike a patent, copyright, or trademark, the right of publicity bears many of the hallmarks of a personal tort right like defamation. And personal torts are usually not territorial in nature. For example, in defamation cases United States courts select a single law to govern all defamatory statements made about a person in different jurisdictions.

At least one leading case has refused to apply the territoriality rule to the right of publicity. In *Cairns v. Franklin Mint Co.*, 292 F.3d 1139

(9th Cir. 2002), the court was faced with a right of publicity claim by the estate of the late Princess Diana against a company that sold memorabilia with her name and likeness. The sales in question had occurred in California. The court applied California's default choice of law rule for determining rights in personal property (Cal. Civil Code § 946) and found that the law of Great Britain, Diana's domicile at death, governed her right of publicity. Because the law of Great Britain did not provide a post-mortem right of publicity, the court held the estate could not recover on its publicity claim.

7. The American Law Institute has proposed a set of principles governing jurisdiction and choice of law in intellectual property disputes. AMERICAN LAW INSTITUTE, INTELLECTUAL PROPERTY: PRINCIPLES GOVERNING JURISDICTION, CHOICE OF LAW, AND JUDGMENTS IN TRANSNATIONAL DISPUTES (Discussion Draft, 2006). Section 301 of the proposal expressly preserves the principle of territoriality:

> (1) Except as provided in Chapter Three [a special rule dealing with widespread simultaneous infringement], the laws applicable to determine the existence, validity, duration, attributes, and infringement of intellectual property rights and remedies for their infringement are:
>
> > (a) for registered rights, the law of each State of registration.
>
> > (b) for other intellectual property rights, the law of each State for which protection is sought.

8. Suppose plaintiff sues defendant for copyright infringement under United States law, but all of the allegedly infringing acts occurred outside the United States. Should defendant move to dismiss for lack of subject-matter jurisdiction, or is the proper response a motion to dismiss for failure to state a claim or motion for summary judgment? See *Litecubes, LLC v. Northern Light Prods., Inc.*, 523 F.3d 1353 (Fed. Cir. 2008). The difference does matter, as it may affect, for example, plaintiff's ability to sue in a different court.

B. CHOICE OF LAW ISSUES

The principle of territoriality forces a party who desires to protect a single invention, work, or mark in more than one nation to obtain separate domestic rights in each nation. But exactly how "separate" are these rights in practice? Although United States law provides the basic right to sue for acts of infringement that occur in the United States, that does not necessarily mean that United States law will govern every issue in the case even when the lawsuit was filed in the United States. Some issues, such as the legal capacity of an organization to sue or be sued, may obviously be governed by foreign law. In addition, when the invention or authorship of the work occurred in a foreign nation, a court may look to foreign law even for some issues relevant to the patent or copyright itself.

Consider, for example, *Itar–Tass Russian News Agency v. Russian Kurier, Inc.*, 153 F.3d 82 (2d Cir. 1998). In *Itar–Tass*, a Russian language newspaper in the United States reprinted over 500 articles that were first distributed by Tass, the Russian News Agency. Tass and some of the individual newspapers sued in the United States. The court held that United States law governed whether the reprinting constituted infringement. However, applying a federal common law choice-of-law rule, it looked to Russian law to determine whether Tass and the individual newspapers owned any sort of copyright interest:

> Copyright is a form of property, and the usual rule is that the interests of the parties in property are determined by the law of the state with "the most significant relationship" to the property and the parties. The Restatement recognizes the applicability of this principle to intangibles such as "a literary idea." Since the works at issue were created by Russian nationals and first published in Russia, Russian law is the appropriate source of law to determine issues of ownership of rights.

As Russian law gave copyright rights to Tass, but not to the individual papers (Russian law has no work made for hire doctrine), the court dismissed the claims of the papers and allowed that of Tass to proceed.

Another consequence of the territoriality principle in the modern global economy is that an intellectual property owner may often find that a single defendant has infringed her rights in several different nations. Of course, each of those infringements will be governed primarily by a separate law. But does that mean that the person must bring separate enforcement actions in each of the nations involved? If a single defendant is involved, it might prove far more convenient to bring all of the claims in the defendant's nation of residence. Or, given the significant expansion of personal jurisdiction concepts in several nations over the past half-century, the plaintiff might be able to obtain personal jurisdiction over all of the infringements in plaintiff's nation of residence. Does anything prevent a court from hearing all of the claims, including those arising under foreign law?

VODA v. CORDIS CORP.

476 F.3d 887 (Fed. Cir. 2007)

GAJARSA, Circuit Judge.

This is an interlocutory appeal by Cordis Corp. from a decision of the U.S. District Court for the Western District of Oklahoma assuming supplemental subject matter jurisdiction pursuant to 28 U.S.C. § 1367 over the foreign patent infringement claims of Jan K. Voda, M.D. ("Voda")....

I. Background

The plaintiff-appellee Voda is a resident of Oklahoma City, Oklahoma. The defendant-appellant Cordis is a U.S.-based entity incorporated in Florida....

The patents at issue relate generally to guiding catheters for use in interventional cardiology. The details of the technology are not essential here....

Voda sued Cordis U.S. in the United States District Court for the Western District of Oklahoma alleging infringement of his three U.S. patents.... Cordis U.S. answered by asserting noninfringement and invalidity of the U.S. patents.

Voda then moved to amend his complaint to add claims of infringement of the European, British, Canadian, French, and German foreign patents....

Cordis U.S. opposed Voda's attempt to amend its complaint to add foreign patent infringement claims on the basis that the district court lacked subject matter jurisdiction over such claims....

III. Discussion

A. *Asserted Statutory Basis*

1. Authorization

Section 1367(a) provides the statutory authority for district courts to exercise supplemental jurisdiction over certain claims outside their original jurisdiction.

> Except as provided in subsections (b) and (c) or as expressly provided otherwise by Federal statute, in any civil action of which the district courts have original jurisdiction, the district courts shall have supplemental jurisdiction over all other claims that are so related to claims in the action within such original jurisdiction that they form part of the same case or controversy under Article III of the United States Constitution....

[*Mars, Inc. v. Kabushiki–Kaisha Nippon Conlux,* 24 F.3d 1368 (Fed. Cir. 1994)] is the first and only case of this court that expressly evaluates whether supplemental jurisdiction under § 1367(a) extends to infringement claims based on foreign patents. In *Mars,* we applied the "common nucleus of operative fact" rubric to determine whether § 1367(a) authorized supplemental jurisdiction over an infringement claim based on a Japanese patent. We held that "the district court erred in assuming that it had 'power' to hear the Japanese patent infringement claim under section 1367(a)." [The court then found *Mars* distinguishable. In *Mars*, there were many differences between the foreign and domestic claims, including differences in the governing laws as well as the allegedly infringing devices sold in each nation. In this case, by contrast, while the laws differed, the infringing devices were much more similar. However, because the district court had not explored the similarity between the claims in sufficient depth, the court declined to decide the case based on lack of power under § 1367(a).]

2. Discretion

Section 1367(c) provides:

The district courts may decline to exercise supplemental jurisdiction over a claim under subsection (a) if—

(1) the claim raises a novel or complex issue of State law,

(2) the claim substantially predominates over the claim or claims over which the district court has original jurisdiction,

(3) the district court has dismissed all claims over which it has original jurisdiction, or

(4) in exceptional circumstances, there are other compelling reasons for declining jurisdiction.

. . . The district court's order contained no § 1367(c) analysis. We find that considerations of comity, judicial economy, convenience, fairness, and other exceptional circumstances constitute compelling reasons to decline jurisdiction under § 1367(c) in this case and therefore, hold that the district court abused its discretion by assuming jurisdiction.

a. Treaties as the "supreme law of the land"

[The court discussed various international treaties relating to patent, which, as discussed in Chapter 1.C, preserve the territoriality principle.] Permitting our district courts to exercise jurisdiction over infringement claims based on foreign patents in this case would require us to define the legal boundaries of a property right granted by another sovereign and then determine whether there has been a trespass to that right.

Based on the international treaties that the United States has joined and ratified as the "supreme law of the land," a district court's exercise of supplemental jurisdiction could undermine the obligations of the United States under such treaties, which therefore constitute an exceptional circumstance to decline jurisdiction under § 1367(c)(4). Accordingly, we must scrutinize such an exercise with caution.

b. Comity and relations between sovereigns

In this case, ... considerations of comity* do not support the district court's exercise of supplemental jurisdiction over Voda's foreign patent infringement claims. First, Voda has not identified any international duty, and we have found none, that would require our judicial system to adjudicate foreign patent infringement claims. [W]hile the United States has entered into the Paris Convention, the Patent Cooperation Treaty (PCT), and the Agreement on Trade-related Aspects of Intellectual Property Rights ("TRIPS"), nothing in those treaties contemplates or allows one jurisdiction to adjudicate the patents of another. Second, Voda has not shown that it would be more convenient for our courts to assume the supplemental jurisdiction at issue. Third, with respect to the rights of our citizens, Voda has not shown that foreign courts will inadequately protect his foreign patent rights....

Fourth, assuming jurisdiction over Voda's foreign patent infringement claims could prejudice the rights of the foreign governments. None of the parties or *amicus curiae* have demonstrated that the British, Canadian, French, or German governments are willing to have our courts exercise jurisdiction over infringement claims based on their patents.

In addition, the local action doctrine informs us that exercising supplemental jurisdiction in this case appears to violate our own norms of what sovereigns ordinarily expect. Courts derived the local action doctrine from the distinction between local and transitory actions beginning with *Livingston v. Jefferson* [15 F. Cas. 660 (C.C.D. Va. 1811) (No. 8411)], written by Justice John Marshall riding Circuit.... In short, the local action doctrine served to prevent courts from adjudicating claims for trespass or title to real property.

The territorial limits of the rights granted by patents are similar to those conferred by land grants. A patent right is limited by the metes and bounds of the jurisdictional territory that granted the right to exclude.... It would be incongruent to allow the sovereign power of one to be infringed or limited by another sovereign's extension of its jurisdiction. Therefore, while our Patent Act declares that "patents shall have the attributes of personal

Eds. United States courts are not required to give full faith and credit to judgments of foreign courts. However, under the doctrine of "comity," United States courts will enforce foreign judgments and the factual findings made by foreign courts if the procedure utilized is fundamentally fair, and if the law applied by the foreign court is not blatantly inconsistent with domestic law. Comity is not nearly as strict a requirement as full faith and credit.

property," 35 U.S.C. § 261, and not real property, the local action doctrine constitutes an informative doctrine counseling us that exercising supplemental jurisdiction over Voda's foreign patent claims could prejudice the rights of the foreign governments.

. . . Patents and the laws that govern them are often described as complex. . . . Cordis U.S. and one of the *amicus curiae* assert, and Voda does not dispute, that the foreign sovereigns at issue in this case have established specific judges, resources, and procedures to "help assure the integrity and consistency of the application of their patent laws." Therefore, exercising jurisdiction over such subject matter could disrupt their foreign procedures. . . .

Accordingly, comity and the principle of avoiding unreasonable interference with the authority of other sovereigns dictate in this case that the district court decline the exercise [of] supplemental jurisdiction under § 1367(c).

c. Judicial economy

Because of our lack of institutional competence in the foreign patent regimes at issue in this case, more judicial resources could be consumed by the district court than the courts of the foreign patent grants. Indeed, adjudication of Voda's British, Canadian, European, French, and German patent claims may substantially predominate his U.S. patent claims. . . .

Voda and one *amicus curiae* point out that consolidated multi-national patent adjudication could be more efficient. While there may be merit in that argument, no international treaty establishes full faith and credit, nor have we found any analogous agreement that would require foreign countries to recognize or obligate the enforcement of our judgments regarding foreign patents. In this case, Voda's amended complaint asks not only for damages and fees but also for "such other and further relief as this Court deems just and proper." Therefore, the additional time and resources required by our courts may result in incomplete adjudication of the claims, prolonging and extending the expenditures by all. . . .

e. Fairness

Lastly, the act of state doctrine* may make the exercise of supplemental jurisdiction over foreign patent infringement claims fundamentally unfair. As "a 'principle of decision binding on federal and state courts alike,' " the act of state doctrine "requires that, in the process of deciding, the acts of foreign sovereigns taken within their own jurisdictions shall be deemed valid." *W.S. Kirkpatrick & Co. v. Envtl. Tectonics Corp., Int'l*, 493 U.S. 400, 406, 409

---

* *Eds.* The act of state doctrine limits the ability of United States courts to question the exercise of sovereign authority by a foreign government.

(1990) (citation omitted). In this case, none of the parties or *amicus curiae* have persuaded us that the grant of a patent by a sovereign is not an act of state. *But see Mannington Mills, Inc. v. Congoleum Corp.*, 595 F.2d 1287, 1293–94 (3d Cir. 1979) (stating that Third Circuit was "unable to accept the proposition that the mere issuance of patents by a foreign power constitutes [] an act of state" under abstention analysis). Therefore, assuming arguendo that the act of state doctrine applies, the doctrine would prevent our courts from inquiring into the validity of a foreign patent grant and require our courts to adjudicate patent claims regardless of validity or enforceability. Given the number of U.S. patent cases that we resolve on validity or enforceability as opposed to infringement grounds, exercising such jurisdiction could be fundamentally unfair to the alleged infringer where, as one *amicus curiae* points out, "the patent is in fact invalid and the defendant would be excused from liability on that basis in a foreign forum." Voda has not shown in this case that the validity of the foreign patents would not be at issue. Indeed, Cordis U.S. asserts otherwise.

   f.   Section 1367(c) abuse of discretion

   In summary, several reasons in this case would compel the district court to decline supplemental jurisdiction under § 1367(c): limitations imposed by treaties that are the "supreme law of the land" and considerations of comity, judicial economy, convenience, and fairness. The district court undertook none of this analysis. Accordingly, we hold that the district court abused its discretion in exercising supplemental jurisdiction. . . .

B. *Alternate Statutory Basis*

   The parties also dispute on appeal whether diversity jurisdiction under § 1332 provides an alternate and independent basis for the district court to hear Voda's claims of foreign patent infringement. However, Voda has not pled diversity, and it is not clear whether the district court would permit such a pleading to be made at this stage in the proceedings. We therefore decline to decide whether the district court could properly exercise jurisdiction based in diversity. . . .

IV.   Conclusion

   We vacate the order of the district court granting Voda leave to amend his complaint to add infringement claims based on foreign patents pursuant to the supplemental jurisdiction statute 28 U.S.C. § 1367 and remand for further proceedings consistent with this opinion.

NEWMAN, Circuit Judge, dissenting.

I respectfully dissent, for the question here presented is not related to federalism and the federal/state relationship, or to pendent jurisdiction of state law issues; nor are disputes about foreign patents so unique as to call up the other theories collected by the panel majority to support this ousting of United States parties from access to United States courts. . . .

A foreign country is not a "state" in the constitutional context, and the judicial application of foreign law plays no role in the jurisdictional balance represented by federalism. The rules governing federal jurisdiction of supplemental state claims are irrelevant to whether a United States court has the authority and can exercise its discretion to decide questions that require the application of foreign law. Courts in the United States have always had the authority to decide questions that require application of foreign law. . . . Yet the panel majority holds that a United States court cannot do so, in its sound discretion, when the issue concerns patents. . . .

I cannot agree. It is inappropriate for the Federal Circuit to create this unique exception to the authority of American courts to resolve controversies that require the application of foreign law.

Access of a nation's citizenry to dispute resolution in the nation's courts is fundamental to a nation ruled by law. This court's new rule carves an inapt exception into judicial authority, judicial obligation, and judicial discretion. Such special treatment of patent issues is flawed as a matter of precedent, procedure, and policy. . . .

The panel majority also invokes the "Act of State" doctrine as justification for barring the district court from choosing to decide the issues of Voda's foreign patents. . . .

Whether a particular governmental action is properly viewed as an act of state has been explained in a variety of contexts; the common thread is whether the issue is one that is normally consigned to the executive branches, such that an international dispute is resolved by political negotiations between diplomats; or whether the issue is more suitable to the individual review that is given to litigants in judicial proceedings dealing with specific facts. The fundamental criterion is whether the governmental action is a significant public act or whether it is a ministerial function, accompanied by whether the proposed judicial review is directed to the public interests of the nation as served by the governmental act, or is a private effort to enforce a private claim.

Clearly, the grant of a patent is not an Act of State, whether done by the United States or by a foreign country. . . .

Courts in other countries have not refrained from applying foreign patent law, including United States law. A Japanese court recently applied the United States doctrine of equivalents in a suit between Japanese companies that included questions of infringement of United States patents, in *K.K. Coral Corp. v. Marine Bio K.K.*, Case No. 1943(wa)/2002 (Tokyo D. Ct., Oct. 16, 2003). All nations have recognized their obligation to provide a judicial forum to address disputes involving their citizens; no warrant has been shown to remove foreign patents from this purview. . . .

From my colleagues' extreme limitation and bar on the district court's exercise of discretion to receive and resolve foreign patent issues, I respectfully dissent.

Notes and Questions

1. One of the majority's concerns is that hearing foreign patent claims would present a possible affront to foreign nations. Which is more insulting—hearing (and possibly misconstruing) a foreign patent claim, or completely refusing to enforce a foreign patent because it was granted by a foreign government? Do considerations of claim and issue preclusion affect your answer?

2. *Diversity as an option. Voda* deals only with supplemental jurisdiction under 28 U.S.C. § 1367 (2006). In Part III.B of its opinion, the Court leaves open the possibility that a court could hear a foreign patent claim pursuant to its diversity jurisdiction under § 1332. Unlike supplemental jurisdiction, courts do not have free-ranging discretion to refuse to exercise diversity jurisdiction. At least one recent decision relied on this difference in holding that a federal district court may exercise its diversity jurisdiction to adjudicate foreign patent claims. *Baker–Bauman v. Walker*, No. 3:06cv017, 2007 WL 1026436 (S.D. Ohio Mar. 29, 2007).

On the other hand, in certain circumstances a court will not exercise diversity jurisdiction even when the requirements of § 1332 are met. Two doctrines are of special relevance to foreign intellectual property claims. First, under the doctrine of *forum non conveniens*, a federal court may dismiss a case that should, based on considerations of fairness and convenience, be litigated in a foreign court. Second, the doctrine of "abstention" provides that a court may (and in some situations must) refuse to hear a claim based on state law because of concerns about undue interference with the role of the states. Should either of these doctrines cause a court to refuse to exercise diversity jurisdiction over a foreign patent or copyright claim? Note that the court in *Baker–Bauman* considered neither doctrine, in part because the parties did not argue them.

Another district court decision may provide a partial answer. In *Fairchild Semiconductor Corp. v. Third Dimension (3D) Semiconductor, Inc.*, 589 F. Supp. 2d 84 (D. Me. 2008), the court held, after extensive analysis, that neither *Voda* nor the doctrine of *forum non conveniens* prevented it from exercising diversity jurisdiction over a case involving two Chinese patents. However, unlike *Voda* and *Baker–Bauman*, *Fairchild* was not a suit for patent infringement. Instead, the case involved a suit by a patent licensee seeking a declaration that it owed no royalties under the license agreement because the product it was making did not fall within the scope of the licensed Chinese patents. To the court, the fact that it was not being asked to enforce the patents was very important.

3.   In the *Fairchild* case discussed in the prior note, the court also placed great emphasis on the fact that the licensee was not challenging the validity of the foreign patents, but merely asking the court to interpret their scope. Do you see why allowing one court to declare a foreign patent invalid could seriously jeopardize the international intellectual property system?

The European Union follows a similar rule. Council Regulation 44/01 gives European courts broad jurisdiction over parties residing in or actions occurring within their borders, regardless of the legal source of the underlying right. Council Regulation 44/01, On Jurisdiction and the Recognition and Enforcement of Judgments in Civil and Commercial Matters, 2001 O.J. (L 12) 1. However, in certain matters the courts of a particular nation have exclusive jurisdiction. Article 22(4) deals with registered intellectual property rights, providing that the courts of the nation in which registration occurs have exclusive jurisdiction over all "proceedings concerned with the registration or validity of patents, trade marks, designs, or other similar rights required to be deposited or registered. . . ." The omission of copyrights was deliberate. As you will see below, the international treaty system provides that a party can obtain a copyright without the need to register.

The ALI proposal discussed above in Section A diverges from the norm on this issue. Under § 211(a) of the proposal, any court may adjudicate foreign intellectual property claims. That jurisdiction even extends to matters of validity of the underlying right. However, § 211(2) contains an important limit on this power. Any adjudication concerning validity of a foreign intellectual property right applies only between the actual parties to the case, not to others. In other words, even if the court finds the patent valid, other alleged infringers may be free to challenge the same patent when they are sued. Whether that exception would prevent a court from applying principles of nonmutual issue preclusion to a decision declaring a patent or copyright invalid remains to be seen.

4.   Does *Voda* prevent a court from exercising jurisdiction over a foreign *copyright* claim? How relevant is it that most nations, like the United States, use regular courts to adjudicate copyright claims, as compared to the specialized patent tribunals mentioned in *Voda* (and discussed in more depth in Chapter 1.E)?

5. 28 U.S.C. § 1338 (2006) gives federal courts exclusive jurisdiction over patent and copyright claims. However, under that provision federal courts have exclusive jurisdiction only over claims arising under United States law. Does *Voda* or any of the additional considerations raised in these notes have any effect on a *state* court's ability to hear a foreign patent case? Would it matter if the state court was asked to declare a foreign patent invalid? Of course, case law dealing with the supplemental or diversity jurisdiction statutes, and the federal doctrines of abstention or *forum non conveniens*, have no direct application to the state courts.

C. THE TREATY REGIME

Both *Subafilms* and *Voda* mention the treaty regime that governs the field of international intellectual property. These treaties are a direct result of the territorial principle discussed in the prior sections. Because intellectual property rights are circumscribed by national borders, a party who wants to protect a particular invention, work, or mark in more than one nation must obtain a new patent, copyright, or trademark in each nation. This model was at first perfectly acceptable, as the legal monopoly represented by an intellectual property right was considered an obstacle to trade. In the late 1800s, however, views began to change. As international trade grew in scope, nations came to realize that recognizing intellectual property rights could in fact enhance trade. These nations have over the past 150 years entered into a number of multilateral treaties designed to allow someone with rights in one nation to obtain similar rights in other nations.

1. COMMON FEATURES OF THE TREATIES

With a few very limited exceptions, these treaties do not create "international intellectual property rights." Instead, they preserve the territorial model of separate domestic rights. The main focus of the treaties is to make it easier for a person to obtain rights for a single invention, work, or mark in multiple locations. To the extent the treaties succeed, they allow a party with valuable intellectual property in one nation to expand its business and move into other nations, where it can avail itself of similar protections.

The treaties employ three basic strategies to ease the process of obtaining foreign intellectual property rights. The first is *simplifying and unifying procedure*. Instead of requiring a party to undergo a complex and idiosyncratic process in each and every nation, the treaties try to make the process more uniform and simple in each nation.

Second, the treaties attempt to *harmonize the substantive laws* to a significant extent in all nations. The process of marketing an invention or work in multiple nations can be quite difficult if the intellectual property laws are inconsistent. In some situations, in fact, an act required by one nation for protection may result in forfeiture of intellectual property protection in other nations. The harmonization provisions try to iron out these differences. They do so generally not by mandating particular language for national laws, but instead by setting *minimum standards* for each nation to meet as it sees fit. Member nations implement these standards by amending their domestic intellectual property laws to make them comply. Note that these minimum standards may require a nation to make significant changes to its law, some of which may be at odds with that nation's intellectual property policy.

Third, many of the treaties *bar discrimination based on nationality*. (The term "national" in the treaties includes both citizens of a nation and non-citizens who owe their primary allegiance to that nation.) Even if the processes are streamlined and unified, and the national laws made completely uniform, the ends of the international intellectual property system could be readily frustrated if a nation were free to deny intellectual property rights to nationals of other treaty members. It is important, however, to distinguish discrimination based on nationality from discrimination based on origin of the work. While barring the former, the treaties do allow some discrimination based on place of origin of the work.

A final common feature worth noting is that the treaties themselves generally do not operate as law in all nations. Many nations recognize that some treaties are "self-executing," which means that the treaties operate as law. In others (including the United States), however, international treaties are generally considered non-self-executing. These jurisdictions, therefore, need to modify its domestic law in a way that satisfies the minimum standards set forth in the treaties. The different ways in which international treaties take legal effect can create problems for intellectual property right holders.

Certain international organizations have also been created to oversee and administer the various treaties. Most of the treaties discussed below are administered by the World Intellectual Property Organization ("WIPO"). WIPO has become a highly visible organization in the field, and its website (www.wipo.int) often proves to be a valuable starting point for research on international intellectual property issues. On the other hand, the most comprehensive (and arguably most important) treaty, the TRIPS Agreement, is administered not by WIPO but by the World Trade Organization ("WTO"). The different agendas of WIPO and the WTO give the TRIPS Agreement a very different "flavor" than that of the other treaties.

2.   THE MAIN TREATIES

a.   *The Paris Convention*

Originally enacted in 1883, the Paris Convention for the Protection of Industrial Property is the oldest of the multilateral intellectual property treaties. It has been revised several times. The treaty establishes a Union of nations, which at present comprises approximately 170 nations (hereinafter "Union members"). All the major industrialized nations are Union members. Since 1967, WIPO has administered the Paris Convention.

The Paris Convention deals with "industrial property", including patents, trademarks, trade names, product designs, utility models, as well as other protections against unfair competition. Like other treaties, the Paris Convention does set a number of minimum standards for national laws on these subjects, especially trademark laws. But harmonization is not the Convention's only, or perhaps even the most important, feature. Two other key features of the treaty have played a very important role in the development of international intellectual property law.

The first of these features is *non-discrimination*. Article 2(1) provides that a Union member must give to all nationals of every Union member the same rights and remedies that it provides to its own nationals. Article 3 extends this same protection to people who are nationals of non-members, but who have established a domicile or an ongoing presence in a Union member. Similarly, Article 2(2) prevents a Union member from establishing domicile or residency requirements as a condition to the grant of intellectual property rights.

The second key feature deals with *priority*. The basic territorial model of intellectual property rights has an inherent problem. Suppose a party obtains a patent in the United States, and the patented product proves wildly successful. If people in other nations learn of the success, they may be able to obtain domestic patents in their respective countries, thereby thwarting any hopes the United States party might have of expanding into those nations.* The Paris Convention deals with this problem by creating a "priority period": a window of opportunity for the party to seek protection in other nations. The priority period commences on the date the person first files for protection in any Union member. This priority period is one year in the case of patents, and six months for trademarks and product designs. To illustrate how the priority

---

* Of course, this option is available only if the nation in question would not consider the United States invention or patent application as "prior art" in the patent process. In some nations, including the United States, foreign patent applications do qualify as prior art. 35 U.S.C. § 102 (2006).

works, suppose a party files a patent application in Nation X on January 3, 2010. In November of that year, she files a patent application for essentially the same invention in Nation Y. Both X and Y are members of the Paris Union. Because the party filed within the one-year priority period for patents, her application in Nation Y "relates back" to her January 3 filing date in X. Nothing that happens after that date in Y affects her ability to obtain a patent in Y. Thus, even if someone else had filed an application for the same invention in Y in February of that year, the party would be entitled to the patent in Y.

The priority system, with its focus on *filing*, had one very significant consequence in the common law nations. Like the United States, many of the common law nations required use, rather than simple registration, as a condition to obtaining trademark rights. In fact, a party could often obtain significant protection without bothering to register. The Paris Convention system, however, puts people in nations with a use-based trademark system at a significant disadvantage. Consider the following example. Suppose an American company comes up with a mark on January 1. Because federal trademark laws do not allow a party to register a mark until it has been used in commerce, the American could not immediately file for registration. Suppose further that on February 1, a German comes up with an identical mark for the same type of product. Because Germany does not require use prior to filing, the German could file immediately. Moreover, the German would have six months from the date of filing in Germany to register the mark in the United States. And if the German does file in the United States before the American company has the chance to use the mark, the German *would have priority* over the American, even in the United States.

This state of affairs, of course, proved unacceptable to the use-based nations. Many use-based nations, including the United States and Canada, have dealt with the problem by allowing a party to file a paper evidencing an "intent to use" a mark. As long as the party actually uses the mark within a prescribed period, her priority in that nation dates back to the date the intent to use application was filed. In our example, the intent to use provision would give the American company the chance to file something on or shortly after January 1, thereby giving it priority (assuming it eventually does use the mark) over the German company.

Although the Paris Convention's priority system gives a party a limited ability to "bootstrap" intellectual property rights in one nation into rights in other Union members, the Convention makes it clear that patents and trademarks in each nation are separate and independent (Articles 4*bis* and 6). Therefore, for example, the mere fact that the original patent application is denied in one nation is not in and of itself reason to deny other patent applications, even if the other applications will take advantage of the rejected application's filing date. Similarly, a finding in one member that a patent is invalid does not automatically affect patents granted or pending in other nations.

Finally, Articles 10*bis* and 10*ter* deal with the issue of unfair competition. Unlike the case of patents, design rights, and trademarks, these provisions do not create any sort of priority. Indeed, because the right to be free from unfair competition is not an exclusive "intellectual property" right, any rules of priority would be nonsensical. These provisions instead speak in very broad terms, requiring nations to protect those doing business within their borders from acts "contrary to honest business practices", and to provide effective remedies against such acts. To date, these provisions have had little impact.

b. "Procedural" Corollaries to the Paris Convention: The Patent Cooperation Treaty, Madrid Agreement and Protocol, and Hague Agreement

While the Paris Convention harmonizes governing law to some degree—especially with respect to the reasons a nation may refuse to grant certain rights—it does nothing to harmonize *procedures* in force in the Union members. The party seeking protection must still file and prosecute applications in every nation in which she seeks protection. Most nations strictly limit the languages that can be used for patent or trademark applications, meaning that the multinational applicant may be forced to hire translators. The processes involved can be very different, and in some instances fatally inconsistent. Therefore, obtaining multiple patents, trademarks, and design rights can still prove to be a cumbersome and expensive process.

Three additional multilateral treaties—the Patent Cooperation Treaty, Madrid Agreement and Protocol, and the Hague Agreement Concerning the International Registration of Industrial Designs ("Hague Agreement")—help to iron out these procedural problems. Each of these treaties is best thought of as a corollary to the Paris Convention, as it helps make more effective the basic priority system established by Paris.

Patent Cooperation Treaty ("PCT"). The basic goal of the PCT is to facilitate the many national patent filings envisioned by Paris. The treaty obligates all member nations to harmonize their patent application procedures. Once harmonization occurs, the party then files a *single home-state application*, which designates all nations in which patent protection is sought. That single application serves as an application in all of the designated nations.

Note what the Patent Cooperation Treaty does *not* do. Although it allows for a single *application*, the party must still undertake a separate patent *prosecution* in all of the designated nations. The party may also have to incur translation costs, as well as other expenses to deal with issues of local procedure. Therefore, the system does not reduce the time and expense of obtaining separate patents to the degree one might anticipate. Nevertheless, the ability "to get one's foot in the door" by filing a single application in a major language, coupled with the harmonization of patent procedures, makes the PCT both appealing and fairly effective. WIPO reports that in 2008 alone, almost 164,000 PCT applications were filed.

Madrid Agreement and Protocol. The Madrid Agreement and Protocol focus on trademarks, service marks, and other indicia of origin. The original Madrid Agreement was enacted in 1891, and has been amended over a half dozen times. However, certain features of the original agreement proved unacceptable to a number of major industrialized nations, including the United States, United Kingdom, Japan, and all the Nordic countries. To bring these nations into the fold, the Madrid Protocol was adopted in 1989. This Protocol tempered many of the more controversial provisions of the Agreement, making the Madrid System more palatable to the holdout nations. The United States joined the Madrid system shortly thereafter, but is still working on implementing the requirements.

Like the PCT, the main goal of the Madrid Agreement and Protocol is to simplify the process by which a party obtains protections for the same mark in multiple nations. However, the process differs from the PCT in a fundamental way. Under the PCT, the party files a single application, but then must deal with multiple, parallel prosecutions. Under Madrid, by contrast, the first step is to obtain a *domestic* trademark registration, often called the "home country" registration. Once that home country registration is obtained, the party then files a single "international application" with WIPO, designating the additional nations in which she seeks registration. Unless a particular nation rejects the registration within the designated time (one year for Madrid Agreement nations, 18 months for Madrid Protocol members), the mark must be registered.

This requirement of a threshold home registration is the source of one of the most important, and controversial, features of the Madrid system—the procedural mechanism of "central attack." Under this mechanism, if the party's home country registration is cancelled, all other registrations stemming from that home country registration will also be cancelled. The Madrid Protocol minimizes the impact of this mechanism somewhat, giving the party three months to convert the foreign registrations into ordinary domestic registrations in those other nations.

Hague Agreement. The Hague Agreement is the corollary treaty dealing with the third main area covered by the Paris Convention—namely, product designs. In its basics, the system works much like the PCT. A party who seeks protection in multiple nations may first file a single international application with WIPO. If he succeeds, WIPO grants an international registration. That registration does not grant any substantive rights, but it does allow the party to pursue domestic registrations in multiple Hague members, taking advantage of the filing date of the international application. Hague also streamlines and harmonizes the domestic registration process.

However, the Hague Agreement has not been as widely embraced as either the PCT or the Madrid Agreement and Protocol. In fact, it is confined mainly to Europe, with only a handful of non-European nations taking part. The primary problem with the agreement stems from the lack of any significant harmonization of national design laws (See Chapter 5.A). Indeed, some nations do not have even a rudimentary design protection scheme in place. Paris and Hague do not even define the general nature of what a design law should look like, much less the particulars of what designs are protected and the form protection should take. Without some uniformity in the underlying law, Hague's harmonized procedure is of little use. In the European Union, by contrast, design law is highly harmonized, making the Hague registration process feasible within that particular system.*

c. The Berne Convention

The Berne Convention for the Protection of Literary and Artistic Works was enacted in 1886, shortly after the original Paris Convention. Its main focus is copyright and related rights. Like Paris, Berne has been amended a number of times over the years, and is administered by WIPO. Currently, approximately 160 nations are members of the Berne Convention.

Berne has a very different feel than Paris. It strongly reflects the exalted view of the "author" that prevailed in Europe in the late 1800s. As a result, Berne goes much further than the other treaties in establishing a very high baseline of protection. Various provisions of Berne specify the sorts of works that must be protected, the rights that must be afforded authors of these works, and the

---

* Within the last few years, Europe has adopted a European Community-wide design system, making domestic design registrations—and accordingly the Hague registration procedure—far less important. See Chapter 5.

scope of any exceptions and limitations to the rights. Although a comprehensive catalog of these provisions is beyond the scope of this book, a few examples help to illustrate Berne's broad scope. Article 2 of Berne indicates that copyright is to be available for "literary and artistic works," which are defined as

> every production in the literary, scientific and artistic domain, whatever may be the mode or form of its expression, such as books, pamphlets and other writings; lectures, addresses, sermons and other works of the same nature; dramatic or dramatico-musical works; choreographic works and entertainments in dumb show; musical compositions with or without words; cinematographic works to which are assimilated works expressed by a process analogous to cinematography; works of drawing, painting, architecture, sculpture, engraving and lithography; photographic works to which are assimilated works expressed by a process analogous to photography; works of applied art; illustrations, maps, plans, sketches and three-dimensional works relative to geography, topography, architecture or science.

While nations are allowed to exempt certain types of works within this broad sphere from protection (for example, political speeches under Article 2*bis*(1)), the allowable exceptions are clearly spelled out and fairly narrow. However, nations may require that a work be fixed as a condition to granting protection.

Berne is also fairly specific regarding the rights that authors must be able to claim. In addition to ordinary rights such as the right to reproduce (Article 9) and perform in public (Article 11), Berne also requires some more controversial rights. Primary among the latter set of rights are the right to translate a work (Article 8) and the "moral rights" of paternity and integrity (Article 6*bis*). Berne also mandates a minimum term of life of the author plus fifty years for most of these rights.

Like Paris, Berne also allows an author with rights in one nation to obtain similar rights in other nations. Mechanically, however, Berne is a model of simplicity. Berne requires all nations to grant at least the minimum level of protection to any eligible work.* Moreover, Article 5(2) provides that the "enjoyment and exercise of these rights shall not be subject to any formality." That innocuous language has rather remarkable consequences. Basically, at the moment the author fixes a work in any Berne nation, she is *automatically protected in every other Berne nation from that point*

---

* The eligibility requirements for Berne are set out in Articles 3 and 4, and are quite complicated. Eligibility turns on the nationality of the author and place of publication.

forward. A nation cannot require a foreign author to register or deposit the work in that nation in order to obtain protection. Because of this automatic protection, Berne has no need for the sort of priority rules set out in Paris. Nor is there any need for "corollary" treaties analogous to the PCT or the Madrid system.

This system of automatic protection, coupled with the very high level of protection, caused some nations to balk at joining Berne. Instead, they joined the Universal Copyright Convention, a less onerous alternative developed under the auspices of UNESCO.) The United States was one of the more notable holdouts. While the United States joined the Paris Union in 1887, it did not join Berne until 1988. Similarly, China and the Russian Federation did not join Berne until 1992 and 1995, respectively.

d.   The European Patent Convention

Although the procedural treaties discussed earlier, like the PCT, the Madrid Agreement and Protocol, and the Hague Agreement, are all multilateral by nature, there are regional treaties and initiatives covering different parts of the world. Examples of these instruments or institutions include the Andean Pact, the Benelux Convention on Trademarks, the Eurasian Patent Convention, the European Patent Convention (EPC), MERCOSUR as well as initiatives facilitated by the French-speaking AIPO (African Intellectual Property Organization) and English-speaking ARIPO (African Regional Industrial Property Organisation).

Because the decisions by the European Patent Office (EPO) will be covered in later chapters, this section discusses the EPC in greater detail. In 1973, the EPC was signed and has a current signatory list of thirty-five European nations. The EPC created two organizations: first, the EPO and the supervisory Administrative Council. This system allows a patentee to file for a single patent, called a European Patent, through the EPO. This alternative does not displace the patent offices of EPC member nations, who continue to maintain their individual patent offices for patentees who choose to file on an individual country-by-country basis. Further, patent applicants may choose to combine EPO procedures with those available under the PCT.

The EPO is comprised of various divisions, which include the receiving section, the examining divisions and opposition divisions. In addition, the EPO has an appellate structure that includes Boards of Appeal of at least three individuals, and Enlarged Boards of Appeal of five persons. These Boards include a mix of legally and technically qualified persons.

Examination before the EPO takes place in two phases. First, the EPO considers whether the request for a patent meets with the substantive requirements of the law. During this first phase, the receiving section prepares and sends the applicant a search report and preliminary opinion that considers whether these requirements are met. At that juncture, upon the patent applicant's request, an examining division undertakes a substantive examination to decide whether the application will be granted. If the request for a patent is granted, it is subject to opposition proceedings filed by third parties who claim that the EPC's patentability requirements have not been met. Alternatively, a patentee may file a request to limit or revoke the patent. EPO decisions made throughout these processes may be appealed to an EPO Board of Appeal. A technical board of appeal typically decides appeals against decisions of the examining and opposition divisions. If appropriate and on limited grounds, an Enlarged Board of Appeal may provide a final stage review of an adverse decision.

A European Patent is effective within all of the thirty-five signatory members of the EPC, as well as some additional countries under cooperation agreements. Several countries require a translation and/or the payment of a fee before the right to enforce attaches. Currently, the EPO does not have a mechanism to resolve infringement disputes. Rather, patent enforcement must be undertaken in the courts of the member nations. Although the European patent law of the member states has been harmonized, variations still exist. As one former jurist explained:

> It is true that national judges apply the same European rules, but there is no guarantee that they apply the same European rules in the same way. Divergences could emerge not only between judicial decisions in the various countries but also between national judicial decisions and the case law of the Boards of Appeal of the EPO. Unity of law and legal certainty are missing. Unity and legal certainty are not enhanced by the fact that national judges are only part of the national procedural laws vary from country to country in many ways.... The result is that inevitable differences exist as to the quality, the speed and the cost of patent litigation in Europe.

Jan J. Brinkhof, *Patent Litigation in Europe: Two Sides of the Picture*, 9 FED. CIR. B.J. 467, 468 (2000). Moreover, parties engaged in infringement actions in different European nations may incur duplicative expenses. Observing some of these issues, proposals have been put forth for a single system to decide validity and infringement. For example, the European Commission was recently authorized to begin negotiations to create a Unified Patent Litigation System within the European Community.

e.   TRIPS Agreement

The Agreement on Trade-related Aspects of Intellectual Property Rights ("TRIPS") is the most comprehensive intellectual property treaty. It became effective on January 1, 1995, and is currently in force in more than 150 nations. TRIPS covers virtually all areas of intellectual property, and also touches upon issues of unfair competition.

TRIPS is also arguably the most influential intellectual property agreement. Unlike the other treaties, TRIPS is part of the broader complex of agreements overseen by the WTO. Through the single undertaking approach, membership in the WTO subjects a nation to the terms of all WTO agreements, including TRIPS. This feature also means that TRIPS can be enforced by trade sanctions within the mandatory dispute settlement process. Although sanctions are rarely imposed for violations of TRIPS, the threat of such sanctions has provided a significant incentive for nations to comply with their obligations.

While TRIPS starts from the premise that intellectual property is a trade issue, its substantive provisions are not radically different from those of the treaties discussed above. Most fundamentally, TRIPS, like Paris and Berne, establishes minimum levels of protection (and certain maximum standards). And these minima are often similar to those in the earlier treaties. Indeed, in the field of copyright TRIPS incorporates most of the provisions of Berne (except the requirement of moral rights protection). The agreement likewise preserves the basic principles of territoriality and national treatment, and focuses on harmonization of national laws.

TRIPS is also designed to move intellectual property law into the modern age. Some of the provisions recognize unique rights that have developed in various nations, such as rights in performances and sound recordings (Article 14) and the right to protect geographical indications (Articles 22 to 24; see Chapter 4.G). Another major focus is technological progress. Many of the harmonization provisions deal with how traditional intellectual property laws and principles should apply to new technologies like computers and life forms. For example, Article 10(1) requires that WTO members protect computer software under copyright law as a literary work. Article 27(3) allows a nation to deny patent protection to certain medical procedures, as well as plants and animals. Articles 35 to 38 mandate a form of protection for integrated circuits and the "mask works" from which they are made.

Because TRIPS is part of a broader trade agreement, it also incorporates certain notions not present in Paris or Berne. Perhaps the most important is the notion of *most-favored nation* treatment. This principle of non-discrimination means that, to the extent a member provides an advantage to one country, the same treatment must in most cases be provided to all. For example, a country that offers patent protection for surgical methods (a technology that a nation may exclude from patent protection under Article 27) developed in one nation must also extend similar protection to surgical method inventions made in other nations.

Given the breadth of the rights conferred, TRIPS understandably gives nations some ability to create limitations and exceptions to intellectual property rights, in order to reflect peculiar local conditions. The most generally-applicable, and controversial, of these exception provisions are the so-called "three step tests." These tests allow limited exceptions to copyrights (Article 13), patents (Article 30), and design protection (Article 26(2)). The common thread to these provisions is that a limitation or exception is acceptable only if (1) it is limited or specific; (2) it does not cause too great a conflict with "the normal exploitation" of the protected invention, design, or work; and (3) it does not "unreasonably prejudice the legitimate interests" of the right holder. However, the actual wording of these exceptions differs in subtle, but potentially significant, ways. For example, a nation may limit or make exceptions to copyright rights only in "certain special cases," while the patent and design protection tests speak in terms of "limited exceptions." Similarly, the copyright test appears to bar *any* conflict with normal exploitation, while the patent and design sections prevent only unreasonable conflict. To complicate matters still further, the trademark provisions set out a similar "two-step" test, which focuses only on "the legitimate interests of the owner of the trademark and third parties." For an example of how the WTO construes a three-step test, see the Panel Decision concerning § 110(5) of the United States Copyright Act in Chapter 3.

The TRIPS Agreement also contains detailed provisions governing intellectual property *enforcement*, an issue largely ignored in earlier treaties. In addition to the usual civil remedies, the agreement mandates border seizures and even criminal penalties under certain circumstances. These enforcement provisions have proven especially valuable. Part of the problem in enacting an effective international intellectual property regime is that some nations with large intellectual property piracy industries would enact powerful laws, but refuse to enforce them. Failure to comply with the enforcement provisions in TRIPS, like violations of its minimum substantive standards, creates the possibility of trade sanctions.

The high levels of protection required by TRIPS can prove difficult for a nation with an underdeveloped or emerging technical or artistic sector. In recognition of this phenomenon, TRIPS contains special provisions for "developing" and "least developed" nations. The agreement's preamble recognizes "the special needs of the least-developed country Members in respect of maximum flexibility in the domestic implementation of laws and regulations in order to enable them to create a sound and viable technological base." TRIPS allows these nations some flexibility in implementation. For example, Article 66 of TRIPS allows least developed countries an additional ten years (beyond the one year allowed for all nations) to implement the agreement "[i]n view of the[ir] special needs ..., their economic, financial and administrative constraints, and their need for flexibility to create a viable technological base." Recently, the time for these members to comply with the TRIPS provisions concerning the protection of patent and trade secret in pharmaceutical products was extended to January 1, 2016. The transitional period in other areas has also been extended to July 1, 2013.

Other TRIPS provisions recognize the needs of developing countries in implementing intellectual property systems. For example, Article 7 states:

> The protection and enforcement of intellectual property rights should contribute to the promotion of technological innovation and to the transfer and dissemination of technology, to the mutual advantage of producers and users of technological knowledge and in a manner conducive to social and economic welfare, and to a balance of rights and obligations.

Article 8(1) declares: "Members may, in formulating or amending their laws and regulations, adopt measures necessary to protect public health and nutrition, and to promote the public interest in sectors of vital importance to their socio-economic and technological development, provided that such measures are consistent with the provisions of this Agreement." Articles 66 and 67 further obligate developed countries to encourage technology transfer, as well as technical and financial cooperation to establish intellectual property laws and supporting agencies. Other provisions in the TRIPS Agreement establish additional limitations and exceptions.

Notwithstanding these concessions, the past few years have witnessed an increasing debate over the desirability of the TRIPS regime (and by implication, the earlier intellectual property treaties as well). This debate is often dubbed the "North–South Debate," pitting the developed "North" against the less-developed "South." The crux of this debate is whether the system proves to be a net benefit or a net burden to the South. Opponents of TRIPS emphasize how the requirement of strong intellectual property protection can drive up the costs to the South of much needed technology, information, and especially medicines. The net result, this argument continues, is a transfer of wealth to the North, further inhibiting development of the South.

To many, language like that in Articles 7 and 8 is too vague and aspirational. The Doha Development Round of Trade Negotiations ("Doha Round") advanced a far more comprehensive proposal, recognizing the special needs of the developing and least-developed worlds. Whether this ambitious proposal will ever be adopted remains to be seen.

D. TRIPS AND ITS INTERNATIONAL IMPACT: INDIA AS A CASE STUDY

1. INDIA IN A PRE–TRIPS WORLD

The impact of TRIPS on developing nations can be examined by using India as a case study. As background, India's first patent system derived from its colonial years, when the British East India Company first introduced patent laws there. At the turn of the twentieth century, a number of Indian physicians and chemists began to establish manufacturing facilities within the country to make antibiotics, synthetic drugs, vaccines, and drugs derived from plants and animals. During the middle part of the century, the Indian government allowed foreign manufacturers to establish manufacturing facilities, in some instances making the same drugs that were already being produced by Indian pharmaceutical manufacturers.

After gaining independence in 1947, the Indian government engaged in a series of studies to reassess its needs. India's Planning Commission issued the First Five Year Plan in 1950, which observed that the country had a high poverty rate, inadequate food supplies and a high rate of epidemic disease. Another prominent study concluded that foreign patent holders outnumbered Indian patentees by a rate of nine to one. N. RAJOGAPALA AYYANGAR, REPORT ON THE REVISION OF THE PATENTS LAW 12 (1959). Known as the Ayyangar Report, this study observed that the patent system enacted during India's colonial years did not operate for the optimal benefit of the country as an independent sovereign. More specifically, the report observed that foreign companies frequently engaged in a practice to obtain patents outside their country of origin solely to minimize competition on a worldwide scale:

> These patents are therefore taken out not in the interests
> of the economy of the country granting the patent or with
> a view to manufacture there but with the main object of
> protecting an export market from competition from rival

manufacturers particularly those in other parts of the world.

Id. at 13. Concerned about fostering invention within India, the Ayyangar Report relied on the experience of certain European countries, primarily Germany, to provide a model for limiting the patentability of chemical inventions to processes:

> The rise of the German chemical industry dates from 1877 and in the course of the next 30 years it came to occupy the foremost position in Europe. This phenomenon was attributed by acute observers in great part to the provision of the German patent law which confined patent grants to process claims, and thus left an open field of research in new methods of manufacture.

Id. at 24. Under such rules, an inventor could claim the right to patent a novel and inventive way to make a particular chemical compound, but not the compound itself. In operation, this patent system meant that those who devised a noninfringing design around a patented method or process were free to make any chemical compound by these alternative means.

The Ayyangar Report stated that a system that denied protection for chemical products best served the interests of India as a whole. As Justice Aayangar declared, "I have considered the matter with utmost care and have reached the conclusion that the chemical and pharmaceutical industry of this country would be advanced and the tempo of research in that field would be promoted if the German system of permitting only process claims were adopted." *Id.* at 36–37. Further, the Ayyangar Report considered whether food and medicines should be the subject of patents, and concluded that "the denial of product claims is necessary in order that such important articles of daily use as medicine and food which are vital to the health of the community should be made available to everyone at reasonable prices and that no monopoly should be granted in respect to such articles." *Id.* at 41.

In 1970, India passed a comprehensive series of patent statutes that incorporated the recommendations from the Ayyangar Report. Specifically, section 5 of India's 1970 Patent Act excluded protection for "substances intended for use, or capable of being used, as food or as medicine or drug," and for "substances prepared or produced by chemical processes." This act authorized patents for "the methods or processes of manufacture" of pharmaceuticals, so long as all other patentability requirements were met. In effect, this allowed pharmaceutical inventors to obtain patents only for the process to create medicines and drugs, but not for the substances themselves. Under this regime, an originator's chemical formulation for a pharmaceutical product could be freely duplicated within

India if one were able to recreate the pharmaceutical by a different process than that claimed in the originator's patent. Further, methods and processes for food or medicines were limited to five years, compared to fourteen years for all other inventions. *Id.* § 53(a).

Further, the 1970 Act required that patents be worked within the country, and recognized that patents were "not granted merely to enable patentees to enjoy a monopoly for the importation of the patented article." *Id.* § 83. The law specifically recognized that "patents are granted to encourage inventions and to secure that the inventions are worked in India on a commercial scale" and provided for government revocation if appropriate. *Id.* § 82. Moreover, the statute authorized the government to grant a compulsory license upon an application if "the patented invention is not available to the public at a reasonable price and praying for the grant of a compulsory licence to work the patented invention." *Id.* § 84. According to one scholar, India's patent laws had a dramatic effect on the market for pharmaceuticals within its borders:

> In the wake of the new legislation, India's generic drug industry flourished as indigenous firms made huge gains in market share against the MNCs [multinational corporations]. A number of MNCs left India or chose not to invest there given the lack of patent protection. At the same time, scientists employed by the generic firms became skilled in process chemistry and reverse engineering. Drug prices in India fell dramatically. For example, the price in 1998 of the Indian equivalent of ranitidine, the active ingredient in Glaxo's Zantac anti-ulcer medicine, was over 100 times less than the price of Zantac on the U.S. market.

Janice M. Mueller, *The Tiger Awakens: The Tumultuous Transformation of India's Patent System and the Rise of Indian Pharmaceutical Innovations*, 68 U. PITT. L. REV. 491, 514 (2006).

2. INDIA AND TRIPS COMPLIANCE

Article 27(1) of the TRIPS Agreement provides that members must provide patent protection for "any inventions, whether products or processes, in all fields of technology, provided that they are new, involve an inventive step and are capable of industrial application."* This provision stood in conflict with India's then-in-force 1970 Patent Law, which had subject matter exclusions for certain

---

* Although Article 27(3)(a) of the TRIPS Agreement authorizes countries to exclude patent protection for inventions that concern "diagnostic, therapeutic and surgical methods for the treatment of humans or animals," it is commonly understood that this exemption does not allow nations to exclude patent protection for pharmaceuticals.

pharmaceutical and agricultural inventions, as well as for chemical product claims.

India entered into TRIPS effective January 1, 1995. Under Article 65(4) of the Agreement, India, as a developing country member, was permitted until January 1, 2005 to extend "product patent protection to areas of technology not so protectable in its territory on the general date of application." Nevertheless, Article 70(8) required India to "provide as from the date of entry into force of the WTO Agreement a means by which applications for patents for such inventions can be filed" as of January 1995 to preserve priority dates. Although India attempted to comply with this provision by a Presidential decree that created a "mailbox" for receiving, dating and then storing patent applications for pharmaceutical and agricultural chemical products, applications in this "mailbox" were not slated for examination by India's patent office until TRIPS became effective in that nation.

As discussed earlier in this Chapter 1.C, TRIPS includes a mandatory enforcement mechanism. Specifically, Article 64 mandates that all disputes arising under the Agreement be settled by the WTO dispute settlement procedure. During 1996, the United States filed a complaint before the WTO Dispute Settlement Body, asserting that India's mailbox procedure failed to comply with Article 70(8) of the TRIPS Agreement. (The European Communities filed a similar complaint later.) The United States prevailed in the WTO panel decision, and India appealed the decision to the WTO Appellate Body. A short excerpt from the Appellate Body's decision illustrates India's efforts to grapple with TRIPS requirements.

Appellate Body Report
India—Patent Protection for Pharmaceutical and Agricultural Chemical Products
WT/DS50/AB/R (Dec. 4, 1997)

India is *entitled*, by the "transitional arrangements" in paragraphs 1, 2 and 4 of Article 65, to delay application of Article 27 for patents for pharmaceutical and agricultural chemical products until 1 January 2005. In our view, India is obliged, by Article 70.8(a), to provide a legal mechanism for the filing of mailbox applications that provides a sound legal basis to preserve both the novelty of the inventions and the priority of the applications as of the relevant filing and priority dates. No more.

But what constitutes such a sound legal basis in Indian law? To answer this question, we must recall first an important general rule in the *TRIPS Agreement*. Article 1.1 of the *TRIPS Agreement* states, in pertinent part:

> ... Members shall be free to determine the appropriate method of implementing the provisions of this Agreement within their own legal system and practice.

Members, therefore, are free to determine how best to meet their obligations under the *TRIPS Agreement* within the context of their own legal systems. And, as a Member, India is "free to determine the appropriate method of implementing" its obligations under the *TRIPS Agreement* within the context of its own legal system.

India insists that it has done that. India contends that it has established, through "administrative instructions", a "means" consistent with Article 70.8(a) of the *TRIPS Agreement*. According to India, these "administrative instructions" establish a mechanism that provides a sound legal basis to preserve the novelty of the inventions and the priority of the applications as of the relevant filing and priority dates consistent with Article 70.8(a) of the *TRIPS Agreement*. According to India, pursuant to these "administrative instructions", the Patent Office has been directed to store applications for patents for pharmaceutical and agricultural chemical products separately for future action pursuant to Article 70.8, and the Controller General of Patents Designs and Trademarks ("the Controller") has been instructed not to refer them to an examiner until 1 January 2005. According to India, these "administrative instructions" are legally valid in Indian law, as they are reflected in the Minister's Statement to Parliament of 2 August 1996. And, according to India:

> There is ... *absolute certainty* that India can, when patents are due in accordance with subparagraphs (b) and (c) of Article 70.8, decide to grant such patents on the basis of the applications currently submitted and determine the novelty and priority of the inventions in accordance with the date of these applications. (emphasis added)

India has not provided any text of these "administrative instructions" either to the Panel or to us. ...

We must look at the specific provisions of the Patents Act. Section 5(a) of the Patents Act provides that substances "intended for use, or capable of being used, as food or as medicine or drug" are not patentable. "When the complete specification has been led in respect of an application for a patent", section 12(1) *requires* the Controller to refer that application and that specification to an examiner. Moreover, section 15(2) of the Patents Act states that the Controller "shall refuse" an application in respect of a substance that is not patentable. We agree with the Panel that these provisions of the Patents Act are mandatory. And, like the Panel, we are not persuaded that India's "administrative instructions" would prevail over the contradictory mandatory provisions of the Patents Act.

We are not persuaded by India's explanation of these seeming contradictions. Accordingly, we are not persuaded that India's "administrative instructions" would survive a legal challenge under the Patents Act. And, consequently, we are not persuaded that India's "administrative instructions" provide a sound legal basis to preserve novelty of inventions and priority of applications as of the relevant filing and priority dates.

For these reasons, we agree with the Panel's conclusion that India's "administrative instructions" for receiving mailbox applications are inconsistent with Article 70.8(a) of the TRIPS Agreement.

Notes and Questions

1. Subsequently, India remedied the circumstances at issue in the WTO's decision. India's patent system was amended to legislatively enact the mailbox rule for applications for substances directed for uses as a medicine or drug. *See* The Patents (Amendment) Act, No. 17 of 1999, § 1(2), India Code (1999) (deeming the mailbox provisions retroactive to January 1, 1995). In addition, this amendment incorporated a system to grant exclusive marketing rights for pharmaceutical substances that were the subject of mailbox applications that were found to satisfy all other patentability requirements. *Id.* ch. IV.A. These rights provide a form of temporary protection to applicants until the time of examination. This legislation was passed over domestic opposition, including accusations that the legislation failed to account for India's economic sovereignty. *See* Meetali Jain, *Global Trade and the New Millennium: Defining the Scope of Intellectual Property Protection of Plant Genetic Resources and Traditional Knowledge in India*, 22 HASTINGS INT'L & COMP. L. REV. 777, 800 n.118 (1999) (describing the controversy). Under this amended statute, applications for pharmaceutical inventions were neither examined nor published, although their priority was preserved. In 2006, soon after India implemented patent protection for pharmaceutical substances, the nation amended the patent laws to allow protection for pharmaceutical substances. The Patents (Amendment) Act, No. 15 of 2005, § 4, India Code (2005). India's Patent Office has now begun to issue drug patents.

2. How has the change to the Indian patent law affected the country's position as the "pharmacy for the developing world"? Consider this statement by Médecins San Frontières (Doctors without Borders):

> The previous Indian Patent Act did not allow patents on pharmaceutical products and thus enabled Indian companies to make their own generic versions of medicines. Generic production has been crucial for the supply of affordable medicines in the developing world, especially for newer drugs such

as antiretrovirals (ARVs) for the treatment of HIV. It has resulted in competition between producers, which has reduced the price of many ARVs from as much as US $15,000 to as little as US $150 per person per year. In addition, due to the lack of product patents on each separate drug, Indian generic manufacturers have been able to combine three different AIDS medicines in one single pill. The availability of these generic fixed-dose combinations has dramatically simplified AIDS treatment in resource-limited settings.

MÉDECINS SAN FRONTIÈRES, CAMPAIGN FOR ACCESS TO ESSENTIAL MEDICINES, PROGNOSIS: SHORT-TERM RELIEF, LONG-TERM PAIN (2005). As a result of changes to India's patent system, this organization predicts that for new medicines, a "lack of competition will lead to steep increases in the prices of any new medicines, be it ARVs, antibiotics, or new cancer treatments."

Some researchers estimate that it costs somewhere between $403 to $802 million to develop a drug to the point of marketing approval. Joseph A. DiMasi, Ronald W. Hansen & Henry G. Grabowski, *The Price of Innovation: New Estimates of Drug Development Costs*, 22 J. HEALTH ECON. 151 (2003). Pharmaceutical companies have maintained that robust patent protection is necessary to recoup the cost of their investment and to ensure availability of funding for new drugs. This figure has been disputed. For example, consumer advocacy group Public Citizen has issued a report that estimates the figure to be much closer to $110 million even for the most expensive types of research. Moreover, this report observes that the National Institutes of Health, a taxpayer funded agency, annually spends billions of dollars on health care research projects that provide key findings to pharmaceutical companies. PUBLIC CITIZEN, RX R&D MYTHS: THE CASE AGAINST THE DRUG INDUSTRY'S R&D "SCARE CARD" 8 (2001) (stating that "U.S. taxpayer-funded researchers conducted 55 percent of the published research projects leading to the discovery and development" of the five top selling drugs of 1995).

Nonetheless, there is significant evidence that pharmaceutical drug development is an expensive endeavor. Indeed, many commentators have maintained that strong patent protection was the most justified in the pharmaceutical area. How can the problem of access and drug development costs be resolved? For more discussion about how the WTO attempts to address this difficult issue, see Chapter 2.E.

3. Section 3(d) of the Indian patent law excludes from patentability

the mere discovery of a new form of a known substance which does not result in the enhancement of the known efficacy of that new substance or the mere discovery of any new property or new use for a new substance or the mere use of a known process, machine or apparatus unless such known process results in a new product or employs at least one new reactant.

Newly developed pharmaceutical substances therefore may be patented only if they possess an enhanced "efficacy"—or improved therapeutic effect on the body—compared to existing formulations. Moreover, subsequently discovered uses of known pharmaceutical substances are barred from patentability entirely. Thus, under the 2005 India Patent Act, one could not obtain a patent for a newly discovered method of treating HIV using the chemical compound zidovudine, at a time when this substance was already known to treat cancer.

Article 3(d) of the 2005 Act appears targeted to minimize "evergreening." A pharmaceutical company engages in evergreening when it files a series of patent applications to cover different attributes of the same product or variations of the initial substance (such as an improvement to the first formulation) in order to extend patent protection for multiple subsequent terms. If this strategy is successful, generic drug companies must wait until the last of these patents expire to enter the market for that particular formulation. While pharmaceutical companies have asserted that these practices are the natural result of incremental innovation, generic drug companies and consumer advocacy groups question whether these improvements are sufficiently significant to warrant subsequent patents. *See* COMM'N OF THE EUROPEAN COMMUNITIES, PHARMACEUTICAL SECTOR INQUIRY FINAL REPORT 351–67 (2009).

In a challenge filed by pharmaceutical manufacturer Novartis against this provision of India's patent law, the Madras High Court of India declined to determine whether this provision complied with TRIPS. The Court stated:

> When such a comprehensive dispute settlement mechanism is provided as indicated above and when it cannot be disputed that it is binding on the member States, we see no reason at all as to why the petitioner, which itself is a part of that member State, should not be directed to have the dispute resolved under the dispute settlement mechanism referred to above.

If this issue is presented to the WTO's Dispute Settlement Body, what should the outcome be?

4. One of this book's authors posits that TRIPS's undue focus on setting minimum standards (as compared to both minimum and maximum standards) distorts the operation of the intellectual property systems within individual nations:

> By having an undue focus on the floor, countries ignore the fact that policymakers may not be able to protect their own industries and nationals by balancing the additional protection through the inclusion of exceptions and public interest safeguards. Indeed, such exceptions would likely be viewed with disfavor by their richer and more powerful trading partners (and the multinational corporations that heavily lobbied those countries).

Second, it has made it difficult for countries to take a holistic perspective and offer package legislation that includes strengthened protection and public interest offsets, especially when the rules are scrutinized by the WTO dispute settlement panels.

Peter K. Yu, *The International Enclosure Movement*, 82 IND. L.J. 827, 902–03 (2007). Do you agree?

Additional implications for a uniform approach to intellectual property protection are observed in Annette Kur & Henning Grosse Ruse–Khan, *Enough Is Enough—The Notion of Binding Ceilings in International Intellectual Property Protection* (Max Planck Institute for Intellectual Property, Competition & Tax Law, Research Paper No. 09–01, 2008), *available at* http://ssrn.com/abstract=1326429:

> Economic theory suggests that IP protection should be tailored to the domestic level of development: Depending on whether a country has—in any given field of production—a comparative advantage in either innovation or imitation, overall welfare gains will be the highest if the domestic IP policy is responsive and tailored to this advantage. That means if the domestic industrial and technological capacity is sufficient to innovate, relatively stronger protection may offer tailored incentives for further innovation. If the respective capacity is merely adequate to imitate, laxer protection allowing some of this imitation will be beneficial for technological advancement and learning.

What remedy exists if the TRIPS minimum standards prove to be too high and unworkable for developing nations?

5. Compare these perspectives with the following excerpt:

> TRIPS ... will benefit the people of the world, who will have more new pharmaceuticals than they otherwise would have had (because the payments are higher to inventors of such pharmaceuticals). There will, of course, be winners in India as well—the inventors who develop a local industry that creates rather than copies pharmaceuticals, as well as those who do not have to emigrate to work in the cutting edge pharmaceutical industry. Once India develops a viable and competitive world-class pharmaceutical industry, then there will be more winners than losers in India. After some period of time, even more world citizens will be advantaged by TRIPS. The users of patented drugs, which have no satisfactory unpatented substitutes, will have to admit that, in the absence of a worldwide patent system, the drug that may save their life may not have been developed.

Martin J. Adelman & Sonia Baldia, *Prospects and Limits of the Patent Provision in the TRIPS Agreement: The Case of India*, 29 VAND. J. TRANSNAT'L L. 507, 532 (1996). Which is the better view? What are possible solutions to establish an incentive structure for domestic development under TRIPS? Is the answer the same for patent, as for copyright, trademark and trade secret?

E. LIMITED FLEXIBILITIES: "GENERAL" VERSUS "SPECIALIZED" INTELLECTUAL PROPERTY COURTS

Intellectual property law is generally viewed as complex. Not only is the governing law complicated, but many of the cases deal with complicated technologies. These two factors raise the question of whether countries should adopt specialized intellectual property courts to enforce intellectual property rights. Article 41 of TRIPS sets forth certain minimum requirements that member states should adhere to, such as the establishment of effective enforcement proceedings, including remedies, and the preference for written decisions on the merits of cases. Nevertheless, Article 41(5) states explicitly that members are not required to "put in place a judicial system for the enforcement of intellectual property rights distinct from that for the enforcement of law in general." While some countries have established specialized administrative bodies, trial courts and appellate courts to handle selected intellectual property law cases, others have not. A survey by the Intellectual Property and Entertainment Law Committee of the International Bar Association considered the various approaches of 85 different countries in structuring their court system to address intellectual property law cases and the merits of "general" versus "specialized" courts.

International Bar Association, Intellectual Property & Entertainment Law Committee
International Survey of Specialised Intellectual Property Courts and Tribunals
(2007)

The survey indicates that:

The following jurisdictions have developed specialised courts that exclusively hear IP cases: Korea, Malaysia, Thailand, Turkey, and the United Kingdom. [The specialised intellectual property courts in Korea, Turkey and the United Kingdom are quite different from one another.]

In Korea, the Intellectual Property Tribunal (IPT) is the court of first instance for the settlement of industrial property-related disputes and is independently operated within the Korean Intellectual Property Office (KIPO).... Although civil courts may decide issues of enforceability, only the IPT may decide issues of validity concerning patents, utility models, trademarks, and designs. In addition to invalidation actions, the IPT also has exclusive first instance jurisdiction over confirmation of scope trials and appeals of final rejection of applications for registration of IP rights. Infringement actions before the courts and invalidation actions before IPT will often run in parallel. Only after a trial decision is given from the IPT is an applicant/agent allowed to appeal to a higher court, such as the Patent Court and the Supreme Court.

There are eight IP courts in different cities in Turkey, including Istanbul, Izmir and Ankara. Five of them are criminal and three of them are civil IPR courts.... Twelve specialised courts for disputes concerning intellectual, industrial and commercial property will be established in Adana, Ankara, Bursa, Eskisehir, Istanbul, Beyoglu, Izmir, Karsiyaka, Kadikoy, Kayseri, Konya and Mersin....

The United Kingdom has two specialist courts of first instance: The Patents Court, which is part of the Chancery Division of the High Court, and the Patents County Court. Appeals from both courts go to the Court of Appeal. The judges in the Patents Court and Patents County Court are all specialists. There is a specialist patents judge in the Court of Appeals, who normally sits (with two other judges) to hear appeals in patent cases....

The following jurisdictions have developed specialised tribunals that exclusively hear IP cases: Australia, China, Jamaica, Kenya, New Zealand, Singapore, the United Kingdom, and Zimbabwe....

[For example, i]n Singapore, the Copyright Tribunal is a forum for resolving disputes between copyright owners and users of copyright materials. The Tribunal's jurisdiction is set out in Part VII of the Copyright Act (Cap 63). The Copyright Tribunal has the power to refer to the High Court any matter that comes before it for the determination on a point of law. This may be done on its own volition or at the request of any party to the matter. The copyright secretariat is located within the Intellectual Property Office of Singapore (IPOS)....

In the United Kingdom, the Copyright Tribunal is to decide, when the parties cannot agree between themselves, the terms and conditions of licences offered by, or licensing schemes operated by, collective licensing bodies in the copyright and related rights area. It has the statutory task of conclusively establishing the facts of a case and of coming to a decision which is reasonable in the light of those facts. Its decisions are appealable to the High Court only on points of law. In general, only the person seeking a copyright licence can refer disputed matters to the Tribunal.

The following jurisdictions have courts of general jurisdiction with specialised divisions that exclusively hear IP cases or specialist judges with IP backgrounds and expertise in IP cases: Australia, Brazil, Belgium, Canada, Denmark, Finland, France, Germany, Hong Kong, Hungary, India, Iran, Israel, Italy, Japan, New Zealand, Norway, Pakistan, Panama, Romania, Sierra Leone, Singapore, Slovakia, Slovenia, Spain, South Africa, Sweden, Taiwan, and the Netherlands. . . .

[For example, i]n Rio de Janeiro, there are eight State Courts with specialised divisions in Bankruptcy, Corporate, and Industrial Property Laws. Any patent, trademark, industrial design, utility model, or unfair competition lawsuit must be filed before one of these eight courts.

[In Germany, e]ach German state has one district court with a patent panel. Specialised patent panels, consisting of one presiding judge and two assisting lawyers in district courts, hear patent infringement cases. The District Courts of Dusseldorf, Munich, and Mannheim have great expertise in patent matters. In [that country], infringement cases are dealt with exclusively in civil courts. "The infringement courts do not have jurisdiction to deal with validity issues. Patents can be revoked or invalidated only by the Patent Office and the Federal Patent Court. The Federal Supreme Court, Bundesgerichtshof, as the last and final instance, deals with patent infringement and validity." . . .

[In Taiwan, there are] established professional tribunals at the district courts of Taipei, Taichung, Tainan, and Kaohsiung [and there are] professional divisions at other district courts to process IP infringement cases. . . .

The following jurisdictions have commercial courts or divisions that hear IP cases in addition to other business disputes: Austria, Ireland, Portugal, Spain, Switzerland, and the Philippines.

The following jurisdictions have appellate courts that exclusively hear IP cases and also hear other types of appeals: Brazil, Chile, China, Colombia, Finland, France, Germany, Japan, Korea, Panama, Portugal, Sweden, the Netherlands, the United Kingdom, and the United States. . . .

[For example, i]n Finland, the Helsinki Court of Appeal has exclusive jurisdiction over industrial property matters. There is also a dedicated department within the Court for IP matters. Copyright matters, on the other hand, are dealt with on a geographical basis. Thus, centralised handling of copyright matters first occurs when the case reaches the Supreme Court, if the case ever proceeds this far. . . .

The European Patent Organisation ... is also currently on its way to creating a European patent court. A working party mandated by the governments of the contracting states of the European Patent Convention elaborated with the support of the organization a draft for an optional European Patent Litigation Agreement (EPLA) and a draft statute for a European Patent Court. EPLA was established with an aim to create an integrated judicial system for the litigation of European patents with a uniform procedure and a central European patents court which would replace the current system according to which European Patents after being granted have to be litigated individually in national courts (where the protection has been sought/where challenges have been made)....

If the EPLA is ratified, a common specialised patent court would be created. The EPLA is independent and should not be confused with the approach of the European Union to create a community patent with its own jurisdictional system....

Benefits of Specialised IP Courts

Expertise

Judges may produce more reasoned and practical decisions owing to their experience in IP issues. The fact that the specialist judge is familiar with the particular area of law will frequently enable the court, at an early stage, through case management at a directions hearing, to ensure that only the core issues are pursued and, if necessary, that discovery is tailored to the particular case. The judge may, in the more informal atmosphere of this particular process, express some preliminary views about the overall merits of the case, and this may point the way to a settlement or a reduction in the number of matters at issue.

Consistency of legal doctrine in the IP field. This comprehensive understanding of and familiarity with the surrounding case material can be expected to provide greater consistency in the decision-making process and should bring with it the advantage to the litigants of a more predictable outcome of the proceedings. Consistency in decision-making is of extreme importance. Inconsistency in decision-making leads to a lack of confidence in the system and court authority will diminish.

Dynamism. IP courts are more able to keep up with new IP issues and laws. As many IP laws are subject to constant evolution, judges and lawyers should be able to rapidly assess the new amendments and apply the changes. Constantly evolving subject matter, such as IP law, requires expertise in the field in order to make it work. Specific training in IP issues is more attainable as expertise and resources are concentrated within the judiciary....

Effectiveness

Quicker and more effective decision-making process. The time that otherwise would be lost in dealing with aspects of the case in order to educate the judge will be saved, thereby shortening hearings and reducing costs for litigants, courts, and administrative staff. Specialisation theoretically reduces delay because judges become familiar with the case patterns and the legal issues raised by the cases before them. Judges who hear the same types of cases regularly come to recognise fact patterns and issues more quickly and accurately than those who encounter cases only occasionally. As a result, they can control the lawyers more easily, see possibilities for settlement, and write better decisions. Their increased opportunity to see trends may also put them in a better position than judges who see a mix of cases to develop the law to suit evolving conditions.

Better understanding of IP issues by judges. Even though each case would have a different technology at issue, specialised judges would be more efficient at resolving IP cases through their consistent exposure to the substantive law.

Establishment of rules and procedures that are unique to IP issues in nature, ie appointing associate judges or assessors to assist and provide technical knowledge.

Reduced risk of judicial errors, which contributes to the effectiveness of the administration of justice.

Reduced caseload. Specialist courts reduce the caseload of overburdened generalist courts. If a rash of cases in a specialist field emerges at a particular time, or if, for example, there is new legislation in the particular field requiring thorough interpretation by the court, then the specialist court will relieve the general court of this burden and thereby ensure that the stream of litigation is not impeded.

Efficiency

IP courts are more likely to manage the challenges of complex IP cases more efficiently and more precisely. Appeals may be made directly to the highest court, bypassing the courts of appeal. More cost effective due to efficiency and faster adjudication of cases. As many IP rights have acquired a multinational aspect, judicial cognisance of judicial findings in other jurisdictions may be recognised and relied on by specialised IP courts while generally not permitted in general courts. Court proceedings may be shortened as exhibits and experts may be unnecessary.

It should be noted that there are also likely to be benefits to the jurisdictions that create specialised IP courts as well as to its litigants. For example, an increase in foreign direct investment may be realised by countries that create specialised IP courts. Additionally, litigation costs for plaintiffs and defendants may decrease as exhibits and experts needed to establish facts in general courts may be unnecessary.

Potential Downsides of Having Specialised IP Courts

It is important to stress, however, that potential benefits carry possible downsides. These have been identified through the survey as:

Costs of maintaining IP courts may be high. Costs of training judges, court personnel, and public prosecutors may be high. A lack of a substantial caseload may not justify the creation of specialised IP courts in certain jurisdictions. A local presence may not be possible by specialised IP courts and therefore inaccessible to some. Repeat litigators know judges well and are well acquainted with the eccentricities of the specialised court's rules, therefore putting one-time litigants at a disadvantage.

Loss of generalists' overviews. Generalist judges come to cases without preconceptions and are able to apply fresh perspectives to the problems at hand. This suggests that the particular skill a judge brings to the court is his or her ability to attach appropriate weight to the facts and to make a judgment on such assessment.

Informality. This means the kind of familiarity among those administering justice may lead to undue reduction of formality.

Isolation. The creation of a specialised court carries with it the risk that it may lead the particular area of law in a direction away from the development of the general law.

Overlap with other areas of law. This is the case where, for example, an IP case, whether relating to patent, trademark or other matters, raises, outside the specific issue of IP, questions of contract. This situation may require a generalist judge to try the whole case, rather than a specialist judge, who might be tempted to develop inappropriate general principles of law to meet his or her particular view.

Geographical availability. Specialised courts will usually require long-distance travel either by the judges or the parties. This will inevitably increase costs.

Notes and Questions

1. Do you think specialized courts, in one or more of the forms described above, should be preferred over general courts in intellectual property law cases? Why or why not?

2. Given the level of complexity in the differences between the approaches of different countries in their court systems, how do the

divergent approaches impact the harmonization of substantive rules? What about procedural rules that may impact the outcome of cases? More fundamentally, can we meaningfully compare the different approaches when national court systems differ not only in their basic structures, but also their perceived functions?

3.   Specialized courts exist within the United States, at least at the trial court level, in bankruptcy, family and tax law. Why would policymakers choose to use specialized courts for these areas? Are there similarities or differences among intellectual property, family and bankruptcy laws? Problems in the environmental law field can be quite technical and often involve complex technologies. Are there specialized courts to adjudicate environmental law cases?

4.   The European Patent Litigation Agreement did not garner enough support for acceptance in the EU. A new proposal for a "European and Community Patents Court" is under consideration by the EU Council of Ministers. The proposal would create a unified court system that would have jurisdiction over litigation concerning European and Community patents. In a study, Dietmar Harhoff found:

> Avoiding duplication of infringement and revocation cases is likely to generate large benefits for the European economy. The results obtained here suggest that *currently* between 146 and 311 infringement cases are being duplicated annually in the EU Member States. By 2013, this number is likely to increase to between 202 and 431 duplicated cases. Total private savings from having access to a unified Patent Court in 2013 would span the interval between EUR 148 and 289 million.

DIETMAR HARHOFF, ECONOMIC AND COST-BENEFIT ANALYSIS OF A UNIFIED AND INTEGRATED EUROPEAN PATENT LITIGATION SYSTEM 5 (2009), *available at* http://ec.europa.eu/internal_market/indprop/docs/patent/studies/litigation_system_en.pdf. Notably, Professor Harhoff also found that the costs for litigating a patent suit with a value of €250,000 differs substantially between the United Kingdom at €150,000–1,150,000 and Germany at €50,000 *for each party. Id.* at 12.

Chapter 2

PATENTS

A. PATENT ELIGIBLE SUBJECT MATTER: COMPUTER PROGRAMS AND BUSINESS METHODS

Patent eligibility has become one of the most controversial topics in global patent law. Unlike the United States Patent Act of 1952, the European Patent Convention (EPC) specifically excludes certain subject matter from patent eligibility, including "discoveries, scientific theories, and mathematical methods; aesthetic creations; schemes, rules and methods for performing mental acts, playing games or doing business, and programs for computers; and presentations of information." EPC art. 52(2). However, these categories of material are excluded "only to the extent to which a European patent application or European patent relates to such subject-matter or activities *as such*." *Id*. art. 52(3) (emphasis added).*

In the Unites States, the standard of what is patent eligible subject matter is evolving. In In re *Bilski*, 545 F.3d 943 (Fed. Cir. 2008), an *en banc* decision, the Federal Circuit sets forth the machine or transformation test for processes. The United States Supreme Court recently granted *certiorari* to hear the case, and it is unclear how the Supreme Court will address the issue. In Europe, the patentability of software and business methods is equally controversial. Notably, the European Parliament overwhelmingly rejected an European Community Directive on the Patentability of Computer-implemented Inventions, which would have clarified the patent eligibility of software. The interpretation

---

* Article 57 of the EPC, titled "Industrial Application," is sometimes discussed by courts in cases concerning eligibility of patent protection. That Article states: "An invention shall be considered as susceptible of industrial application if it can be made or used in any kind of industry, including agriculture."

of Article 52(2)(c), particularly the provision concerning "doing business" and "programs for computers," has proven difficult for courts and patent offices alike. There is also a recent divergence in continental Europe and the United Kingdom over their approach toward the patentability of software. The division has appeared to have led the president of the European Patent Office (EPO) to send out questions to the Enlarged Board of Appeal asking for clarification of the scope of patent eligible subject matter relating to software.

Several recent U.K. cases concerning software patentability have been decided. In 2006, the Court of Appeal of England and Wales decided *Aerotel Ltd. v. Telco Holdings Ltd.*, [2006] EWCA (Civ) 1371, which appeared to limit patentability for software. After *Aerotel*, the U.K. Intellectual Property Office released a practice note, stating that product patent claims in computer programs would not be allowed in light of that decision. The Office subsequently proceeded to deny all product claims covering computer programs. Posting of David Pearce to IPKat, http://ipkitten.blogspot.com/2008/01/high-court-allows-computer-program.html (Jan. 25, 2008, 19:08). In early 2008, the High Court of Justice of England and Wales held in *Astron Clinica Ltd v. Comptroller Gen. of Patents, Designs and Trade Marks*, [2008] EWHC (Pat) 85, that it was improper for the Patent Office to deny all product claims on computer programs. Later that year, the High Court weighed in again on the patentability of software in the *Symbian* case below.

SYMBIAN LTD. v. COMPTROLLER GENERAL OF PATENTS, DESIGNS AND TRADEMARKS

High Court of Justice of England and Wales
[2008] EWHC (Pat) 518

Mr Justice Patten.

This is an appeal by Symbian Limited ("Symbian") against the decision of the Comptroller General of Patents (dated 30 July 2007) refusing UK Patent Application No. GB 0325145.1 on the ground that the invention is excluded from patentability under s. 1(2) of the Patents Act 1977 ("the 1977 Act"). The Hearing Officer ... confirmed the objection to patentability raised by the examiner which was that each of the claims related to a program for a computer.

The inventions

Most modern computer operating systems embody a dynamic link library (DLL). The DLL is a collection of small programs or files, any one of which can be called up as required by an executable program (EXE) running on the computer at the relevant time. DLL files are used to perform a variety of functions. A common example is allowing the EXE program to communicate with a specific device such as a printer. . . .

[The claimed invention] therefore has an application to a wide range of electrical devices including any form of computer, various forms of cameras and communication devices such as mobile and smart phones and other products which combine communications, image recording and computer functionality within a single device.

. . . [T]he DLL contains a number of functions and modules which may be common to a number of different software and hardware operations available to the user of the device. A function stored in the DLL can be activated by means of a call from the application requiring the particular functionality. The effective management of this process is necessary for the efficient operation of the computer because application programs each require functionality for their own purposes and are therefore in competition with each other to use the resources of the computer in order to perform the specific function which the owner of the device has accessed.

Each file in the DLL occupies a particular position or ordinal. There are essentially two ways in which an application can call for a particular file and link to it. The first is by reference to the ordinal number (link-by-ordinal); the second is by reference to the name (link-by-name). . . .

Under the link-by-name system a call to the function by the application program involves its name being looked up in a table which lists the assigned function name with its respective ordinal number. The ordinal number is then accessed by the application seeking to utilise that function. In this system it is possible to modify application code without regard to the order of functions in the DLL. Although the look-up table will need to correctly associate DLL files with their name and ordinal number, the location of the file in the DLL will be unimportant.

By contrast, the link-by-ordinal number system is faster and requires less processing power and memory. Names are longer in comparison to ordinals and require additional code for their definition. Moreover, ordinal linking does not require a name ordinal look-up table to be stored on the device thereby saving memory and reduces the amount of processing power used in the look-up operation. Ordinal linking would therefore be the preferred method in many DLL based operating systems particularly those for use in smart phones which have restricted physical resources. It is, however, more difficult to administer because the application code has to include the correct location in the DLL of the functions to be accessed. Any changes to the DLL can affect the application code and impede the access to the DLL file which the application is seeking. Ultimately, this can lead to the wrong function being allocated and to the failure of the program.

The link-by-ordinal system, although faster and more efficient is therefore more vulnerable to modifications of the DLL. As mentioned earlier, these commonly occur when there are updates to the functionality of the device.

According to the specification the invention seeks to overcome these problems and to optimise the use of an ordinal number linking system in the DLL by providing an interface which contains suitable mapping between the functions and their ordinals within the DLL thereby eliminating the possibility of malfunction caused by a change in the ordinal position of a particular DLL file due to the modification of the DLL library by the addition of a new DLL file.

The invention involves the division of the DLL into two sections: one containing fixed functions whose ordinals cannot be changed; the other containing functions which can be modified or moved by third party additions to the functionality of the device....

Claim 1 reads:

"A method of operating a computing device having an operating system and a dynamic link library containing a plurality of functions accessible by an executable program, each function in the dynamic link library being associated with an ordinal number, the method comprising:

Providing the dynamic link library as a first part and an extension part each containing one or more of the plurality of functions;

Causing the executable program to link to functions in the first part directly by means of the associated ordinal numbers; and

Causing the executable program to link to functions in the extension part indirectly via a further library containing additional functions"

Claim 9 relates to software arranged to cause a computing device to operate in accordance with the method set out in claims 1–8....

The law

Art. 52 of the EPC (which is given effect to by s. 1(2) of the 1977 Act) provides as follows:

"(1) European patents shall be granted for any inventions, [in all fields of technology] which are susceptible of industrial application, which are new and which involve an inventive step.

(2) The following in particular shall not be regarded as inventions within the meaning of paragraph 1: . . .

> c. schemes, rules and methods for performing mental acts, playing games or doing business, and programs for computers; . . . .

(3) The provisions of paragraph 2 shall exclude patentability of the subject-matter or activities referred to in that provision only to the extent to which a European patent application or European patent relates to such subject-matter or activities as such." . . .

To understand the background to the *Aerotel* test it is unnecessary to go further back than the EPO Board of Appeal's decision in *Vicom System Inc's Application* [1987] O.J. EPO 14. It concerned a claim to a method of digitally processing images although there was also a subsidiary apparatus claim to a computer program to operate that technology. The Board said:

"16. In arriving at this conclusion the Board has additionally considered that making a distinction between embodiments of the same invention carried out in hardware or in software is inappropriate as it can fairly be said that the choice between these two possibilities is not of an essential nature but is based on technical and economical considerations which bear no relationship to the inventive concept as such. Generally speaking, an invention which would be patentable in accordance with conventional patentability criteria should not be excluded from protection by the mere fact that for its implementation modern technical means in the form of a computer program are used. Decisive is what technical contribution the invention as defined in the claim when considered as a whole makes to the known art. Finally, it would seem illogical to grant protection for a technical process controlled by a suitably programmed computer but not for the computer itself when set up to execute the control."

Both claims were upheld. . . .

[T]he Court of Appeal accepted the reasoning of the Board of Appeal in *Vicom* that not all computer programs were to be excluded from patentability. The key to exclusion is Art. 52(3): i.e. are they merely programs for computers as such. The technical contribution test established in *Vicom* therefore moves the essential enquiry away from the fact that one is dealing with an invention based on a computer program to a consideration of the kind of technical effect which the program produces in the device in which it operates.... [The court then reviews the *Gale* and *Fujitsu* cases which follow the *Vicom* approach.]

[D]ecisions of the Court of Appeal achieved an obvious measure of consistency with the decisions of the EPO in *Vicom* and in *IBM/Computer Program Product T 1173/97*, [1999] O.J EPO 609, which emphasize that the intention of Art. 52(2) and (3) is not to exclude all computer programs from patentability. Thereafter the paths separate. In the trilogy of cases (*Pension Benefit System Partnership(2000) T 931/9; Hitachi/Auction Method (2004) T258/03 and Microsoft/Data Transfer (2006) T424/03*) there was a departure from the approach in Vicom with its emphasis on technical contribution. The Board in all three cases accepted that an apparatus claim (in the programmed computer) was not excluded by Art. 52(2) as a computer program: the so-called "hardware approach". It was, they said, therefore unnecessary to resort to the criterion of technical contribution in order to determine whether the invention was excluded matter. They therefore rejected the approach of the Court of Appeal in *Gale* and of the Board in *Vicom* with its emphasis on substance over form.

In *Aerotel* Jacob LJ rightly described the various decisions of the EPO Board of Appeal as mutually contradictory and declined to follow any of the later trio of decisions....

The Hearing Officer's Decision

The Hearing Officer focussed on the method claim 1 of each set of claims on the basis that in substance each of these claims relate to a method of operating a computer which is broadly the same. She then went through the *Aerotel* four step test [which includes: (1) construe the claim; (2) identify the contribution; (3) determine if the contribution lies solely in the excluded subject matter; and (4) check the contribution if it is actually technical].

Step 1: Construing the claim

This is not a problem in the present case. As explained earlier, the substance of the claim is the re-organisation of the DLL into two parts and the provision of a library interface for the extension DLL so as to improve the linking of any EXE program running on the computer with the available functions contained in the DLL files. No issues of construction arise.

Step 2: Identify the contribution

Symbian's case before the Hearing Officer was that the contribution made by the invention lay in the improved reliability of a computing device enabled by the provision of a novel interface. This enabled the EXE program to access available functionality regardless of additions or amendments made by the updates to the DLL and its ordinal numbers.

The Hearing Officer assessed the contribution in these terms:

"... Whilst the use of the 'interface' may well lead to improved reliability, it seems to me that this is an advantage of the method claimed rather than the actual contribution in the sense set out in paragraph 43 of the *Aerotel/Macrossan* judgement. In my view, the contribution made by the invention as claimed in all the claim sets lies in the interface which enables an executable program to access the functionality available on the computing device, regardless of any additions or amendments made to the available functionality by a third party. Does the contribution fall solely within the excluded subject matter? ..."

In physical terms that is right. But the assessment of the contribution made by the computer program used to carry the invention into effect does seem to me to involve some reference to and consideration of the problems which the invention solves albeit by the interposition and use of the interface. This would include improvements in reliability consequent upon the modifications to the operating system. To use the words of Jacob LJ it has to encompass the problem said to be solved; how the invention works; and what its advantages are....

Step 3: Does the contribution lie solely in excluded subject matter?

This is the "as such" test. The Hearing Officer was referred to the treatment of *Gale* in *Aerotel* and in particular to paragraph 92 of the judgment in which Jacob LJ said this:

"So what *Gale* decided is that the computer program exclusion extends not merely to the code constituting a program, but that code as embodied on a physical medium which causes a computer to operate in accordance with that code. More is needed before one is outside the exclusion—as for instance a change in the speed with which the computer works. A technical effect which is no more than the running of the program is not a relevant technical effect. And *Gale* clearly decides that merely putting a new program on a known memory device is not enough to escape art 52(2)."

So is this invention no more than the running of the program? Having regard to the earlier authorities the answer has to be that it depends on what the program does and not merely how it does it.

The mere fact that it involves the use of a computer program does not exclude it: see *Aerotel*.... This point was made in its clearest form in paragraph 16 of the decision in *Vicom* ... which underpins all of the current English authority on this point....

The key elements in [the Hearing Officer's] reasoning appear to be that the use of the new interface to obtain better linking between the EXE program and the updated DLL does not involve a change in the role of the DLL but only in the way in which it is accessed in the new piece of software. This is nothing more than a computer program and is therefore, she decided, excluded from patentability. Nowhere in this analysis does she ask herself in terms what the technical contribution made by the invention is although that is perhaps implicit in her analysis at Step 2. She clearly therefore takes the view that an improved method of accessing files in the DLL (although creating improvements in the reliability of the computer as a functioning machine) cannot amount to a relevant technical contribution because it is confined to the improvement of one piece of software by another. Having excluded the invention as part of Step 3 she regards Step 4 as redundant.

... In a case such as this where the only potential application of Art. 52(2) is in relation to a computer program care needs to be taken not to pre-judge the issue of technical contribution or even to exclude it by concentrating too much on the fact that the invention is program based. Clearly one needs to avoid treating any computer program as some kind of technical advance. But I fail to see why a program which has some novel technical effect on an important component in the computer's operating system should not qualify as doing more than merely operating as a computer program notwithstanding its effect is to solve what on one view is a software problem affecting the functionality and reliability of the computer. I think this is what Pumfrey J had in mind when he referred in *Shoppalotto[.com Ltd's Patent Application*, [2005] EWHC (Pat) 2416] to a patentable invention as providing a solution to a concrete technical problem.

Without an effective operating system a computer is nothing. It is simply inaccurate to label all programs within the computer as software and on that basis to regard them as of equal importance in relation to its functionality. The end result of the invention (as claimed) is that it does (to use the test in *Gale*) solve a technical problem lying within the computer....

In the present case there is a perceived technical shortcoming caused by modification to the DLL as a result of updates to the computer's functionality. This is not a case where the invention is limited to the processing of data. If an increase in the speed at which the computer works can take the program out of Art. 52(3)

... it is difficult to see why the improved reliability of the machine brought about by the re-organisation of the DLL in its operating system does not.

Conclusion

I think that the Hearing Officer took too narrow a view of the technical effect of the invention and was wrong to exclude it from patentability on the basis that it amounted to no more than a computer program. The appeal will therefore be allowed.

Notes and Questions

1.   The *Symbian* decision excerpted above was later affirmed by the Court of Appeal of England and Wales. *Symbian Ltd v. Comptroller Gen. of Patents, Designs and Trademarks*, [2008] EWCA (Civ) 1066.

2.   What does the *Symbian* court mean by "[i]t is simply inaccurate to label all programs within the computer as software and on that basis to regard them as of equal importance in relation to its functionality"? Would software that increases the reliability and speed at which certain share prices are calculated satisfy the *Symbian* test? Will application of the test outlined in *Symbian* lead to predictable and consistent results?

3.   Do the method claims in *Symbian* satisfy the United States' most recent patent eligible subject matter test for processes?

4.   *Aerotel* outlined some "additional considerations" which were driving the United Kingdom and the rest of Europe to broaden the scope of patentable subject matter:

> First, there has been some political pressure on Europe to remove or reduce the categories of non-inventions. Part of that has come ... from the fact that TRIPS (the Agreement on Trade Related Intellectual Property Rights) (1994) does not have the same explicit categories of non-invention as the EPC. It says (Art. 27(1)): "Subject to the provisions of paragraphs 2 and 3 [which roughly correspond to the Art. 53 exceptions] patents shall be available for any inventions, whether products or processes, in all fields of technology, provided that they are new, involve an inventive step and are capable of industrial application.... [P]atents shall be available and patent rights enjoyable without discrimination as to ... the field of technology". Some of the Art. 52(2) excluded categories are not fairly within the description "field of technology" and so not within TRIPS (e.g. aesthetic creations) but others seem to be within it—the paradigm example being computer programs. Hence the pressure.... Secondly, there is pressure from would-be patentees on patent offices. People are applying for what are, or arguably are, business method and computer program patents in significant numbers.... This pressure in part stems

from the fact that, following *State Street* (business methods) and *Alappat* (computer programs) people have been getting patents for these subject-matters in the USA. Since they can get them there, they must as a commercial necessity apply for them everywhere. If your competitors are getting or trying to get the weapons of business method or computer program patents you must too. An arms race in which the weapons are patents has set in. The race has naturally spread world-wide.... Fourthly, despite the fact that such patents have been granted for some time in the US, it is far from certain that they have been what Sellars and Yeatman would have called a "Good Thing." The patent system is there to provide a research and investment incentive but it has a price. That price (what economists call "transaction costs") is paid in a host of ways: the costs of patenting, the impediment to competition, the compliance cost of ensuring non-infringement, the cost of uncertainty, litigation costs and so on. There is, so far as we know, no really hard empirical data showing that the liberalisation of what is patentable in the USA has resulted in a greater rate of innovation or investment in the excluded categories. Innovation in computer programs, for instance, proceeded at an immense speed for years before anyone thought of granting patents for them as such....

5. Does the current test for patent eligible subject matter for processes in the United States alleviate some of the policy concerns pushing for broader patent eligible subject matter in Europe?

* * *

The *Symbian* case cites the following European Patent Office decision as adopting a different approach from the United Kingdom courts to the patentability of software under Article 52(3) of the EPC.

MICROSOFT CORP.'S APPLICATION

EPO Technical Board of Appeal
Case T 0424/03–3.5.01 (Feb. 23, 2006)

The appellant requests that the decision under appeal be set aside and a patent be granted....

Claim 1 reads:

"1. A method in a computer system (10) having a clipboard for performing data transfer of data in a clipboard format, said method comprising the steps of:

providing several clipboard formats including a text clipboard format, a file contents clipboard format and a file group descriptor clipboard format, selecting data that is not a file for a data transfer operation,

using the file contents clipboard format to hold said data by

converting said selected data into converted data of said file contents clipboard format and storing the converted data as a data object,

using the file group descriptor clipboard format to hold a file descriptor holding descriptive information about the data that is to be encapsulated into a file during the data transfer operation,

completing the data transfer by

providing a handle to said data object,

using said handle to paste said data of said data object to a data sink,

using said descriptive information to enable the computer system to create a file at the data sink and

encapsulating the data object into said file.''

Method claims 2 to 4 depend on claim 1. Claim 5 is directed to a computer readable medium having computer executable instructions adapted to cause the computer system to perform the method of one of claims 1 to 4. . . .

The Board concurs with the appellant in considering the claimed method as an invention within the meaning of Article 52(1) EPC.

Claim 1 relates to a method implemented in a computer system. T 258/03—*Auction method/Hitachi* (OJ EPO 2004, 575) states that a method using technical means is an invention within the meaning of Article 52(1) EPC. A computer system including a memory (clipboard) is a technical means, and consequently the claimed method has technical character in accordance with established case law.

Moreover, the Board would like to emphasise that a method implemented in a computer system represents a sequence of steps actually performed and achieving an effect, and not a sequence of computer-executable instructions (i.e. a computer program) which just have the potential of achieving such an effect when loaded into, and run on, a computer. Thus, the Board holds that the claim category of a computer-implemented method is distinguished from that of a computer program. Even though a method, in particular a method of operating a computer, may be put into practice with the help of a computer program, a claim relating to such a method does not claim a computer program in the category of a computer program. Hence, present claim 1 cannot relate to a computer program as such.

The Board also considers the claimed method steps to contribute to the technical character of the invention.

These steps solve a technical problem by technical means in that functional data structures (clipboard formats) are used independently of any cognitive content in order to enhance the internal operation of a computer system with a view to facilitating the exchange of data among various application programs. The claimed steps thus provide a general purpose computer with a further functionality: the computer assists the user in transferring non-file data into files.

Claim 5 is directed to a computer-readable medium having computer-executable instructions (i.e. a computer program) on it to cause the computer system to perform the claimed method. The subject-matter of claim 5 has technical character since it relates to a computer-readable medium, i.e. a technical product involving a carrier (see decision T 258/03—*Auction method/Hitachi* cited above). Moreover, the computer executable instructions have the potential of achieving the above-mentioned further technical effect of enhancing the internal operation of the computer, which goes beyond the elementary interaction of any hardware and software of data processing (see T 1173/97—*Computer program product/IBM*; OJ EPO 1999, 609). The computer program recorded on the medium is therefore not considered to be a computer program as such, and thus also contributes to the technical character of the claimed subject-matter. . . .

The Board concludes that the application and the invention to which it relates meet the requirements of the EPC.

Notes and Questions

1. Microsoft appealed the refusal to issue the patent by the EPO's Examining Division to its Technical Board of Appeal, which authored the preceding decision. The Technical Board of Appeal also hears appeals from the Opposition Division. Third parties may file oppositions within nine months of the "publication of the grant of the patent." HECTOR MACQUEEN, CHARLOTTE WAELDE & GRAEME LAURIE, CONTEMPORARY INTELLECTUAL PROPERTY POLICY: LAW AND POLICY 369 (2007). Opposition proceedings are considered "a valuable social device which gives access to the patent system to groups who may have a legitimate concern about how well the granting authorities are striking the balance of interests at stake." Michael Spence described the opposition and appeals processes as follows:

> EPO opposition proceedings are determined by an Opposition Division made up of three technical examiners. During these proceedings a patent applicant may make amendments to a patent specification to save it, provided . . . that those amend-

ments do not add matter to that disclosed in the specification or extend the scope of the patent. An appeal from the decision of an Opposition Division lies with a Technical Board of Appeal. If a Board of Appeal decides that an appeal raises an important point of law it can refer the point to the Enlarged Board of Appeal. Similarly, if the President of the EPO believes that two Boards of Appeal have given conflicting decisions on a question of law, she may refer that question to the Enlarged Board of Appeal.

MICHAEL SPENCE, INTELLECTUAL PROPERTY 147 (2007).

2. Under the EPO approach in *Microsoft*, what is excluded as computer software *as such*? How does the EPO's analysis of this question differ from that of the *Symbian* court? Consider the following:

> The EPO does not grant patents for computer programs or computer-implemented business methods that make no technical contribution. Programs for computers as such are excluded from patentability by virtue of Art. 52(2)(c) and (3) EPC. According to this patent law, a program for a computer is not patentable if it does not have the potential to cause a "further technical effect" which must go beyond the inherent technical interactions between hardware and software.

> On the other hand, a CII [Computer Implemented Invention] (even in the form of a computer program) that can provide this further technical effect can be patentable, subject to the other patentability requirements, such as novelty and inventive step. In this case, it would be recognised as providing a technical solution to a technical problem.

> Let us demonstrate the effects of CII legislation with some real-life cases. The truth of the matter is this: Inventions that use computer programs to provide a business process—not a technical process—are not patentable.

> A patent application for an Internet auction system was not granted because the system used conventional computer technology and computer networks—which meant it made no inventive technical contribution to the level of existing technology. Such a system may provide business advancement to its users, but that is not the type of advancement required by the EPO. [*See Hitachi/Auction Method*, Case T258/03–3.5.01 (EPO (Technical Bd. App.), Apr. 21, 2004)]

> On the flip side, the problem of improving signal strengths between mobile phones is a technical problem, even if it is solved by modifications to the phone software rather than its hardware. Such an invention would obtain a patent, provided that the solution is also novel and inventive.

> In this respect, the granting practice of the EPO differs significantly from that of the United States Patent and Trade-

mark Office (USPTO), where patent protection for software is granted, even if it does not solve a technical problem.

EPO, *Patents for Software?*, http://www.epo.org/topics/issues/computer-implemented-inventions/software.html (last updated Dec. 12, 2008). Is a claimed process for online retailing that includes the use of a computer patentable under the EPO test? If the claim includes technical and non-technical elements, is it patentable under the EPO test? *See Comvik/Two Identities*, Case T0641/00–3.5.01 (EPO (Technical Bd. App.), Sept. 26, 2002) ("[I]t is legitimate to have a mix of technical and 'non-technical' features (*i.e.* features relating to non-inventions within the meaning of Art. 52(2) EPC) appearing in a claim, even if the non-technical features should form a dominating part.").

3. Some commentators have noted the EPO's increasing emphasis on technical character:

> What is emerging in the EPO is a shift of focus towards novelty and inventive step, bypassing the exclusions altogether. The Office is less concerned with excluded matter so long as technical character can be found. Indeed, the advice of EPO examiners is now to move beyond a consideration of technical character and to proceed directly to consider questions of novelty and inventive step. The rationale is that in assessing inventive step the examiner must establish which technical problem has been solved by the invention. If no technical problem can be found then the implication is that no technical character is present.

HECTOR MACQUEEN, CHARLOTTE WAELDE & GRAEME LAURIE, CONTEMPORARY INTELLECTUAL PROPERTY POLICY: LAW AND POLICY 529 (2007). Is this approach consistent with the current United States approach to recognizing the patentability of computer programs? Do you think the EPO should bypass the exclusions and focus on novelty and inventive step? Why or why not? Should patent eligible subject matter be a threshold question that must be answered before addressing novelty and inventive step?

4. The President of the EPO recently referred the following questions to be addressed by the Enlarged Board of Appeals of the EPO in an effort to seek clarity in the patentability of software:

> 1. Can a computer program only be excluded as a computer program as such if it is explicitly claimed as a computer program?

> 2.(a) Can a claim in the area of computer programs avoid exclusion under Art. 52(2)(c) and (3) merely by explicitly mentioning the use of a computer or a computer-readable data storage medium?

> 2.(b) If question 2(a) is answered in the negative, is a further technical effect necessary to avoid exclusion, said effect going beyond those effects inherent in the use of a computer

or data storage medium to respectively execute or store a computer program?

3.(a) Must a claimed feature cause a technical effect on a physical entity in the real world in order to contribute to the technical character of the claim?

3.(b) If question 3(a) is answered in the positive, is it sufficient that the physical entity be an unspecified computer?

3.(c) If question 3(a) is answered in the negative, can features contribute to the technical character of the claim if the only effects to which they contribute are independent of any particular hardware that may be used?

4.(a) Does the activity of programming a computer necessarily involve technical considerations?

4.(b) If question 4(a) is answered in the positive, do all features resulting from programming thus contribute to the technical character of a claim?

4.(c) If question 4(a) is answered in the negative, can features resulting from programming contribute to the technical character of a claim only when they contribute to a further technical effect when the program is executed?

Communication from the Enlarged Board of Appeal Concerning Case G 3/08, [2009] O.J. EPO 32. For additional commentary see Posting of David Pearce to IPKat, http://ipkitten.blogspot.com/2008/10/epo-enlarged-board-referral-on-software.html (Oct. 24, 2008, 19:54).

* * *

The next excerpt addresses patent protection for business method inventions in China, which includes a discussion of China's approach to patent eligible subject matter.

Zhang Yurong & Yu Xiang
The Patent Protection for Business Method Inventions in China
30 EUR. INTELL. PROP. REV. 412 (2008)

There has been a misconception that the protection for business methods by patents is prohibited in China. As a matter of fact, the Chinese Patent Law and its Implementing Regulations do not expressly prohibit business method patents. In the examination practice, [the State Intellectual Property Office ("SIPO")] takes a cautious approach towards the examination of business method patents. . . . In the current proceeding for the patent examination, the examiners of the SIPO evaluate the patentability of an invention involving business methods according to Guidelines for Examination . . . (hereinafter, "Guidelines 2006") entered into force on July 1, 2006. . . .

Statutory subject matter

In order to be patented under Chinese patent law for an invention, it must be considered patentable subject matter. Rule 2.1 of the Implementing Regulations of the Patent Law defines an invention as a new technical solution relating to a product, a process or improvement thereof. Therefore, the technical nature of an invention is a prerequisite for its qualifying for a patent. Based on this principle and other legal, political and social considerations, the Chinese Patent Law excludes some types of subject matter from patent protection. . . .

Art. 25.1 of the Patent Law expressly excludes five categories of subject matter from patent protection. This list includes the following:

- scientific discoveries;

- rules and methods for mental activities;

- methods for the diagnosis or for the treatment of diseases;

- animal and plant varieties; and substances obtained by means of nuclear transformation.

Since business method patents are often related to the rules and methods for mental activities under Rule 25.1(2) of the Patent Law, they are always considered to be un-patentable subject matter. . . .

Technical solution

. . . [A]ny application for a patent for an invention containing a computer program should satisfy the "three-element criteria". The invention which is used for solving technical problems by technical measures and may achieve a technical effect shall be the object of patent protection. This has been clarified also in the Guidelines 2006, in which it is stated that "an invention application relating to computer programs is the subject matter of patent protection only if it constitutes a technical solution". When, then, does an invention constitute a technical solution? According to the Guidelines 2006:

> ". . . if the solution of an invention application relating to computer programs involves the execution of computer programs in order to solve technical problems, and reflects technical means in conformity with the laws of nature by computers running programs to control and process external or internal objects, and thus technical effects in conformity with the laws of nature are obtained, the solution is a technical solution as provided for in Rule 2.1 and is the subject matter of patent protection."

According to such criterion, the examination for an invention relating to computer programs is even stricter than it used to be in determining whether or not the invention is a technical solution.

Rules and methods for mental activities are not patentable for involving no technical characteristic. According to the Guidelines 2006:

> " 'Mental activities' refer to human thinking movements ... Because they do not use technical means or apply the laws of nature, nor do they solve any technical problem or produce any technical effect, they do not constitute technical solutions. Rules and methods for mental activities not only fail to comply with Rule 2.1, but fall to be the circumstance as provided in Article 25.1(2)." ...

The current examination procedures for business method patents in China

... A business method application relating to computer programs is the patentable subject matter only if it constitutes a technical solution....

SIPO has set out a two-part test to determine whether or not a patent application on software-related business method should be granted.

- The first step: determining whether the claimed solution belongs to the rules and methods for mental activities under Art. 25.1(2) of the Patent Law. The method of determining is to consider whether the solution includes technical features. If only the solution includes technical features, it will be excluded from Art. 25.1(2) of the Patent Law.

- The second step: if the solution is excluded from Art. 25.1(2), it will further be examined whether it constitutes the "technical solution" of Rule 2.1 of the Implementing Regulations. The concrete way of determining is to identify whether it satisfies the "three-element criteria", namely, solving technical problems, using technical measures and producing a technical effect....

As far as China is concerned, Guidelines 2006 stipulate computer programs per se do not constitute the subject matter for patent protection. A business method invention application relating to computer programs is the subject matter of patent protection only if it constitutes a technical solution. Namely, it should meet the norm of the "three-element criteria". Moreover, the Guidelines 2006 also clarify that the three elements—solving technical problems, using technical measures and producing a technical effect—must be met simultaneously, which is different from the requirement for technical effect adopted by the EPO. Similarly, the Guidelines 2006 also deleted the "technical contribution" principle for determining whether an invention belongs to rules or methods for mental activities, which shows that SIPO has followed EPO.

Compared with the "technical character" of EPO, the examination principles of the "technical solution" and the "three-element criteria" of SIPO are much stricter. Therefore, the patentability standards for statutory subject matter in China are even higher than EPO, which adds to the difficulty in obtaining patent protection for business method inventions in China.

Notes and Questions

1. Why do you think China has adopted a stricter approach to patent eligible subject matter than the EPO? Are there historical, economic, or social considerations within China that would induce China to adopt a stricter approach to patentability? If the EPO's general approach to determining whether an invention falls within patent eligible subject matter is to analyze whether the invention satisfies novelty or nonobviousness, is China's approach really that different from that of the EPO?

2. This article was written before China adopted the Third Amendments to its patent law in 2008. These amendments took effect in October 2009. As of this publication, China has yet to adopt Implementing Regulations for the Third Amendments, which may raise new issues not addressed by the article.

B. MORAL UTILITY

The United States Patent Act contains no express authorization to withhold patent protection for lack of moral utility, although our courts and the United States Patent and Trademark Office have recognized that protection for an invention may be denied if "injurious to the well-being, good policy, or sound morals of society." *Lowell v. Lewis*, 15 F. Cas. 1018, 1019 (C.C.D. Mass. 1817) (No. 8568). The TRIPS Agreement expressly authorizes members to withhold patent protection. Article 27 states in pertinent part:

> Members may exclude from patentability inventions, the prevention within their territory of the commercial exploitation of which is necessary to protect *ordre public* or morality, including to protect human, animal or plant life or health or to avoid serious prejudice to the environment, provided that such exclusion is not made merely because the exploitation is prohibited by their law.

What exactly does this provision mean? Is a member state authorized to exclude from patentability an invention that runs afoul of public morality concerns? Does Article 27 actually envision a uniform worldwide rule, or does this text allow for variations in local views of morality and *ordre public*? The term *"ordre public"* is a term of art that is different from "public order." What does it mean?

European patent practice incorporates express authorizations for assessing inventions in light of public policy concerns, primarily with respect to biological inventions. Like the United States, the EPO supports the patentability of living things, including animals. In *HARVARD/Transgenic animal* (T–315/03), [2005] E.P.O.R. 31, the EPO found that certain claims to a transgenic mouse are patentable, and recognizing that "the law is clear: there is no excluded or excepted category of 'animals in general.' " However, ethical concerns have been raised for particular inventions when "living things" include human or human-derived material.

Article 1 of the Charter of Fundamental Rights of the European Union states: "Human dignity is inviolable. It must be respected and protected." Article 53 of the EPC provides that "European patents shall not be granted" for "inventions the commercial exploitation of which would be contrary to *ordre public* or morality. . . ." Additionally, Rule 28 of the EPC provides the following specific exclusions from patentability of biotechnological inventions:

(a) processes for cloning human beings;

(b) processes for modifying the germ line genetic identity of human beings;

(c) uses of human embryos for industrial or commercial purposes;

(d) processes for modifying the genetic identity of animals which are likely to cause them suffering without any substantial medical benefit to man or animal, and also animals resulting from such processes.

A biotechnological invention that falls within the enumerated categories of Rule 28 of the EPC is deemed unpatentable. Notably, these categories are not exhaustive. If a biotechnological invention does not fall within one of these categories, the patent claim must be assessed under Article 53 of the EPC. *See HARVARD/Transgenic animal* (T–315/03), *supra*.

Provisions corresponding to both Article 53 and Rule 28 of the EPC are stated in Article 6 of the European Parliament and Council Directive 98/44, Legal Protection of Biotechnological Inventions, 1998 O.J. (L 213) 13. These authorities are considered in the following case, which evaluates an invention relating to stem cell research.

WARF/STEM CELLS

EPO Enlarged Board of Appeal
[2009] E.P.O.R. 15

The present invention concerns *inter alia* human embryonic stem cell cultures which at the filing date could be prepared exclusively by a method which, necessarily involved the destruction of the human embryos from which they are derived, said method not being part of the claims. Rule 28 EPC provides, *inter alia*: "Under Article 53(a), European patents shall not be granted in respect of biotechnological inventions which, in particular, concern ... (c) uses of human embryos for industrial or commercial purposes". The question thus is whether the present invention falls under the prohibition of this provision....

On its face, the provision of Article 6(2)(c) of the Directive and thus also Rule 28(c) EPC is straightforward and prohibits the patenting if a human embryo is used for industrial or commercial purposes. Such a reading is also in line with the concern of the legislator to prevent a misuse in the sense of a commodification of human embryos and with one of the essential objectives of the whole Directive to protect human dignity. This concern is also evidenced by the selective policy of the Community in funding stem cell research. The Appellant argues that the very fact that the Community funds such research shows that the legislator did not want to exclude activities such as those underlying the present invention and which include the use (and destruction) of human embryos. However, Council press release 11554/06 (Presse 215) of 24 July 2006, states on page 7 that as regards Community Research "... the Commission confirmed that it will continue the current practice and will not submit to the Regulatory Committee proposals for projects which include research activities which destroy human embryos, including for the procurement of stem cells. The exclusion of funding for this step of research will not prevent the Community funding of subsequent steps involving human embryonic stem cells." This selective funding in no way supports the Appellant's position.

Against a reading of Rule 28(c) EPC being applicable to the invention in this case, the Appellant has put forward several arguments. Firstly it argues for a very specific meaning of embryo, as being embryos of 14 days or older, in accordance with usage in the medical field.

Neither the European Union legislator nor the EPC legislator have chosen to define the term "embryo", as used in the Directive or now in Rule 28 EPC. This contrasts with the German law where embryo is defined as including a fertilized egg, or the UK law

Section 1(1)) where embryo includes the two cell zygote and an egg in the process of fertilisation. The European Union and the EPC legislators must presumably have been aware of the definitions used in national laws on regulating embryos, and yet chose to leave the term undefined. Given the purpose to protect human dignity and prevent the commercialization of embryos, the Enlarged Board can only presume that "embryo" was not to be given any restrictive meaning in Rule 28 EPC, as to do so would undermine the intention of the legislator, and that what is an embryo is a question of fact in the context of any particular patent application.

Secondly the Appellant contends that, in order to fall under the prohibition of Rule 28(c) EPC, the use of human embryos must be claimed.

However, this Rule (as well as the corresponding provision of the Directive) does not mention claims, but refers to "invention" in the context of its exploitation. What needs to be looked at is not just the explicit wording of the claims but the technical teaching of the application as a whole as to how the invention is to be performed. Before human embryonic stem cell cultures can be used they have to be made. Since in the case referred to the Enlarged Board the only teaching of how to perform the invention to make human embryonic stem cell cultures is the use (involving their destruction) of human embryos, this invention falls under the prohibition of Rule 28(c) EPC. To restrict the application of Rule 28(c) EPC to what an applicant chooses explicitly to put in his claim would have the undesirable consequence of making avoidance of the patenting prohibition merely a matter of clever and skilful drafting of such claim.

In a case like the present one, where the teaching to obtain the embryonic human stem cells claimed is confined to the use (involving their destruction) of human embryos, the argument raised by the Appellant, namely that the exclusion from patentability would go much too far if one would consider all the steps preceding an invention for the purposes of Rule 28(c) EPC, is not relevant.

The Appellant further argues that the use of human embryos to make the claimed human embryonic stem cell cultures is not a use "for industrial or commercial purposes", as required by Rule 28(c) EPC, but some other form of use not prohibited by this Rule. A claimed new and inventive product must first be made before it can be used. Such making is the ordinary way commercially to exploit the claimed invention and falls within the monopoly granted, as someone having a patent application with a claim directed to this product has on the grant of the patent the right to exclude others from making or using such product. Making the claimed product remains commercial or industrial exploitation of the invention even where there is an intention to use that product for further research. On the facts which this Board must assume making the claimed product involves the destruction of human embryos. This use involving destruction is thus an integral and essential part of the industrial or commercial exploitation of the claimed invention, and thus violates the prohibition of Rule 28(c) EPC.

In the context of the terms "for industrial or commercial purposes" used in Rule 28 EPC and Article 6(2)c) of the Directive, the Appellant has also pointed to the legislative history of the Directive and argued that the replacement of the terms "methods in which human embryos are used" by "uses of human embryos for industrial or commercial purposes" meant a narrowing of the provision, excluding inventions such as the present one from its scope.

However, this Board cannot detect such a narrowing. The reason given in Point 37 of the Common Position for this amendment is that a distinction was wanted between the uses of human embryos for industrial or commercial purposes, which were excluded from patentability, and inventions for therapeutic or diagnostic purposes applied to the human embryo and useful to it, the latter not being excluded from patentability. To clarify this exception from the exception, a new Recital 42 was introduced into the Directive. Thus, if anything, these reasons point in the direction of the opinion of this Board that in the present case human embryos are used for industrial or commercial purposes, since patentability was only considered if the invention was to the benefit of the embryo itself. That this is not the case here is evident, since the embryos used to perform the invention are destroyed.

... [I]t is important to point out that it is not the fact of the patenting itself that is considered to be against *ordre public* or morality, but it is the performing of the invention, which includes a step (the use involving its destruction of a human embryo) that has to be considered to contravene those concepts....

For the reasons given above, the Enlarged Board of Appeal comes to the conclusion that the legislators (both the legislator of the Implementing Regulations to the EPC and of the Directive) wanted to exclude inventions such as the one underlying this referral from patentability and that in doing so, they have remained within the scope of Article 53(a) EPC and of the TRIPS Agreement. In view of this result, it is not necessary nor indeed appropriate to discuss further arguments and points of view put forward in these proceedings such as whether the standard of *ordre public* or morality should be a European one or not, whether it matters if research in certain European countries involving the destruction of human embryos to obtain stem cells is permitted, whether the benefits of the invention for humanity should be balanced against the prejudice to the embryo, or what the point in time is to assess *ordre public* or morality under Article 53(a) EPC. The legislators have decided, remaining within the ambit of Article 53(a) EPC, and there is no room for manoeuvre.

[The Panel next considered whether] it is of relevance that after the filing date the same products could be obtained without having to recur to a method necessarily involving the destruction of human embryos (here: e.g. derivation from available human embryonic cell lines).

When assessing whether a claim contravenes Rule 28(c) EPC, technical developments which became publicly available only, after the filing date cannot be taken into consideration. It cannot be relevant whether later either the applicant himself or others made something further available that would then have allowed the product to be made in an innocuous manner. Similarly to the case of an invention which is insufficiently described in the application as filed to be carried out, lack of any disclosure in the application as filed putting the skilled person in possession of a way to carry out the invention complying with Rule 28(c) EPC cannot be cured by the occurrence of subsequent technical developments. Any other conclusion would lead to legal uncertainty, and risk being to the detriment of any third party who later provided an innocuous way to carry out the invention. . . .

In view of the questions referred, this decision is not concerned with the patentability in general of inventions relating to human stem cells or human stem cell cultures. It holds unpatentable inventions concerning products (here human stem cell cultures) which can only be obtained by the use involving their destruction of human embryos.

Notes and Questions

1. *WARF/Stem Cells* considers patentability that necessarily results in the destruction of an embryo by applying the categorical exclusions of Rule 28(c) EPC. In contrast, Article 53 of the EPC prohibits patenting of "inventions the commercial exploitation of which would be contrary to *ordre public* or morality," which does not include similar mandatory categories.

In *Howard Florey/Relaxin*, [1995] E.P.O.R. 541, the Opposition Division of the EPO relied on Article 53(a) to assess objections to the patentability of DNA derived from the tissue obtained from pregnant women. Rejecting an objection that this invention was an offense against human dignity to make use of a female pregnancy for a technical process oriented to make a profit, the Opposition Division explained:

> [T]he patenting of the DNA would indeed be abhorrent to the overwhelming majority of the public if it were true that the invention involved the patenting of human life, an abuse of pregnant women, a return to slavery and the piecemeal sale of women to industry. However, the Opposition Division emphatically rejects these arguments.
>
> With regard to the isolation of mRNA from tissue taken from pregnant women, the proprietor stated that the women who donated tissue consented to do so within the framework of necessary gynaecological operations. There is no reason to perceive this as immoral. Indeed, human tissue or other material, such as blood, bone, and so on, has been widely used for many years as a source for useful products, often proteins but now also RNA or DNA, which are unavailable elsewhere.

Additionally, *Howard Florey/Relaxin* rejected the view that patenting DNA derived from human sources was akin to patenting human life, observing that "DNA is not 'life,' but a chemical substance which carries genetic information and can be used as an intermediate in the production of proteins which may be medically useful."

Compare the *WARF/Stem Cells* approach, which applied Rule 28(c) of the EPC without balancing any medical benefits from the invention, observing "there is no room for manoeuvre." With respect to Article 53(a), what competencies must courts and patent examiners possess to assess such evidence? *See generally* Cynthia M. Ho, *Splicing, Morality and Patent Law: Issues Arising from Mixing Mice and Men*, 2 WASH. U. J.L. & POL'Y 247, 283 (2000) ("The evolution of the morality preclusion demonstrates that including a morality component into the patentability scheme is analogous to opening a Pandora's box.").

2.   To what degree can a decision maker separate personal moral views on difficult questions of application? In *HARVARD/Transgenic animal* (T–315/03), *supra*, the Board of Appeals emphasized the role of the Opposition Division in considering challenges to particular patents on moral grounds:

> [An appellant argues] that it was not established that the opinion of the four members of the Opposition Division was representative (of, the Board assumes, European society). The Board agrees with the respondent that the Opposition Division was under no obligation to establish any such thing. The Opposition Division was not required to form its own opinion and then somehow establish that such opinion was representative of a wider group. Quite the contrary, the task of the Opposition Division was to assess whether or not the exploitation of the invention conformed with conventionally-accepted standards of conduct in European society. The Opposition Division had to make that decision, as with all decisions

between opposing parties, only on the basis of the evidence placed before it by the parties in support of their arguments and with no consideration for personal opinions. Similarly it is the task of the Board to decide, in the light of the evidence before the first instance and any further evidence permitted on appeal, whether the first instance decision made that assessment correctly. The actual opinion or opinions of the members of the Opposition Division (or the Board) are irrelevant.

Is such a division possible in difficult cases? What safeguards might be built into the system to assist in making such division?

3. *WARF/Stem Cells* observed that the fact that the cells used to practice the invention originated in human embryos was sufficient to deny the patent, although the patent claim did not specify the source of the cells. Consider a similar issue addressed in *Howard Florey/Relaxin*, where the invention derived from the human tissue from pregnant women:

> A patent confers on its proprietor the right to exclude for a limited period of time third parties from commercially using the patented invention. It cannot be overemphasised that patents covering DNA encoding human H2–relaxin, or any other human gene do not confer on their proprietors any rights whatever to individual human beings, any more than do patents directed to other human products such as proteins, including human H2–relaxin. . . . The whole point about gene cloning is that the protein encoded by the cloned gene—in this case human H2–relaxin—is produced in a technical manner from unicellular hosts containing the corresponding DNA; there is therefore no need to use human beings as a source for the protein. The only stage at which a woman was involved was at the beginning of the making of the invention, as a (voluntary) source for the relaxin mRNA.

How far may a claimed invention be removed from its human source to invoke moral utility concerns? The *Howard Florey/Relaxin* approach has been argued to rely on one of a "cadre of techniques which fall short of actually addressing the substance of the objection." Amanda Warren–Jones, *Morally Regulating Innovation: What Is Commercial Exploitation?*, 2008 INTELL. PROP. Q. 2, 193–212.

4. Recently, the United States Patent and Trademark Office rejected an application for a biotechnological invention on moral utility grounds. *See* Office Action on U.S. Patent Application No. 08/993,564 (filed Dec. 03, 2002). The application sought protection for a chimeric embryo that incorporated both human and non-human cells. The rejection observed that humans are "not eligible for patents." Additionally, the rejection recognized that "the exclusionary rights con-

veyed by a patent would be difficult to apply at best to humans in view of the constitutional rights of human persons."

By contrast, a patent for claims directed to mice implanted with human tissue was allowed according to the EPO Opposition Division. *R. v. Leland Stanford/Modified Animal*, [2002] E.P.O.R. 2. The medical benefits of the invention included the only available animal model for testing for HIV–I infection, and for testing of anti-AIDS therapies prior to conducting human trials. The court balanced the benefits of the invention in assessing patentability:

> [I]t is undeniable that the production of chimeric animals containing human organs grown from human cells isolated from aborted foetuses or deceased persons, whether children or adults, instinctively appears distasteful, if not immoral, to many people at first glance. On the other hand, the medical benefits conferred by the invention are not in dispute among the parties to the present proceedings ... , and the use of donated human material for research is widely accepted provided consent was given, which there is no reason to doubt in the present case.... The practice of each individual embodiment of every invention in the medical field is subject to approval by the appropriate regulatory bodies in the Contracting States; in consequence, it is possible for every state to authorise only those embodiments deemed acceptable in that state.

In light of the conflict between the applicable standards, is a worldwide, harmonized standard under Article 27(2) of TRIPS possible?

C. PRIORITY, PRIOR ART, GRACE PERIOD, AND BEST MODE

The main difference between the United States patent system and those of other countries is the first-to-invent system. The United States Congress has considered legislation to move the United States patent system closer to a first-to-file system. The first-inventor-to-file system, for example, has been advanced to provide a compromise between the two systems. There remain significant differences in Europe and the United States between the use of prior art for determining novelty. There are additional concerns over the so-called grace period. The first excerpt is from the Senate Report accompanying the proposed 2007 Patent Reform Act. Although Congress failed to pass the bill, this report remains relevant and provides the context of efforts to modify United States patent law, as well as the fundamental policy questions such modifications have raised.

1. PRIORITY: FIRST-TO-INVENT VERSUS FIRST-TO-FILE

The Patent Reform Act of 2007

S. Rep. No. 110–259 (2008)

First inventor to file; grace period; and prior art

There are three significant, practical differences between the [first-to-invent and first-to-file] systems. The first concerns the rare instance in which two different people file patent applications for the same invention. In a first-to-file system, the application with the earlier filing date prevails and will be awarded the patent, if one issues. In the first-to-invent system, a lengthy, complex and costly administrative proceeding (called an "interference proceeding") must be conducted to determine who actually invented first. . . .

The second difference involves prior art. A patent will not issue if it is not new, or if it would have been obvious to someone in the relevant area of technology. . . . In the first-to-file system, prior art[, commonly other patents and printed publications] includes all art that exists prior to the filing date—again, an objective inquiry. In contrast, in a first-to-invent system, prior art is measured from the more amorphous date of invention.

Third, in some first-to-file systems, prior art can include the inventor's own disclosure of his invention prior to the filing date of his application. . . . Thus, inventors in first-to-file systems must keep their inventions secret prior to filing applications for them, thereby sacrificing a significant part of one of the benefits of the patent system—disclosure of inventions. Although some first-to-file systems do provide the inventor with a grace period, some do not. In contrast, the United States' first-to-invent system provides the inventor with a grace period of one year. . . .

The first-to-file system is used in every patent system, other than the United States, because it has the advantages of simplicity, efficiency and predictability. A first-to-file system avoids costly interference proceedings, provides better notice to the public, simplifies the prior art scheme that may preclude a patent from issuing, and provides more certainty to the patent system [and] encourages the prompt filing of patent applications. . . .

United States' applicants, who also want to file abroad, are forced to follow and comply with two different filing systems. Maintaining a filing system so different from the rest of the world disadvantages United States' applicants, the majority of which also file in other countries.

Notes and Questions

1. Does the first-to-invent system help small inventors? Consider the following excerpt:

> Since small inventors—and particularly individual inventors—have led the fight against patent harmonization, it seems particularly important to determine whether small inventors in fact benefit from the first to invent system. An important recent study by Gerald Mossinghoff ... studied all 2,858 interference decisions between 1983 and 2000 in order to determine whether small inventors were actually more likely to prevail in priority disputes. He found that the first to invent system did not benefit small inventors on average....
>
> We [studied] one other aspect of the dispute that has relevance ... : on whose behalf the interference proceeding was initiated. Initiation matters because it is the party on whose behalf the interference is being initiated ... who might be thought to be the one who stands to benefit from the interference system....
>
> The results are striking. Of the 94 initiating parties for which status data were available, only 17 (or 18%) were individuals or small businesses, while 72 (77%) were large entities. By contrast, of the 145 respondents in an interference for which data was available, 63 (or 43%) were individuals or small businesses, while 77 (53%) were large entities. These findings are significant because they suggest that interference proceedings are more often used by large entities to challenge the priority of small entities, not the reverse.... This makes some intuitive sense. Large, sophisticated entities are more likely to understand the patent system, including the rather arcane interference process, and use it to their advantage. Small entities tend to be less sophisticated about patents, and may not take full advantage of interferences.

Mark A. Lemley & Colleen V. Chien, *Are the U.S. Patent Priority Rules Really Necessary?*, 54 HASTINGS L.J. 1299 (2003).

2. In light of the limitations imposed by the Intellectual Property Clause of the United States Constitution (Article I, Section 8, Clause 8), could the United States move to a first-to-file system—and if so, how?

2. PRIOR ART

This section addresses some issues concerning prior art in the international context. For purposes of § 102(b) of the United States Patent Act, prior art does not include a public use of the invention or the invention on sale outside of the United States. Section 102(a) also does not include public knowledge or use outside of the United States as prior art. Foreign prior art is relevant in the United States only if the invention was either patented abroad or described in a printed publication. Thus, an inventor may be able to obtain a patent in the United States for an invention that may have been on sale, in public use, or in public knowledge outside of the United States. *But see* 35 U.S.C. § 102(f) (2006) ("A person shall be entitled to a patent unless . . . he did not himself invent the subject matter to be patented").

As discussed in the next excerpt, commentators argue that §§ 102(a)–(b) allow for the patenting of some inventions, at one level of development or another, including some forms of "traditional knowledge," that are in public use or on-sale outside of the United States. Notably, there is not a universal definition of "traditional knowledge." For a discussion of the difficulties in defining traditional knowledge, see WIPO INTERGOVERNMENTAL COMMITTEE ON INTELLECTUAL PROPERTY, GENETIC RESOURCES, TRADITIONAL KNOWLEDGE, AND FOLKLORE, TRADITIONAL KNOWLEDGE—OPERATIONAL TERMS AND DEFINITIONS (2002). The following is one definition:

> WIPO currently uses the term "traditional knowledge" to refer to tradition-based literary, artistic or scientific works; performances; inventions; scientific discoveries; designs; marks, names and symbols; undisclosed information; and all other tradition-based innovations and creations resulting from intellectual activity in the industrial, scientific, literary or artistic fields. "Tradition-based" refers to knowledge systems, creations, innovations and cultural expressions which: have generally been transmitted from generation to generation; are generally regarded as pertaining to a particular people or its territory; and, are constantly evolving in response to a changing environment. Categories of traditional knowledge could include: agricultural knowledge; scientific knowledge; technical knowledge; ecological knowledge; medicinal knowledge, including related medicines and remedies; biodiversity-related knowledge; "expressions of folklore" in the form of music, dance, song, handicrafts, designs, stories and artwork; elements of languages, such as names, geographical indications and symbols; and, movable cultural properties. Excluded from this description of TK would be items not resulting from intellectual activity in the industrial, scientific, literary or artistic fields, such as human remains, languages in general, and other similar elements of "heritage" in the broad sense.

WIPO, *Glossary of Terms*, http://www.wipo.int/tk/en/glossary/#tk (last visited July 17, 2009).

* * *

In the following materials, the preceding definition of traditional knowledge or some variation of the concept is used. Another related issue concerns the use of biodiversity resources from a country without attributing the source, obtaining informed consent from the custodians, or sharing any profits made from the commercial exploitation of those resources. This is sometimes referred to as "biopiracy."

Margo A. Bagley
Patently Unconstitutional: The Geographical Limitation on Prior Art in a Small World
87 Minn. L. Rev. 679 (2003)

The novelty requirement, originally unlimited by geography in the first two patent acts, was limited by the Patent Act of 1836 to barring inventions, publicly known, used, or sold in the United States, or described in foreign patents or printed publications anywhere in the world. This distinction apparently arose, at least in part, from a perception that foreign knowledge or use was not sufficiently accessible to the interested public in the United States for it to be deemed to be in the global public domain. . . .

Technological Change and "New Libraries"

The world has grown considerably smaller since the passage of the 1836 Patent Act with its geographical limitation on prior art. The development of technology enabling global travel and information transfer at increasing rates of speed have played a role in creating the global village in which we now live. . . .

For example, over the past few decades the pharmaceutical industry has enormously increased research-related travel and ethnobiological research of indigenous groups. Ethnobiological research refers to studying the knowledge of "indigenous peoples about the utility, diversity and chemical characteristics of plants found in their environment." In 1989, the worldwide market value for drugs derived from medicinal plant knowledge of indigenous peoples was approximately $43 billion. Another study found that 57% of the top 150 prescription drugs contained at least one major active compound now or at one time derived from biological sources. Also, in a different survey of 119 known useful plant-derived drugs, 74% had "the same or related use as the plants from which they were derived." In other words, indigenous groups were using the plants from which the drug was derived to cure the same ailments for which the patented drug is now being prescribed.

In a related development, the past decade has witnessed the formation of several bioprospector contracts between developing countries and transnational corporations. Examples include agreements between the pharmaceutical giant Merck and the Costa Rican government; Bristol–Myers Squibb and the governments of Suriname and Costa Rica; an agreement between Shaman Pharmaceuticals and the Aguaruna Indians of Peru; the launching of a biodiversity research program in Micronesia by Japan; and NIH sponsored initiatives between Monsanto and the Cayetano Peruvian University to study plants from the Andean rain forest. . . .

Importantly, eliminating the § 102(b) geographical limitation will not prevent foreign public knowledge or use from being used in the invention process. Rather, eliminating the limitation will simply mean that the invention that is ultimately patented must be novel and nonobvious in view of that foreign prior art. . . .

A. *Piracy and Biopiracy*

While the changes in research habits noted . . . are yielding beneficial discoveries, they are also, in some cases, causing considerable problems. Where the research culminates in the patenting of information derived from the traditional knowledge or genetic resources of indigenous peoples in developing countries, it is often labeled "biopiracy." The term biopiracy has been defined as "the patenting of plants, genes, and other biological products that are indigenous to a foreign country" without compensating the keepers of those resources and the holders of knowledge appropriated during the ethnobiological research process. . . . As explained by one commentator: "What developing tropical nations are saying is that if the West cries foul over piracy of intellectual property, [such as] computer software, then biopiracy in Western labs of jungle extracts should also be considered a high economic crime."

The geographical limitation contained in § 102(b) facilitates biopiracy by preventing evidence of foreign knowledge or use from being considered in patentability and patent validity proceedings. . . . [T]o the extent biopiracy decimates or prevents the creation of foreign industries . . ., it may increase the need for continuing U.S. aid to developing countries as opposed to helping those countries move towards self-sufficiency. . . .

The Mexican Enola bean controversy illustrates how § 102(b) can serve as a barrier to U.S. trade for foreigners. There, Mexican bean importers (at least one of whom had started her business to capitalize on the free trade opportunities created by NAFTA [North American Free Trade Agreement]) and the farmers they represent, were effectively barred from the U.S. yellow bean import business by the grant of a patent whose acquisition appears to have been facilitated by § 102(b)'s geographical limitation. This is unfortunate in many respects. It negatively impacts the farmers, importers, and their families, as well as the communities in which they operate and, perhaps only marginally, Mexico's ability to increase its gross domestic product, exports, and employed labor force. . . .

B. Policies Underlying Section 102(b)

In addition to facilitating biopiracy, the geographical limitation undermines at least [one of the] well-established policies that justify § 102(b)'s existence[:] "(1) discouraging the removal, from the public domain, of inventions that the public reasonably has come to believe are freely available. . . ." The geographical limitation is problematic from the first policy standpoint in three different scenarios. First, it allows third parties to patent information publicly known or used in a foreign country even though they were not aware of the earlier knowledge or use. Second, it facilitates violations of § 102(f) by making it easier for third parties to patent derived information from foreign sources that they did not themselves invent. Lastly, it allows inventors to make and use their inventions in foreign countries for a potentially unlimited period of time before filing for a U.S. application as long as the inventions are not otherwise patented or described in a printed publication. . . .

C. Harmonization: The Urge to Merge

An additional consequence of an even smaller world is an increase in efforts by nations to harmonize their laws and enter treaties to facilitate world trade. . . .

Probably the most significant regional treaty is the Convention on the Grant of European Patents (EPC), signed in 1973 by a group of countries seeking to create a uniform European patent system. The EPC . . . contains substantive and procedural requirements for obtaining a European patent (valid in all member countries) with only a single application. Article 54 of the EPC, which defines novelty, states in pertinent part,

> 1. An invention shall be considered to be new if it does not form part of the state of the art.

> 2. The state of the art shall be held to comprise everything made available to the public by means of a written or oral description, by use, or in any other way, before the date of filing of the European patent application.

The determination of the nonobviousness of the invention, or the presence of an "inventive step" as denoted in the EPC, is also made with reference to the state of the art as defined in Article 54. Consequently, evidence of foreign public knowledge or use has been admissible in EPO proceedings and infringement litigation for over two decades. In fact, this broad, geographically neutral definition of prior art is what enabled evidence of foreign public use in India to be used to revoke Grace's European patent on neem. . . .

[I]n Japan, applicants cannot patent

[i]nventions which were publicly known in Japan or elsewhere; . . . inventions which were publicly worked in Japan or elsewhere; . . . inventions which were described in a distributed publication or made available to the public through electric telecommunication lines in Japan or elsewhere prior to the filing of the patent application.

A 1998 report prepared by the Planning Subcommittee of Japan's Industrial Property Council identified three key reasons for revising the definition of novelty-destroying information: (1) a perception that granting patents in Japan on technology in the global public domain would delay the development of Japanese industry since Japanese inventors and companies would be unable to use the technology; (2) allowing the patenting of technology in the global public domain gives the impression that Japan is an imitator, not a pioneer in technology development; and (3) while "surveying" (i.e., accessing) foreign known and worked inventions was difficult at the time the old law was enacted in 1959, it has now become relatively easy to access such information so the rule should be "expanded to include the entire world." . . .

Section 102(b) [also] promotes and allows monopoly prices here on goods that could possibly be purchased more cheaply in other countries where the subject matter is not patentable and competition is thus available. . . .

For all of the above reasons, a move by the United States to a definition of prior art inclusive of foreign knowledge or use must be a question of "when," not "if."

Notes and Questions

1. For a response to Professor Bagley, see Craig Allen Nard, *In Defense of Geographic Disparity*, 88 MINN. L. REV. 222 (2003). In that response, Professor Nard argued in favor of keeping geographic difference to provide an incentive to commercialize traditional knowledge and reimbursement to holders of traditional knowledge. Which position do you find more convincing: Professor Bagley or Nard?

2. The United States utility patent covering the Mexican Enola Bean was recently rejected after a reexamination proceeding. That rejection was subsequently affirmed in significant respects by the

Board of Patent Appeals and Interferences—almost 10 years after the patent was first granted by the United States Patent and Trademark Office in 1999. *See* Ex Parte *POD–NERS*, No. 2007–3938, 2008 WL 1901980 (B.P.A.I. Apr. 29, 2008). Is that fair? *See* Press Release, ETC Group, Hollow Victory: Enola Bean Patent Smashed at Last (Maybe) (Apr. 29, 2008), *available at* http://www.etcgroup.org/en/materials/publications.html?pub_id=683 (" 'Mexican and U.S. farmers who suffered damages from this unjust monopoly will never be compensated for their losses.' "). In July 2009, the Federal Circuit affirmed the decision of the Board of Patent Appeals and Interferences. In re *POD–NERS*, No. 2008–1492, 2009 WL 2029976 (Fed. Cir. Jul 10, 2009) (unpublished) (affirming obviousness determination based on prior art publication).

3. Some countries, such as India, have used databases to ensure that their traditional knowledge is prior art and to prevent the patenting of such important knowledge. How effective are these databases? What are their strengths and weaknesses? Note that the creation of these databases is significantly different from introducing intellectual property laws to allow for greater exploitation of traditional knowledge.

Li Xuan
Novelty and Inventive Step: Obstacles to Traditional Knowledge Protection under Patent Regimes: A Case Study in China
29 Eur. Intell. Prop. Rev. 134 (2007)

The protection of Traditional Knowledge (TK) has become one of the major issues in the area of the intellectual property. While some advocate establishing a sui generis regime to protect TK, others consider existing intellectual property (IP) system is appropriate to protect TK. From a social welfare perspective, the establishment of a sui generis regime is not efficient if the existing IP regime is already adequate to protect TK. . . . As China is one of the largest TK holding countries in the world and the Chinese Patent Law has been the longest implemented patent regime on traditional medicinal knowledge protection since 1993, Chinese patent experience on TK protection becomes particularly relevant for the current debate. . . .

Is TK prior art?

It is a disputed question whether TK constitutes prior art. There is no definite answer given the diversified characteristics of TK and national patent regimes. Two steps are needed to examine the novelty of TK. The first step is to examine how TK is made public from a patent examination perspective: i.e. (1) the TK has been published; (2) the TK has been used and known publicly; and (3) the TK has been spread orally. The second step is to examine how prior art is defined in different legal regimes: distinctions are made between means of publicity, geography of publicity, time of publicity, absolute and relative novelty. . . .

[I]n principle, China adopts the similar definition of prior art to that of the United States. However, unlike the United States, where most TK originates from foreign countries, China is one of the largest TK-holding countries where most TK originates from China. Thus how China defines novelty in patent search practice becomes more interesting for the current debate on TK. Would Chinese TK be defined as prior art? Or, would it still be possible for Chinese TK to acquire the patent in spite of novelty requirement?

Chinese novelty examination practice

The above mentioned two-step methodology can be applied to examine the novelty of TK in China. The first step is to examine the means with which TK is made public. In this regard, it is noted that there are two types of traditional medicinal knowledge in China: (1) traditional Chinese medicinal knowledge (TCM); and (2) traditional indigenous knowledge (TIK). TCM is mainly developed and accumulated by the Han people, the ethnic majority in China. Most of TCM are documented in ancient classic medical books written Chinese characters, e.g. Shang Han Lun (Typhus Theory) and Ben Cao Gang Mu (Herbal Systematics). However, the fact that a large amount of TCM is in the form of codified knowledge does not prevent follow-up TK development and evolution on the basis of publicly known TCM while keeping newly developed TCM inventions undisclosed. Therefore TCM can be either documented in publications or kept secret. On the other hand, TIK is mainly developed and accumulated by 55 minority ethnicities in China, such as the Miao, Dong and Zhuang people, among others. The majority of TIK is non-documented and has been disseminated only orally within the certain closed communities in China, primarily because many minority ethnicities do not have their independent written systems, or only have incomplete or non-popularised characters historically. According to the practice of Chinese indigenous communities, TIK is inherited and transmitted through three major channels: ancestors, masters and the community. Among the three channels, inheritance from ancestors is the dominant form. Notably, most TIK was transmitted orally with confidentiality, which implies that the majority of TIK in the indigenous community is not prior art but undisclosed information.

The second step is to examine the practice of prior art search in China. The novelty of a patent application will be examined on the basis of the "technical equivalence" principle. In other words, a patent application for TK loses its novelty only when there exists an identical invention prior to the receipt of the said application.... Currently, in terms of number of patent applications filed by Chinese citizens, TCM ranks the first among various sectors, while the multipleherb prescription is among the most patented TCM. Therefore novelty has not been a real obstacle to the patentability of TCM.

For those undocumented TIK, though the Chinese Patent Office adopts a relative novelty standard whereby a patent will not be granted if the invention was known or used by others in China before the invention thereof by the applicant for patent, Chinese patent examination practices demonstrate that it is more complicated in determining whether TIK constitutes prior art than the case of TCM. For example, in reviewing patent applications, the Chinese Patent Office does not consider some local names of TIK that are only known to indigenous community as publicly known names. On the one hand, although some TIK is known or used in the community, the way this TIK is used does not make it prior art because the TIK is only known to an indigenous community with local names. On the other hand, a significant amount of TIK is not in the public domain, as it is inherited and has been kept secret within close family lineage only. As such, this TIK meets the novelty requirements of patent law and can therefore benefit from the protection of patent law. From the novelty examination practices of TCM and TIK in China, it is considered that novelty requirement is not an obstacle for TIK to be patented.

Notes and Questions

1. According to Li Xuan, in China, novelty will not provide much of a hurdle to patenting TCM (traditional Chinese medicinal knowledge) and TIK (traditional indigenous knowledge). In the next section on inventive step, we will see how that requirement can provide a more substantial hurdle to the patenting of TCM and TIK in China.

2. One of the changes in the recent amendments to the Chinese Patent Law concerns what may be considered prior art:

> Currently, Article 22 of [the Chinese] Patent Law makes use of a two-pronged approach to novelty. That is, while an absolute novelty standard is applied to publications, a relative novelty standard is applied to prior public use or public knowledge. As such, a publication anywhere in the world concerning a relevant invention is deemed as prior art, but prior public use such as sales, offers for sale, and manufacturing outside China is not prior art and does not destroy novelty. The current law, therefore, creates an often exploited loophole by Chinese companies to usurp patent protection in China for another's invention. Such a situation may occur when a product is disclosed to the public at a foreign trade show, but

without any publications, and a third party races to the State
Intellectual Property Office (SIPO) and files a Chinese patent
application on the product. . . .

The . . . Amendment eliminates this loophole by introducing an absolute novelty requirement. Under the amended
Article 22, the territorial restriction on prior public use and
knowledge has been removed, and an invention loses its novelty in China from any prior public disclosure in the world. The
inclusion of an absolute novelty requirement will force patent
practitioners to adjust their patent application strategies. For
jurisdictions which enjoy a grace period, such as in the
U.S. . . . utilization of that period before filing a Chinese
patent application will destroy the novelty of the invention.

Phong Nguyen, *Changing Landscape: Introduction to the Third
Amendment to the Chinese Patent Law*, ABA Bus. L. Sec. eNewsletter
(July 2, 2009), *available at* http://www.abanet.org/buslaw/committees/
CL983500pub/newsletter/200906/nguyen.pdf.

3.   There are several proposals, in one form or another, to modify
international treaties such as TRIPS and the PCT to require disclosure
of the source of biodiversity resources and traditional knowledge. For
example, several countries, including Brazil, have proposed to amend
TRIPS by adding a new Article 29*bis* that mandates disclosure, while
Switzerland has proposed an amendment to the PCT Regulations to
explicitly enable national patent legislation to require such disclosure.
See Peter K. Yu, *Cultural Relics, Intellectual Property, and Intangible
Heritage*, 81 Temple L. Rev. 433, 434–40 (2008). Given that such
disclosure does not result in the denial of the patent, what purpose
does it serve? Does it matter whether the disclosure requirement is
mandatory or optional?

4.   While these proposals have yet to be adopted, individual countries are enacting legislation to protect their biodiversity resources and
traditional knowledge. As previously mentioned, one approach includes
the creation of traditional knowledge databases. Another is exemplified
by the recent amendments to the Chinese Patent Law. Article 26 of the
amended law provides:

With respect to an invention or creation made by relying on
the genetic resource, the applicant shall explain the direct
source and original source of the genetic resource in the
patent application documents. If the applicant cannot explain
the original source, the applicant shall state the reasons.

Article 5 states further:

No patent right shall be granted for any invention or creation
made by relying on the genetic resources the acquisition or use
of which is contrary to the provisions of laws or administrative
regulations.

Would a failure to "explain the direct source and original source of the genetic resource in the patent application" violate Article 5 and result in forfeiture of a patent? Does Article 26 only require disclosure of a genetic resource from China? Why would a country want to know the origin of the genetic resources that were used in developing the patented invention? If you support a disclosure requirement, why is China such an important country to adopt a genetic resources disclosure requirement? Does it matter whether other countries impose a similar requirement? Would such a requirement impede invention and innovation? Are there other concerns?

3. GRACE PERIOD

Phillip W. Grubb
Patents for Chemicals, Pharmaceuticals and Biotechnology: Practice and Strategy

(Oxford University Press 2005)

A grace period may be defined as a period of time before the filing date of an application during which certain types of prior art do not invalidate the application. Depending upon the applicable law, it may refer to any publications of the invention deriving directly or indirectly from the applicant, or be restricted to exceptional situations such as public in breach of confidence. The first type of grace period, allowing a valid application to be filed even after deliberate publication by the inventor, is found for example in Australia, Brazil, Canada, Malaysia, Mexico and the Philippines (12 months) and in Japan, Korea, and Taiwan (6 months). In some of these, for example Brazil, Japan, and Korea, the benefit of the grace period must be claimed on filing, or shortly after, in the others this is not necessary. In Mexico, the grace period applies before the priority application is filed, so that it is possible to publish an invention in the UK, file a British patent application 11 months later, and file a valid Mexican application claiming the UK priority date within the following year. In the other countries this is not possible, the national filing must itself be made within 12 or 6 months of the publication. . . .

It has from time to time been proposed that a grace period should become a feature of the European patent system. It is felt that the present system is unduly harsh to individual inventors and academic scientists who may publish their results before realizing that they may be commercially interesting. On the other hand, the possibility the patent applications could still be validly filed even after an invention had been published would greatly increase the difficulty of estimating whether a manufacturer's proposed action would infringe any other party's patent rights. Applicants publishing their inventions before filing in reliance on a grace period would be faced with complex requirements, different deadlines in different countries, and loss of rights in those countries in which grace periods did not exist. . . .

It is frequently said that the US patent system works well with a grace period, but what the USA has is something different. If the critical date for prior art purposes is the invention date and not the filing date, then a publication by the inventor is not prior art at all. A grace period excludes something from the prior art which *a priori* is within it, but what the USA has is a statutory bar that after 12 months makes something prior art which originally was not. This is logical in the context of a first-to-invent system, but makes no sense in a first-to-file system.

Notes and Questions

1. The United States and Japan have different lengths of grace periods. What are the advantages or disadvantages of each respective period? How would the grace period interact with the priority period under the Paris Convention? Article 30 of the Japanese Patent Act also states the conditions under which a patent applicant can benefit from the grace period, such as the inventor's presentation of her invention in a printed publication or through electronic transmission, and testing of the invention. Should conditions be added to United States patent law—and if so, what conditions?

2. One author describes the differences between Vietnam's and United States' treatment of a grace period:

> Similar to most other first-to-file systems, Vietnam has adopted a disclosure-specific grace period, in which only certain categories of disclosure are qualified to take advantage of a grace period [of six months]. According to the novelty provisions of the United States patent law, there is no restriction on the type of disclosures available during the grace period that will be considered for novelty and non-obviousness. In contrast, Vietnam patent law restricts the disclosure exemptions to three disclosure-qualified categories: abusive disclosure by a third party, display at an international exhibition, and presentation in the form of a scientific report.

Nguyen Nguyet Dzung, *Vietnam Patent Law: Substantive Law Provisions and Existing Uncertainties*, 6 CHI.-KENT J. INTELL. PROP. 138 (2007).

3. Do you think it is likely that the United States will unilaterally adopt a first-to-file system? If so, why? If not, what would the United States ask in return?

4. The adoption of the Bayh–Dole Act in the United States has, among other potential causes, led to an increase of patenting and licensing activities by universities. *See* DAVID C. MOWERY ET AL., IVORY TOWER AND INDUSTRIAL INNOVATION: UNIVERSITY-INDUSTRY TECHNOLOGY TRANS-

FER BEFORE AND AFTER THE BAYH-DOLE ACT 1 (2004). The one-year grace period in the United States allows inventors, including university researchers, to file their patent applications one year after publication of their research results. It takes into account the desire for some United States inventors who are academic researchers to publish their research results. Moreover, academic research can be basic—near the laboratory bench—and knowledge of whether the research will be commercially valuable may not be known at the time of invention. The one-year grace period can provide university researchers and other inventors with the opportunity to determine whether their invention is commercially viable before applying for either a regular or a provisional patent. Many developed countries have adopted or are considering adopting laws similar to the Bayh–Dole Act. Will this provide pressure to adopt a general grace period in Europe or perhaps a longer grace period in Japan? Are academic researchers in Europe and Japan disadvantaged as against academic researchers in the United States? Should the United States have a longer grace period? *See* Margo Bagley, *Academic Discourse and Proprietary Rights: Putting Patents in Their Proper Place*, 47 B.C. L. REV. 217 (2006).

4. BEST MODE

Section 112 of the United States Patent Act states that "[t]he specification . . . shall set forth the best mode contemplated by the inventor of carrying out his invention." This best mode requirement, however, is only optional under the TRIPS Agreement. Article 29(1) provides:

> Members shall require that an applicant for a patent shall disclose the invention in a manner sufficiently clear and complete for the invention to be carried out by a person skilled in the art and may require the applicant to indicate the best mode for carrying out the invention known to the inventor at the filing date or, where priority is claimed, at the priority date of the application.

Why does the United States require patent applicants to disclose "the best mode," even though other countries do not include such a requirement? Is the inclusion of such a requirement beneficial to the country? If so, who are the beneficiaries?

As mentioned earlier, in an increasingly globalized environment, inventors are likely to obtain patents in more than one country. As far as the best mode requirement is concerned, would the inclusion of this requirement in the United States successfully transform the *optional* TRIPS requirement into a *de facto* multilateral requirement—at least for inventors eager to enter the United States market?

D. OBVIOUSNESS: THE INVENTIVE STEP

The analog to the United States requirement of nonobviousness is the requirement for "an inventive step" in the United Kingdom and continental Europe. Article 56 of the EPC provides in part: "An invention shall be considered as involving an inventive step if, having regard to the state of the art, it is not obvious to a person skilled in the art...."

While most European countries are parties to the EPC, they generally apply two different approaches to determining whether the inventive step requirement has been satisfied. In the United Kingdom, the seminal case on obviousness—*Windsurfing International Inc v. Tabur Marine (Great Britain) Ltd*, [1985] R.P.C. 59 (Ct. App.)—generally tackles the inventive step analysis in a similar way to United States courts. The EPO often applies the problem/solution test to determine whether the inventive step requirement has been met. China takes a somewhat similar approach.

The first excerpt includes a U.K. case applying the *Windsurfing* decision, which also adds some additional considerations to the analysis of whether an invention satisfies the inventive step requirement. The case was decided by the late Hugh Laddie, a leading jurist in the U.K. intellectual property field. The second excerpt is an EPO Technical Board of Appeal case using the problem/solution test. The final excerpt discusses the application of China's approach to inventive step and specifically analyzes this requirement in the context of medicinal treatments using traditional knowledge.

HABERMAN v. JACKEL INT'L LTD.

Patents Court
[1999] FSR 685

LADDIE J.

This is the judgment in a patent action concerning the design of feeding devices which are used in the process of weaning young babies off the mother's nipple or away from a feeding bottle. The patent is U.K. Patent G.B. No. 2266045. It was applied for on April 7, 1992 by the first plaintiff, Mrs ... Haberman.... The defendant is Jackel International Limited....

The patent in suit

Mrs Haberman's evidence was that in the summer of 1990 she had an idea for making a non-drip trainer cup which would seal between sips.... In April 1992 she applied for the patent in suit.... As the patent explains, save for the addition of a special valve, the cup is of a conventional design consisting of a cup-shaped container with a bottom and upstanding walls. The lid includes a spout with an opening. As liquid is sucked out of the cup through the spout a partial vacuum will be created inside. To counter this an air inlet port is provided. In this embodiment a valve assembly is used which is connected to the lid by means of a boss which is squeezed through a hole in the lid. The assembly is made of a flexible plastics material and contains two valves. One is formed by a slit in the plastics material which lies underneath the spout. The other is a similar slit underneath the air inlet port. The slit valves are so designed that liquid inside the cup cannot flow out of the spout unless the child applies suction to it. Similarly, liquid is prevented from flowing out of the air inlet port. The specification states that cups to the patented design are cheap and simple to manufacture and adapted for ready use by ordinary members of the public. . . . [The cup covered by the patent is called the "Anywayup Cup."].

Obviousness

In considering the attack of obviousness I bear in mind the decision of the Court of Appeal in *Windsurfing International Inc. v. Tabur Marine* (Great Britain) Ltd [1985] R.P.C. 59. That case sets out a structured approach to the question of obviousness which can simplify analysis. Here there is no difficulty in identifying the inventive concept. It is the use of a simple slit valve to prevent leakage of fluid from the outlet of a training cup. There is also no dispute between the parties as to the relevant common general knowledge at the priority date; it was well known that teats from feeding bottles could and had been made drip resistant by incorporating slit valves in the end and it was also well known that training cups existed, were prone to leak and that this was regarded as a problem. Mrs Haberman's step was to take the known simple valve and apply it to a known simple cup. As it was put in *Windsurfer*, the question is whether, viewed without any knowledge of the alleged invention, the difference between what Mrs Haberman did and the prior art would have been obvious to the skilled man or whether it required any degree of invention. Jackel's position is that no invention is involved here. What Mrs Haberman did was blindingly obvious and had been so for some time.

In all cases where obviousness is in issue the court is trying to look back to what paths would have been seriously considered by a notional skilled but uninventive person in the relevant art at the priority date. The task is made more difficult because the patentee's development is already known to the parties and the court. . . . Many patented inventions operate in accordance with simple principles of physics, chemistry or other sciences. It is normally easy to understand why they work. From this it is but a short step to

thinking that a competent technician in the art would have realised, starting from the same simple principles, why the solution
proposed by the patentee should have worked. So, working from
those principles, the solution must be obvious. In such cases it is
also easy to take the relevant expert witnesses under cross-exami-
nation through a series of logical steps which lead to the solution.
The simpler the solution, the easier it is to explain. The easier it is
to explain, the more obvious it can appear. This is not always fair to
inventors....

Jackel relied on Mr Bernard Sinclair as its expert.... He was
given one of the Jackel cups which is said to infringe and was asked
to put forward design concepts which could be used to render it
spill proof.... In any event, it appears he sat with the defendant's
solicitors for about half an hour thinking up designs. Apparently
from time to time the solicitors asked him whether there were any
additional alternatives which he could think of. Within the half-
hour he had come up with a slit valve design. His evidence is that
this design is obvious....

Here there is no difficulty in understanding what Mrs Haberman has done nor is it difficult to see how anyone in the art could
have arrived at the same design from any of the prior art or, as Mr
Platts–Mills argues, from common general knowledge alone. Since
dripless teats using slit valves were extremely well known and
widely used, surely it was obvious to take the valve system from
them and use it in a trainer cup. A simple experiment would have
been to cut off the top half of one of the numerous dripless teats on
the market and fix it inside the spout of one of the numerous
training cups on the market. This analysis is compelling. Does it
reflect what an ordinary man in the art, steeped in the folklore,
perceptions and prejudices of the trade would have done? ...

To be of value in helping to determine whether a development
is obvious or not it seems to me that the following matters are
relevant:

(a) What was the problem which the patented development
addressed? Although sometimes a development may be the obvious
solution to another problem, that is not frequently the case.

(b) How long had that problem existed?

(c) How significant was the problem seen to be? A problem
which was viewed in the trade as trivial might not have generated
much in the way of efforts to find a solution. So an extended period
during which no solution was proposed (or proposed as a commercial proposition) would throw little light on whether, technically, it
was obvious.... On the other hand evidence which suggests that
those in the art were aware of the problem and had been trying to
find a solution will assist the patentee.

(d) How widely known was the problem and how many were likely to be seeking a solution? Where the problem was widely known to many in the relevant art, the greater the prospect of it being solved quickly.

(e) What prior art would have been likely to be known to all or most of those who would have been expected to be involved in finding a solution? A development may be obvious over a piece of esoteric prior art of which most in the trade would have been ignorant. If that is so, commercial success over other, less relevant, prior art will have much reduced significance.

(f) What other solutions were put forward in the period leading up to the publication of the patentee's development? ... As has been said on more than one occasion, there may be more than one obvious route round a technical problem. The existence of alternatives does not prevent each of them from being obvious. On the other hand where the patentee's development would have been expected to be at the forefront of solutions to be found yet it was not and other, more expensive or complex or less satisfactory, solutions were employed instead, then this may suggest that the *ex post facto* assessment that the solution was at the forefront of possibilities is wrong.

(g) To what extent were there factors which would have held back the exploitation of the solution even if it was technically obvious? For example, it may be that the materials or equipment necessary to exploit the solution were only available belatedly or their cost was so high as to act as a commercial deterrent. On the other hand if the necessary materials and apparatus were readily available at reasonable cost, a lengthy period during which the solution was not proposed is a factor which is consistent with lack of obviousness.

(h) How well has the patentee's development been received? Once the product or process was put into commercial operation, to what extent was it a commercial success. In looking at this, it is legitimate to have regard not only to the success indicated by exploitation by the patentee and his licensees but also to the commercial success achieved by infringers. Furthermore, the number of infringers may reflect on some of the other factors set out above. For example, if there are a large number of infringers it may be some indication of the number of members of the trade who were likely to be looking for alternative or improved products.

(i) To what extent can it be shown that the whole or much of the commercial success is due to the technical merits of the development, *i.e.* because it solves the problem? Success which is largely attributable to other factors, such as the commercial power of the patentee or his license, extensive advertising focusing on features which have nothing to do with the development, branding or other technical features of the product or process, says nothing about the value of the intention.

I do not suggest that this list is exhaustive. But it does represent factors which taken together may point towards or away from inventiveness. Most of them have been addressed in this case.

The evidence of commercial success and longfelt want

There is no dispute that the problem which Mrs Haberman's patent seeks to solve, namely the leakage or fluids from feeding containers, has existed for a very long time. . . . The variety of solutions put forward to meet the leakage problem is impressive not only in number but because they all appear to suffer from significant disadvantages when compared with Mrs Haberman's design. . . . Although the objective of making a leak-proof cup was known, by and large it had not been achieved. . . . These efforts should be set against the simplicity of what Mrs Haberman suggested. All the raw materials were readily available. The simplest of valves, used frequently in the same trade, could be used to make a product which had all the virtues which anyone designing a product would want to achieve. The advantages of the use of such a design would have been immediately apparent, once it was thought of. . . .

It is against that background that the claim to commercial success has to be gauged. Although I will go through some of the evidence in relation to this, I can summarise my conclusions at the outset. Mrs Haberman's product was cheap, simple, effective and a remarkable commercial success. . . . The only reason for that success was the incorporation of the simple slit valve. The success of the new models was also in major part attributable to the use of slit valves. . . .

Sales commenced in about March 1996. By the end of that year the plaintiffs were selling at a rate of about 20,000 cups per month. Only 12 months after launch they were selling at the rate of 685,000 p.a. . . . In 1997, the plaintiffs achieved total sales of over 3/4 million cups. In the first nine months of 1998 sales had reached nearly 2 million cups. Sales have fallen somewhat in the face of recent competition from other cups using slit valves. . . .

[Mr Llewellyn–Jones, a director of one of the plaintiffs who was in charge of selling the Anywayup cup] stated:

At trade exhibitions and stands the cups were energetically thrown and juggled into the air, some were dashed on the ground and on many occasions we shook a cup full of liquid in the face of would-be purchasers to prove that it does not leak.

The point to be made about this evidence is that the only selling feature relied upon was that the product was leak resistant. I have ... noted that its appearance was dull and unexceptional. In other words it was only the effect of Mrs Haberman's design which was used to promote the Anywayup cup and it was only that which achieved the sales. . . .

Belanger

The entry of Playtex into the slit valve market is relevant to the case of obviousness based on Belanger. Mr Platts–Mills did not relinquish his argument of obviousness based on the other prior art. . . . Mr Platts–Mills did pay particular attention to Belanger. It will be recalled that that depicts a drip-proof training cup. The value shown and described is of a multipart design involving springs. . . . [T]he specification states that suitable alternative designs of valves exist in numerous forms and types including ball valves, needle valves and flat-handled valves. Mr Platts–Mills said that it must have been obvious to change from the complex valves depicted in Belanger and use the simple slit valve with which everyone in the trade was familiar. There is much force in this. Yet Belanger, like Mr Tupper before him, did not take this obvious step. Not only does his patent illustrate a complicated valve, all the alternatives he suggests expressly are also complicated. . . .

In addition, I do not think it is fair in this case to get round the impact of long felt want by concentrating only on the prior art which is most close to the priority date of the patent in suit and ignoring the earlier art. The same considerations which should have made the Haberman design obvious over Belanger should also have made it obvious over common general knowledge and, for example, Mr Tupper's 1957 proposal. As Mr Sinclair said, and this was not disputed, the slot at the end of the mouthpiece in the Tupper device was acting as a valve. If it was obvious to change from the multipart valve in Belanger to the Haberman slit valve, the same thought processes should have made it obvious to change from the Tupper slot to a slit valve. Indeed, since the Tupper slot was likely to be viewed as unsatisfactory, the incentive to change might have been greater.

I have not found the decision on validity in this case easy. Mr Platts–Mills' arguments on obviousness are powerful. At times I could not see how this could be anything but obvious. But in the end I have not been persuaded. Mrs Haberman has taken a very small and simple step but it appears to me to be a step which any one of the many people in this trade could have taken at any time over at least the preceding ten years or more. In view of the obvious benefits which would flow from it, I have come to the conclusion that had it really been obvious to those in the art it would have been found by others earlier, and probably much earlier. It was there under their very noses. As it was it fell to a comparative outsider to see it. It is not obvious. . . . Mrs Haberman's patent discloses something sufficiently inventive to deserve the grant of a monopoly.

BASF/METAL REFINING

EPO Technical Board of Appeal

[1979–1985] E.P.O.R. B354 (EPO (Technical Bd. App.) 1983)

European patent application No. 79 101 414.5 . . . filed on 9 May 1979 . . ., claiming priority from the German prior application of 11 May 1978, was refused by the decision of the Examining Division of the European Patent Office dated 17 February 1981, on the basis of the eight claims as filed. . . . Claim 1 is worded as follows: Method for treating melts of pig-iron and steel or steel alloys in a converter, crucible or other vessel, characterised in that the entire oxidising (for carbon elimination) and treatment process is carried out using carbonic acid (Kohlensäure—The German term is traditionally used also to denote carbon dioxide) in one vessel on a continuous basis until the finished steel is produced. . . .

When assessing inventive step for this method, it is not a question of the subjective achievement of the inventor, so that the case history of the invention presented at the oral proceedings is irrelevant. It is rather the objective achievement which has to be assessed. As in the case of novelty, inventive step is an objective concept. Objectivity in the assessment of inventive step is achieved by starting out from the objectively prevailing state of the art, in the light of which the problem is determined which the invention addresses and solves from an objective point of view . . ., and consideration is given to the question of the obviousness of the disclosed solution to this problem as seen by the man skilled in the art and having those capabilities which can be objectively expected of him. This also avoids the retrospective approach which inadmissibly makes use of knowledge of the invention. . . .

If this yardstick is applied to the present case, the inventive step must be considered from the point of view of a practitioner in the steel sector who was already familiar with the publications cited in the lower instance and with the oxygen-blowing process which . . . was introduced into technology thirty years ago. The marked overheating of the melt during the oxidising is regarded as a disadvantage in this method, since the converter lining is thereby damaged, leading to the steel melt becoming contaminated with particles from the lining. . . . A proposed solution to avoid these disadvantages is already described in DD–A–103 266. In order, among other things, to increase the cooling effect of the gases and thus increase the durability of the converter lining . . ., the pig-iron melt is here oxidised with a pulsating oxygen jet surrounded by a blanketing medium, especially steam (Claims 1 to 10), and the steel melt is subsequently scavenged by introducing an inert or low-reactivity pulsating gas jet with surrounding blanketing medium to reduce undesirable gas inclusions (Claim 14). Nitrogen, argon, carbon dioxide or flue gas are used as the scavenging gas (Claim 15).

In the search for a further solution to the known problem the appellant set himself the dual task of both (a) avoiding an overheating of the melt which necessarily leads to a reduction in the service life of the converter lining and to contamination of the melt with converter particles and (b) preventing the formation of red iron-oxide smoke during the oxidising process, in order thereby to dispense with the need for costly filtering equipment. The problem thus defined was determined from an objective point of view on the basis of the result aimed at and actually attained by the invention.

To solve this problem the application proposes essentially the use of carbonic acid as oxidising and scavenging agent.

The skilled practitioner seeking a new solution to this problem in the prior art was aware of the fact that pig-iron melts cool off when oxidises with carbon dioxide (see DE–C–934 772, Claim 1 and page 2, lines 24/25 and 81/82). The cooling off is a result of the endothermic reaction of the carbon contained in the pig-iron with the carbon dioxide oxidising agent to form carbon monoxide. . . . The use of carbon dioxide as an oxidising agent therefore presented itself from the point of view of the skilled practitioner as a solution to sub-problem (a).

FR–A–1 058 181 was able to provide the required suggestion for solving sub-problem (b). This publication imparts the teaching that the formation of the feared red iron-oxide smoke in the treatment of pig-iron melts with oxygen can be significantly reduced by adding to the oxygen blowing gas a compound which undergoes an endothermic reaction through dissociation or reduction (Résumé 1°), e.g. carbon dioxide (Résumé 2°b). On the basis of this teaching it was to be expected that—with a view to solving sub-problem (a)—switching over to carbon dioxide as oxidising agent would lead to complete suppression of the red smoke. Moreover, the close connection between the two sub-problems is already clear from the above-mentioned FR–A–.

If these teachings from the prior art are combined, a man skilled in the art could expect the dual problem posed to be solvable by using carbon dioxide as the oxidising agent. In addition it was clear that—unlike the single-stage process as in the above-mentioned DE–C- and FR–A for which patent applications were filed in

1938 and 1951 respectively—the stringent requirements as to the purity of steel at the date of priority (11 May 1978), particularly with regard to undesirable gas inclusions, could only be met by additional subsequent scavenging of the steel melt with a scavenging gas, as exemplified in the above-mentioned DD–A–103 266. Since the solution of the overall problem posed demanded the use of carbon dioxide for the oxidising, it was obvious, for reasons of simplifying the process, to use the same inexpensive gas as a scavenging gas as well.

Once the development of a method for refining pig-iron by oxidising and subsequent scavenging of the melt by means of carbon dioxide as oxidising and scavenging agent in a single converter became obvious, determination of the amounts of carbon dioxide required for this was purely a matter of routine experimentation. . . .

The appellant, on the other hand, takes the view that by combining these publications a man skilled in the art would not have arrived at the claimed method without inventive effort, because he would have only taken into consideration those embodiments which were particularly emphasised therein. . . . [T]he Board does not share the appellant's view that only those embodiments described as being preferred in a citation are to be considered when assessing the inventive step. In fact, when examining for inventive step, the state of the art must be assessed from the point of view of the man skilled in the art at the time of priority relevant for the application. Consequently all previously published embodiments must be taken into consideration which offered a suggestion to the skilled practitioner for solving the problem addressed, even where the embodiments were not particularly emphasised. It is therefore not a matter of what was regarded as advantageous at that time in the publications constituting the prior art. . . .

The appellant sees the fact that the steel industry has passed by the method as applied for, despite the significant economic contribution it makes to solving the environmental problems in this field, as an indication of the presence of inventive step. . . . Where any such indications are present, the overall picture of the state of the art and consideration of all significant factors may indeed show that inventive step is involved, without however leading to the compelling conclusion that inventive step must generally follow from this situation. The considerable technical effect here claimed provides no basis for the presence of inventive step, if only because it is not surprising, but was on the contrary certainly to be expected in view of the problem facing the skilled practitioner.

The fact that the steel industry has passed by the method as applied for becomes understandable if the question is considered as to whether and when the appellant's method met an urgent need. The appellant has himself stated that the oxygen-blowing process was rational and economically attractive when introduced into technology thirty years ago, but that the advent and especially the tightening of environmental laws over the last few years have raised investment costs for dust-removal and filtering equipment by about 25%, leading to an increase in the price of steel by 5 to 10 DM/t. In the view of the Board this indicates that over a long period of time there was no motive for breaking away from the oxygen-blowing process which had been successfully introduced and more-over involved expensive plant of long service life, and that the need for the appellant's method which from the present-day point of view is environmentally innocuous arose relatively shortly before the date of priority of the present application. A process developed in the light of a need which arose relatively shortly before the application cannot be regarded as involving inventive step if this need could be readily met by an obvious combination of teachings from the prior art. . . .

The appeal . . . is rejected.

Notes and Questions

1. What are the differences between the United States approach to obviousness and the analysis described in *Jackel* to determine inventive step? Is the *Jackel* approach to inventive step helpful in mitigating concerns over hindsight bias? Was the *Windsurfing* test particularly helpful in determining inventive step?

2. The EPO test for determining inventive step includes three steps:

> (1) determining the 'closest prior' art; (2) establishing the 'objective technical problem' to be solved; and (3) considering whether or not the claimed invention, starting from the closest prior art and the objective technical problem, would have been obvious to a skilled person.

HECTOR MACQUEEN, CHARLOTTE WAELDE & GRAEME LAURIE, CONTEMPORARY INTELLECTUAL PROPERTY POLICY: LAW AND POLICY 452 (2007). The commentators quote one English judge's observations concerning the EPO test:

> 'its concentration on the closest prior art, which must stem from a belief that if an invention is not obvious in light of the closest prior art it cannot be obvious in light of anything further away. This runs the risk of offending against the principle that a skilled man must be permitted to do that which is obvious in the light of each individual item of prior art seen in the light of the general common knowledge.'

What do you think should include "the closest prior art?" Is "the closest prior art" always restricted to prior art in the same technical field? *See id.* ("The closest prior art often restricts the search to the same technical field as the invention and looks for the most promising point from which an obvious development towards the invention might be made.").

3.   Phillip Grubb describes the British critique of the problem and solution test:

> The practice in the EPO is to apply the 'problem and solution approach' to inventive step. This derives from Rule 27(1)(c), which states that the invention is to be disclosed in such a way that the technical problem (even if not expressly stated as such) and its solution can be understood. Having established what is the closest prior art, the examiner is supposed to determine what was the technical problem solved by the invention, and then to judge whether or not the solution would have been obvious to the person skilled in the art. This procedure is supposed to make the evaluation of inventive step more objective and rule out *ex post facto* analysis, but the difficulty is that the problem is determined with hindsight in full knowledge of the invention as well as of the prior art, and may have had nothing to do with the problem the inventor was trying to solve. From the British point of view, the determination of this hypothetical 'problem' seems an unnecessary additional step in the more simple analysis of what is the difference between the prior art and the invention, and whether or not this difference (whether or not it is to be considered as a problem) would be obvious to the person skilled in the art. Other Board of Appeal decisions have held that the problem and solution approach is only one possible way of judging inventive step, and its use is not a *sine qua non*.

PHILLIP W. GRUBB, PATENTS FOR CHEMICALS, PHARMACEUTICALS AND BIOTECHNOLOGY: FUNDAMENTALS OF GLOBAL LAW, PRACTICE AND STRATEGY 64–65 (4th ed. 2005). What is the principal difference between the U.K. and the EPO approaches?

4.   Dr. Grubb provides a critique of the United States approach to obviousness prior to the United States Supreme Court's decision in *KSR v. Teleflex*, 550 U.S. 398 (2007):

> One of the greatest difficulties is that, in contrast to British and EPO practice, it is permissible in the US to 'mosaic' together any number of prior art documents and, often with a generous measure of hindsight, to piece together the invention as a sequence of logical steps. Another problem is that, whereas in the EPC the whole contents of an unpublished application can be used to attack novelty but not to allege obviousness, in the USA an earlier-filed application can base both types of attack.

GRUBB, *supra*, at 70. In response to the first problem in the above excerpt, what do you think Grubb's position on *KSR v. Teleflex* would be?

5. One group of commentators describes the so-called "could-would test" applied by the EPO as part of the third step of the EPO test as follows:

> For being obvious, it is not sufficient that a person skilled in the art could have tried to arrive at the claimed invention, but that he would have done so ("could-would-test"). There must have been a suggestion in [the prior art] to apply the information in question that created a reasonable expectation of success for the skilled person to arrive at the claimed subject matter with its intrinsic properties.

ALEXANDER R. KLETT, MATTHIAS SONNTAG & STEPHAN WILSKE, INTELLECTUAL PROPERTY LAW IN GERMANY: PROTECTION, ENFORCEMENT AND DISPUTE RESOLUTION 6 (2008). Does the "could-would test" differ from the approach set forth in *KSR v. Teleflex* and subsequent Federal Circuit case law concerning obviousness? If so, how?

6. In *Conor Medsystems v. Angiotech Pharmaceuticals*, [2008] UKHL 49, the U.K. House of Lords explains how different outcomes may occur based on the "same" patent in different jurisdictions subject to the EPC:

> There is still no European Patent Court. A European patent takes effect as a bundle of national patents over which the national courts have jurisdiction. It is therefore inevitable that they will occasionally give inconsistent decisions about the same patent. Sometimes this is because the evidence is different. In most continental jurisdictions, including the European Patent Office ..., cross-examination is limited or unknown. Sometimes one is dealing with questions of degree over which judges may legitimately differ. Obviousness is often in this category.

Li Xuan

Novelty and Inventive Step: Obstacles to Traditional Knowledge Protection under Patent Regimes: A Case Study in China

29 EUR. INTELL. PROP. REV. 134 (2007)

The principle and standard of inventive step examination in China

According to Art. 22(3) of the Chinese Patent Law, the Chinese standard on inventive step requires both prominent substantive features and a notable progress.... Specifically, in terms of prominent substantive features China introduces the "problem and solution approach" of the European Patent Office (EPO) to assess inventive step. In terms of "a notable progress", effect is considered as a priority factor to determine the inventive step. While international norm focuses on a comparison of the features of the invention versus those of the prior art and taking advantageous effect into consideration as one of the factors to infer inventive step, effect weighs more in Chinese patent examination as it takes a problem, solution and effect as combined substantive conditions. China recognises four conditions as an inventive step: (1) the invention claimed generates better technical effect in comparison to the closest prior art, e.g. quality improvement, output enhancement, energy saving, environment pollution prevention, etc.; (2) the invention claimed provides an alternative technical solution, the technical effect of which basically achieves the present technical level; (3) the invention claimed represents some sort of trend of new technological development; (4) the invention claimed generates an obviously technical advantageous effect in some aspect even if accompanied by a disadvantageous effect in another aspect. The Chinese Patent Examination Guideline emphasises that examination of inventive step shall not only be based on the technical solution per se, but also combined with technical problem and its technical effect as a whole. . . .

The technical difficulties of applying inventive step

TK can hardly be expressed in structural terms

Determining the differences between the prior art and the claims at issue is rather contentious for TK. Differently from chemical pharmaceutical products, which can be generally described in structural terms by specifying their chemical composition, TK or TK-based medicines are usually crude plant materials, such as leaves, flowers, fruits, seeds, stems, wood, bark, roots, rhizomes or other plant parts, which may be used in whole or in fragmented or powdered forms. They are often prepared by steeping or heating herbal materials in alcohol and/or honey, or in other liquids. The production process is usually simple and does not involve any sophisticated know-how or invention novel enough to secure protection under existing patent law. . . .

Chemical pharmaceutical products have long been effectively protected under the product patent, which is the strongest form of patent protection. The existence of an inventive step of chemical pharmaceutical products is judged by taking into account the structural similarity between the claimed invention and the prior art compounds. If the structure of its chemical formula has distinguished features in comparison to the prior art and this compound has demonstrated an acceptable medical indication, the pharmaceutical compound is considered as inventive step. However, it is difficult to apply the same rule to the TK. Unlike chemical pharmaceuticals, as regards TK as crude materials, herbal composition rather than formula becomes decisive to claim inventive step. This substantially increases the difficulties on patent examination because TK is a mixture of many unknown substances. In terms of herbal compositions, the establishment of inventive step needs to be examined on the basis of the addition (or deduction), substitution, combination or modification in quantitative proportion of herbs, respectively. Practically, the determination of the difference between the prior art and the claims of TK at issue is less objective than the case of chemical pharmaceuticals. It is reflected by the fact that the addition and deduction of a herb in the prescription is the most contentious infringement claim in terms of a TK-related judiciary case in China. . . .

Effect as index to assess inventive step

Another technical difficulty is to apply effect as indicator for inventive step examination of TK. A greater than expected effect is an evidentiary factor pertinent to the legal conclusion of inventive step of the claims in general, and effect is considered as a priority factor to determine inventive step in China. However, there are technical difficulties in applying the effect indicator for TK which result from the intrinsic characteristic of TK. The difficulty can be demonstrated through an illustrative case. Suppose there are two prescriptions, A and B, is there inventive step on "A + B" when A is determined as the closest prior art and a mixture of "A + B" has generated an unexpected technical effect of C in comparison to the closest prior art? Supposing there is reliable experimental data demonstrating the technical effect of C, there are two scenarios that lead to two opposite consequences: if the existence of effect C results in the addition of B to A, that is, C is the consequence of A + B, the mixture of A + B shall be considered inventive. In contrast, if the existence of effect C is a newly disclosed result concealed in A and the addition of B does not generate the function of A, the mixture of A + B is obvious comparing to the prior art of A, which shall not be considered inventive. Thus the causation between effect C and A + B is crucial. However, owing to the crude characteristic of TK, it is statistically difficult to establish a quantitative relationship between effect C and A + B or A individually. Therefore this substantially increases the uncertainty of inventive step determination of TK. In addition, when an unexpected technical effect is regarded as a priority factor to overcome a prima facie case of inventive step, a usage TK patent may be wrongfully granted as a product TK patent. For instance, if the applicant only discloses new medical indication of an existing TK product A of prior art, a usage patent is the appropriate protection for the claimed invention. However, the applicant may get a product patent by adding ordinary carrier to A if a notable effect is decisive to infer inventive step. Therefore it is likely to generate an inappropriate discrepancy between the scope of protection and the contribution it made which is in violation of the principle of fairness.

Conclusion

   ... [T]he real obstacle that hinders TK from being patented is inventive step. Unlike chemical pharmaceuticals, the existence of an inventive step of a TK product is judged by applying the product-by-process method instead of structural similarity comparison between the claimed and the prior art compounds. With the product-by-process method, the scope of patent of a TK product is substantially narrowed down to the TK product obtained with the claimed process only. Thus a product patent is de facto not available for a TK invention which does not meet the requirement of Art. 27.1 of TRIPs. This is due to the fact that crude TK can hardly be described in structural terms as a chemical pharmaceutical can but can only be described in terms of herbal compositions. In addition, technically speaking, the causation of an unexpected technical effect of a TK patent application can hardly be established as clearly as in the case of chemical pharmaceuticals, and such a situation increases the uncertainty of acquiring a TK patent. These obstacles should not be attributed to the patent regime per se but they originate from the inherent inadequacy between the patent regime and the characteristics of TK. It is therefore considered necessary to establish a sui generis regime for TK protection.

Notes and Questions

   1. After considering the problems with protecting traditional knowledge by intellectual property protection in Chapter 2.C and the prior excerpt, should traditional knowledge receive sui generis protection? If so, in what form? What are the goals behind such protection? For a discussion of the different goals behind the protection of traditional knowledge, see generally Peter K. Yu, *Cultural Relics, Intellectual Property, and Intangible Heritage*, 81 TEMPLE L. REV. 433, 454–84 (2008).

E. TRIPS, DOHA AND COMPULSORY LICENSING

   From a government's perspective, access to pharmaceutical inventions, including essential medicines, has raised significant public health concerns. For nations with limited financial resources, drug costs pose a grave challenge. As one commentator explains with respect to drug prices for populations within developing nations:

Purchasing AIDS drugs at U.S. prices is not an option for the vast majority of these people. The per capita annual cost of a popular first-line ARV [antiretroviral for treating HIV/AIDS] in the United States is $7215, and the recently introduced Fuzeon (enfuvirtide) costs $20,000 per year. The annual per capita health expenditures in sub-Saharan Africa averages $29.30 and range from $12 (Malawi) to $253 (South Africa). Radically reducing the price of AIDS medications for the poor is thus a necessary condition to extending ARV treatments to millions of afflicted persons worldwide. Indeed, for many patients, the drugs must be free.

Kevin Outterson, *Pharmaceutical Arbitrage: Balancing Access and Innovation in International Prescription Drug Markets*, 5 YALE J. HEALTH POL'Y L. & ETHICS 193, 252 (2005).

At the same time, if new medicines are to be developed, drug companies need to be able to recoup the significant cost of drug development. By excluding competition, patents put these companies in the best position to maximize profit—sometimes through price discrimination (the practice of selling medicines at a higher price in wealthier nations and at lower prices among populations with fewer resources). However, not all companies would engage in price discrimination for every market and formulation.

There are several reasons. For example, the cost of regulatory approval may be high. Some of these companies may also choose to forego distribution in some nations entirely, especially those that do not offer strong intellectual property protection.

Moreover, a drug manufacturer's ability to price discriminate may be undermined by the practice of arbitrage. When engaging in this conduct:

wholesalers in a low-price country divert supplies through international trade channels to nations in which the manufacturer is attempting to maintain high prices, undermining the high prices (and their contribution to research and development expenditures) in the wealthier nations and, if quantitatively substantial, inhibiting the manufacturer's willingness to supply at low prices in the low-income nation.

F.M. Scherer & Jayashree Watal, *Post–TRIPS Options for Access to Patented Medicines in Developing Nations*, 5 J. INT'L ECON. L. 913, 928 (2002). Patentees may forgo low-cost, high-volume sales in poorer countries to reduce the risk that these drugs will re-enter another nation that can afford to pay higher prices, often through parallel importation. They also may want to focus on the more affluent segment of the population in these countries to maximize the profitability of sales made there even though that segment may represent only a minority. Peter K. Yu, *The International Enclosure Movement*, 82 IND. L. J. 827, 844–45 (2007).

To reconcile these diverging needs and concerns, TRIPS provides for a compulsory licensing system, under which a WTO member state is allowed to grant a non-exclusive patent license to a user who makes a commercially reasonable offer that has been refused. For non-commercial public use and in situations where a national emergency or extreme urgency takes place, the government may proceed with authorization even in the absence of an attempted negotiation with the patentee. To prevent arbitrage, Article 31(f) states explicitly that the compulsory license "shall be authorized predominantly for the supply of the domestic market of the Member authorizing such use." This limitation prevents a wholesaler from exporting drugs produced for sale in poorer nations to compete with higher priced sales in wealthier nations.

Thus, in operation, Article 31 struck a compromise between the need to incentivize invention and concerns over public health by allowing local drug manufacturers to develop another's patented formulation so long as reasonable remuneration payments are made to the patentee. As one example, Thailand has issued, to the dismay of the affected rights holders, compulsory licenses for local drug makers to develop generic treatments for HIV/AIDs and heart disease.

Unfortunately, many nations, including a large number of least developed countries, do not have any or sufficient capacity to manufacture or develop drugs. Article 31 is therefore of limited assistance to these countries. First, due to their lack of such capacity, these countries cannot take advantage of the compulsory licensing arrangement provided by the provision. Even worse, the Article 31(f) limitation that a compulsory license be only authorized "predominantly for the supply of the domestic market" has effectively prevented other countries with manufacturing capacity to export the needed drugs to them.

In light of the problem for these countries, WTO members adopted the Declaration on the TRIPS Agreement and Public Health during the Fourth WTO Ministerial Meeting in Doha, Qatar in 2002. World Trade Org., Declaration on the TRIPS Agreement and Public Health, WT/MIN(01)/DEC/2, 41 I.L.M. 755 (2002). Paragraph 6 of the Declaration recognized that "WTO Members with insufficient or no manufacturing capacities in the pharmaceutical sector could face difficulties in making effective use of compulsory licensing under the TRIPS Agreement" and instructed the TRIPS Council to devise an "expeditious solution."

Most recently, the WTO member states accepted a protocol of amendment, which sought to add a new Article 31*bis* to the TRIPS

Agreement. If ratified by two-thirds of the WTO membership, this new provision would relieve certain members of the territorial limits of Article 31(f). Specifically, Article 31*bis* allows WTO member states with insufficient or no manufacturing capacity to import on-patent pharmaceuticals under a compulsory license. To alleviate concerns that such exports may find their way back to the global market at below-market prices, the proposed amendment includes provisions that would deter diversion of the needed drugs.

Some commentators have been critical of the Doha arrangement, arguing that the arrangement would undermine the uniform global system of protection that TRIPS was intended to establish. Alan Sykes writes:

> Any pharmaceutical company contemplating research on diseases of particular interest to developing nations is now on notice that in the event a successful new drug is developed, developing country customers may declare a "national emergency" and thereafter award compulsory licenses without prior negotiation, and at a royalty rate that may be minimal depending on the eventual interpretation of the "adequate remuneration" standard in Article 31. Even if such behavior is not in the collective interest of developing nations, the temptation to engage in it on an individual country basis may be great because the costs to others are externalized.

Alan O. Sykes, *TRIPS, Pharmaceuticals, Developing Countries, and the Doha "Solution,"* 3 CHI. J. INT'L L. 47 (2002).

Meanwhile, Thomas Cotter argues that developing countries are unlikely to abuse this arrangement. Thomas F. Cotter, *Market Fundamentalism and the TRIPS Agreement*, 22 CARDOZO ARTS & ENT. L.J. 307, 335–36 (2004). For example, developing nations do not wish to incur diplomatic reprisals or other adverse impacts that would follow any abuse, such as litigation expenses incurred by a WTO challenge. In addition, as Professor Cotter has noted, "a country's ability to engage in compulsory licensing is constrained by other practical factors—among them the need to have an established industrial sector in place that can engage in reverse engineering and production of the patented invention and the need for an adequate legal and administrative system to oversee the compulsory licensing procedure," circumstances that are simply not present in a number of emerging economies.

Regarding Professor Sykes' argument that the Doha arrangement reduces the incentives for pharmaceutical companies to develop solutions to health afflictions unique to developing countries, Professor Cotter states:

[A] little dose of reality is helpful. Even in the presence of strong patent rights, the developing nations' willingness to pay may be so constrained that little incentive will exist anyway for the pharmaceutical companies to engage in much of this type of research and development. Indeed, most observers who have considered this issue have concluded that it will take much more than strong patent rights to induce this type of research.... Thus, even if the TRIPs Declaration marginally decreases the incentive to engage in research into tropical diseases, there remain (unfortunately) other obstacles that are much more significant; to argue against the Declaration on this ground is to let the tail wag the dog.

This problem is what commentators have described as the "neglected disease" problem. Examples of these diseases include measles, malaria, tuberculosis, sleeping sickness, leishmaniasis, and Chagas disease.

In recent years, some WTO members have introduced legislation to implement the arrangement. Canada, for example, enacted the Canadian Access to Medicines Regime in 2004. Three years later, Canadian drug manufacturer Apotex began shipping Apo–TriAvir, a triple combination HIV/AIDS drug, to Rwanda under this regime. However, Apotex has recently indicated its reluctance to continue to use the regime unless the process is streamlined. Press Release, CAMR Federal Law Needs to Be Fixed If Life–Saving Drugs for Children Are to Be Developed (May 29, 2009), *available at* http://www.apotex.com/ca/en/aboutapotex/pressreleases/20090514.asp. According to Apotex, the company has invested millions of dollars in the research and development of the product and in legal costs incurred in its negotiation with the brand companies. It nevertheless found the system "in its current form ... not workable" for the company and difficult for developing countries.

Whether Article 31*bis* will be ratified is far from assured. Even if it is, it is unclear whether the provision will be widely used by such drug manufacturers as Apotex.

Notes and Questions

1. Why would a patent holder object to broad dissemination and licensing of an invention when compensation is paid? Does the requirement for seeking remuneration raise other unrelated issues—and, if so, what are they? Why would a nation be reluctant to ratify Article 31*bis*? Should Article 31*bis* cover the so-called "lifestyle" drugs, such as Viagra or Rogaine?

2. Before the adoption of Article 31*bis*, countries were presented with four different options:

(i) an authoritative interpretation based on Article 30 [of the TRIPS Agreement];

(ii) an amendment to Article 31 in order to overcome the restriction, under Article 31(f), to the possibility to export products manufactured and/or sold under a compulsory licence;

(iii) a dispute settlement moratorium with regard to the non-respect of the restriction under Article 31(f); or

(iv) a waiver with regard to Article 31(f).

Peter K. Yu, *The International Enclosure Movement*, 82 IND. L. J. 827, 880 (2007) (quoting the European Communities' proposal to the TRIPS Council during its 2002 meeting). Which of these options is the most desirable? Which of these is the least desirable? Why? When considering the rights of patent holders and government obligations to formulate health policy, how should the balance be struck?

Chapter 3

COPYRIGHTS

The Introductory Chapter discusses the different minimum standards established by the TRIPS Agreement and other international treaties (such as the Paris and Berne Conventions). Notwithstanding these treaties, there remain significant differences between the United States copyright system and that of other countries. For example, there are considerable differences between how United States copyright law handles issues such as the protection of moral rights, fair use or fair dealing, the first sale or exhaustion doctrine, the work made for hire arrangement, protection against private copying in the digital environment, and extra-judicial protection for copy-protection measures. This Chapter focuses on some of these key differences.

A. PROTECTION OF DATABASES

One of the key differences between United States copyright law and that of other countries concerns the protection of nonoriginal, noncreative databases. As the United States Supreme Court declared in *Feist Publications, Inc. v. Rural Telephone Service Co.*, "[o]riginality is a constitutional requirement." 499 U.S. 340, 346 (1991). Thus, a compilation—in that case, the white pages of a telephone directory—is not worthy of copyright protection unless information in the compilation is selected, coordinated, or arranged in an original manner. In *Feist*, the Court went out of its way to reject the "sweat of the brow" doctrine, stating that nonoriginal, noncreative databases would not qualify for copyright protection even if a substantial amount of labor and capital have been expended to create those works.

This position contrasts interestingly with that of other countries. Before the U.K. copyright law was amended in 1988, for example, copyright works involving the "skill, labour and judgment," including nonoriginal, noncreative databases, will be protected even if they do not meet the higher "intellectual creation" standard. This lower sweat-based standard posed significant challenges when the European Community sought to harmonize the copyright laws of its member states in the mid–1990s. To reconcile these diverging standards, the European Parliament and Council Directive 96/9 (commonly known as the European Community Database Directive, a portion of which is reproduced below) struck a compromise by offering two tiers of protection—one for original, creative databases that satisfy the "intellectual creation" standard and the other for nonoriginal, noncreative databases that meet only the lower "sweat of the brow" standard.

European Parliament and Council Directive 96/9, On the Legal Protection of Databases

Mar. 11, 1996
1996 O.J. (L 77) 20

Article 1
Scope

1. This Directive concerns the legal protection of databases in any form.

2. For the purposes of this Directive, 'database' shall mean a collection of independent works, data or other materials arranged in a systematic or methodical way and individually accessible by electronic or other means.

3. Protection under this Directive shall not apply to computer programs used in the making or operation of databases accessible by electronic means. . . .

Article 7
Object of protection

1. Member States shall provide for a right for the maker of a database which shows that there has been qualitatively and/or quantitatively a substantial investment in either the obtaining, verification or presentation of the contents to prevent extraction and/or re-utilization of the whole or of a substantial part, evaluated qualitatively and/or quantitatively, of the contents of that database.

2. For the purposes of this Chapter:

(a) 'extraction' shall mean the permanent or temporary transfer of all or a substantial part of the contents of a database to another medium by any means or in any form;

(b) 're-utilization' shall mean any form of making available to the public all or a substantial part of the contents of a database by the distribution of copies, by renting, by on-line or other forms of transmission. The first sale of a copy of a database within the Community by the rightholder or with his consent shall exhaust the right to control resale of that copy within the Community;

Public lending is not an act of extraction or re-utilization.

3.   The right referred to in paragraph 1 may be transferred, assigned or granted under contractual licence.

4.   The right provided for in paragraph 1 shall apply irrespective of the eligibility of that database for protection by copyright or by other rights. Moreover, it shall apply irrespective of eligibility of the contents of that database for protection by copyright or by other rights. Protection of databases under the right provided for in paragraph 1 shall be without prejudice to rights existing in respect of their contents.

5.   The repeated and systematic extraction and/or re-utilization of insubstantial parts of the contents of the database implying acts which conflict with a normal exploitation of that database or which unreasonably prejudice the legitimate interests of the maker of the database shall not be permitted.

Article 8
Rights and obligations of lawful users

1.   The maker of a database which is made available to the public in whatever manner may not prevent a lawful user of the database from extracting and/or re-utilizing insubstantial parts of its contents, evaluated qualitatively and/or quantitatively, for any purposes whatsoever. Where the lawful user is authorized to extract and/or re-utilize only part of the database, this paragraph shall apply only to that part.

2.   A lawful user of a database which is made available to the public in whatever manner may not perform acts which conflict with normal exploitation of the database or unreasonably prejudice the legitimate interests of the maker of the database.

3.   A lawful user of a database which is made available to the public in any manner may not cause prejudice to the holder of a copyright or related right in respect of the works or subject matter contained in the database.

Article 9
Exceptions to the sui generis right

Member States may stipulate that lawful users of a database which is made available to the public in whatever manner may, without the authorization of its maker, extract or re-utilize a substantial part of its contents:

(a) in the case of extraction for private purposes of the contents of a non-electronic database;

(b) in the case of extraction for the purposes of illustration for teaching or scientific research, as long as the source is indicated and to the extent justified by the non-commercial purpose to be achieved;

(c) in the case of extraction and/or re-utilization for the purposes of public security or an administrative or judicial procedure.

Article 10
Term of protection

1.   The right provided for in Article 7 shall run from the date of completion of the making of the database. It shall expire fifteen years from the first of January of the year following the date of completion.

2.   In the case of a database which is made available to the public in whatever manner before expiry of the period provided for in paragraph 1, the term of protection by that right shall expire fifteen years from the first of January of the year following the date when the database was first made available to the public.

3.   Any substantial change, evaluated qualitatively or quantitatively, to the contents of a database, including any substantial change resulting from the accumulation of successive additions, deletions or alterations, which would result in the database being considered to be a substantial new investment, evaluated qualitatively or quantitatively, shall qualify the database resulting from that investment for its own term of protection.

Article 11
Beneficiaries of protection under the sui generis right

1.   The right provided for in Article 7 shall apply to database whose makers or rightholders are nationals of a Member State or who have their habitual residence in the territory of the Community.

2.   Paragraph 1 shall also apply to companies and firms formed in accordance with the law of a Member State and having their registered office, central administration or principal place of business within the Community; however, where such a company or firm has only its registered office in the territory of the Community, its operations must be genuinely linked on an ongoing basis with the economy of a Member State.

3.   Agreements extending the right provided for in Article 7 to databases made in third countries and falling outside the provisions

of paragraphs 1 and 2 shall be concluded by the Council acting on a proposal from the Commission. The term of any protection extended to databases by virtue of that procedure shall not exceed that available pursuant to Article 10.

BRITISH HORSERACING BOARD LTD. v. WILLIAM HILL ORGANIZATION LTD.

European Court of Justice (Grand Chamber)
Case C–203/02, 2004 E.C.R. I–10415

This reference for a preliminary ruling concerns the interpretation of Article 7 and Article 10(3) of Directive 96/9/EC of the European Parliament and of the Council of 11 March 1996 on the legal protection of databases (OJ 1996 L 77, p. 20, 'the directive').

The reference was made in the course of proceedings brought by The British Horseracing Board Ltd, the Jockey Club and Weatherbys Group Ltd ('the BHB and Others') against William Hill Organization Ltd ('William Hill'). The litigation arose over the use by William Hill, for the purpose of organising betting on horse racing, of information taken from the BHB database. . . .

The main proceedings and the questions referred for a preliminary ruling

The BHB and Others manage the horse racing industry in the United Kingdom and in various capacities compile and maintain the BHB database which contains a large amount of information supplied by horse owners, trainers, horse race organisers and others involved in the racing industry. The database contains information on *inter alia* the pedigrees of some one million horses, and 'pre-race information' on races to be held in the United Kingdom. That information includes the name, place and date of the race concerned, the distance over which the race is to be run, the criteria for eligibility to enter the race, the date by which entries must be received, the entry fee payable and the amount of money the racecourse is to contribute to the prize money for the race.

Weatherbys Group Ltd, the company which compiles and maintains the BHB database, performs three principal functions, which lead up to the issue of pre-race information.

First, it registers information concerning owners, trainers, jockeys and horses and records the performances of those horses in each race.

Second, it decides on weight adding and handicapping for the horses entered for the various races.

Third, it compiles the lists of horses running in the races. This activity is carried out by its own call centre, manned by about 30 operators. They record telephone calls entering horses in each race organised. The identity and status of the person entering the horse and whether the characteristics of the horse meet the criteria for entry to the race are then checked. Following those checks the entries are published provisionally. To take part in the race, the trainer must confirm the horse's participation by telephone by declaring it the day before the race at the latest. The operators must then ascertain whether the horse can be authorised to run the race in the light of the number of declarations already recorded. A central computer then allocates a saddle cloth number to each horse and determines the stall from which it will start. The final list of runners is published the day before the race.

The BHB database contains essential information not only for those directly involved in horse racing but also for radio and television broadcasters and for bookmakers and their clients. The cost of running the BHB database is approximately £4 million per annum. The fees charged to third parties for the use of the information in the database cover about a quarter of that amount.

The database is accessible on the internet site operated jointly by BHB and Weatherbys Group Ltd. Some of its contents are also published each week in the BHB's official journal. The contents of the database, or of certain parts of it, are also made available to Racing Pages Ltd, a company jointly controlled by Weatherbys Group Ltd and the Press Association, which then forwards data to its various subscribers, including some bookmakers, in the form of a 'Declarations Feed', the day before a race. Satellite Information Services Limited ('SIS') is authorised by Racing Pages to transmit data to its own subscribers in the form of a 'raw data feed' ('RDF'). The RDF includes a large amount of information, in particular, the names of the horses running in the races, the names of the jockeys, the saddle cloth numbers and the weight for each horse. Through the newspapers and the Ceefax and Teletext services, the names of the runners in a particular race are made available to the public during the course of the afternoon before the race.

William Hill, which is a subscriber to both the Declarations Feed and the RDF, is one of the leading providers of offcourse bookmaking services in the United Kingdom, to both UK and international customers. It launched an on-line betting service on two internet sites. Those interested can use these sites to find out what horses are running in which races at which racecourses and what odds are offered by William Hill.

The information displayed on William Hill's internet sites is obtained, first, from newspapers published the day before the race and, second, from the RDF supplied by SIS on the morning of the race.

According to the order for reference, the information displayed on William Hill's internet sites represents a very small proportion of the total amount of data on the BHB database, given that it concerns only the following matters: the names of all the horses in the race, the date, time and/or name of the race and the name of the racecourse where the race will be held. Also according to the order for reference, the horse races and the lists of runners are not arranged on William Hill's internet sites in the same way as in the BHB database.

In March 2000 the BHB and Others brought proceedings against William Hill in the High Court of Justice of England and Wales, Chancery Division, alleging infringement of their *sui generis* right. They contend, first, that each day's use by William Hill of racing data taken from the newspapers or the RDF is an extraction or re-utilisation of a substantial part of the contents of the BHB database, contrary to Article 7(1) of the directive. Secondly, they say that even if the individual extracts made by William Hill are not substantial they should be prohibited under Article 7(5) of the directive.

The High Court of Justice ruled in a judgment of 9 February 2001 that the action of BHB and Others was well founded. William Hill appealed to the referring court.

In the light of the problems of interpretation of the directive, the Court of Appeal decided to stay proceedings and refer the following questions to the Court of Justice for a preliminary ruling:

'(1) May either of the expressions:

— "substantial part of the contents of the database"; or

— "insubstantial parts of the contents of the database"

in Article 7 of the directive include works, data or other materials derived from the database but which do not have the same systematic or methodical arrangement of and individual accessibility as those to be found in the database?

(2) What is meant by "obtaining" in Article 7(1) of the directive? In particular, are the [facts and matters in paragraph 14] above capable of amounting to such obtaining?

(3) Is "verification" in Article 7(1) of the directive limited to ensuring from time to time that information contained in a database is or remains correct? . . . .'

Preliminary observations

Article 7(1) of the directive reserves the protection of the sui generis right to databases which meet a specific criterion, namely to those which show that there has been qualitatively and/or quantitatively a substantial investment in the obtaining, verification or presentation of their contents.

Under the 9th, 10th and 12th recitals of the preamble to the directive, its purpose, as William Hill points out, is to promote and protect investment in data 'storage' and 'processing' systems which contribute to the development of an information market against a background of exponential growth in the amount of information generated and processed annually in all sectors of activity. It follows that the expression 'investment in ... the obtaining, verification or presentation of the contents' of a database must be understood, generally, to refer to investment in the creation of that database as such.

Against that background, the expression 'investment in ... the obtaining ... of the contents' of a database must, as William Hill and the Belgian, German and Portuguese Governments point out, be understood to refer to the resources used to seek out existing independent materials and collect them in the database, and not to the resources used for the creation as such of independent materials. The purpose of the protection by the sui generis right provided for by the directive is to promote the establishment of storage and processing systems for existing information and not the creation of materials capable of being collected subsequently in a database.

That interpretation is backed up by the 39th recital of the preamble to the directive, according to which the aim of the sui generis right is to safeguard the results of the financial and professional investment made in 'obtaining and collection of the contents' of a database. As the Advocate General notes in points 41 to 46 of her Opinion, despite slight variations in wording, all the language versions of the 39th recital support an interpretation which excludes the creation of the materials contained in a database from the definition of obtaining.

The 19th recital of the preamble to the directive, according to which the compilation of several recordings of musical performances on a CD does not represent a substantial enough investment to be eligible under the sui generis right, provides an additional argument in support of that interpretation. Indeed, it appears from that recital that the resources used for the creation as such of works or materials included in the database, in this case on a CD, cannot be deemed equivalent to investment in the obtaining of the contents of that database and cannot, therefore, be taken into account in assessing whether the investment in the creation of the database was substantial.

The expression 'investment in ... the ... verification ... of the contents' of a database must be understood to refer to the resources used, with a view to ensuring the reliability of the information contained in that database, to monitor the accuracy of the materials collected when the database was created and during its operation. The resources used for verification during the stage of creation of data or other materials which are subsequently collected in a database, on the other hand, are resources used in creating a database and cannot therefore be taken into account in order to assess whether there was substantial investment in the terms of Article 7(1) of the directive.

In that light, the fact that the creation of a database is linked to the exercise of a principal activity in which the person creating the database is also the creator of the materials contained in the database does not, as such, preclude that person from claiming the protection of the sui generis right, provided that he establishes that the obtaining of those materials, their verification or their presentation, in the sense described in paragraphs 31 to 34 of this judgment, required substantial investment in quantitative or qualitative terms, which was independent of the resources used to create those materials.

Thus, although the search for data and the verification of their accuracy at the time a database is created do not require the maker of that database to use particular resources because the data are those he created and are available to him, the fact remains that the collection of those data, their systematic or methodical arrangement in the database, the organisation of their individual accessibility and the verification of their accuracy throughout the operation of the database may require substantial investment in quantitative and/or qualitative terms within the meaning of Article 7(1) of the directive.

In the case in the main proceedings, the referring court seeks to know whether the investments described in paragraph 14 of this judgment can be considered to amount to investment in obtaining the contents of the BHB database. The plaintiffs in the main proceedings stress, in that connection, the substantial nature of the above investment.

However, investment in the selection, for the purpose of organising horse racing, of the horses admitted to run in the race concerned relates to the creation of the data which make up the lists for those races which appear in the BHB database. It does not constitute investment in obtaining the contents of the database. It cannot, therefore, be taken into account in assessing whether the investment in the creation of the database was substantial.

Admittedly, the process of entering a horse on a list for a race requires a number of prior checks as to the identity of the person making the entry, the characteristics of the horse and the classification of the horse, its owner and the jockey.

However, such prior checks are made at the stage of creating the list for the race in question. They thus constitute investment in the creation of data and not in the verification of the contents of the database.

It follows that the resources used to draw up a list of horses in a race and to carry out checks in that connection do not represent investment in the obtaining and verification of the contents of the database in which that list appears.

In the light of the foregoing, the second and third questions referred should be answered as follows:

— The expression 'investment in ... the obtaining ... of the contents' of a database in Article 7(1) of the directive must be understood to refer to the resources used to seek out existing independent materials and collect them in the database. It does not cover the resources used for the creation of materials which make up the contents of a database.

— The expression 'investment in ... the ... verification ... of the contents' of a database in Article 7(1) of the directive must be understood to refer to the resources used, with a view to ensuring the reliability of the information contained in that database, to monitor the accuracy of the materials collected when the database was created and during its operation. The resources used for verification during the stage of creation of materials which are subsequently collected in a database do not fall within that definition.

— The resources used to draw up a list of horses in a race and to carry out checks in that connection do not constitute investment in the obtaining and verification of the contents of the database in which that list appears.

Notes and Questions

1.   Although the European Community Database Directive was promulgated around the time when countries were updating copyright laws in response to challenges created by the Internet, it is important to remember that the directive applies equally to both electronic and nonelectronic databases. Article 1(2) states specifically that the directive covers databases that are accessible by "electronic *or other* means" (emphasis added).

2.   *Sui generis* database rights can be traced back to the "catalogue rule" in Nordic countries, which provides short-term protection for catalogues, tables and similar fact-based compilations. Article 49 of

the Swedish Act on Copyright in Literary and Artistic Works, for example, provides:

> Anyone who has produced a catalogue, a table or another similar product in which a large number of information items have been compiled or which is the result of a significant investment, has an exclusive right to make copies of the product and to make it available to the public.
>
> The right under the first Paragraph lasts until fifteen years have elapsed from the year in which the product was completed.

See generally Gunnar W.G. Karnell, *The Nordic Catalogue Rule, in* PROTECTING WORKS OF FACTS: COPYRIGHT, FREEDOM OF EXPRESSION AND INFORMATION LAW 67 (Egbert J. Dommering & P. Bernt Hugenholtz eds., 1991).

3.   Copyright law, in general, provides incentives for authors to create. The sui generis rights in the European Community Database Directive, however, protect "substantial investment in either the obtaining, verification or presentation of the contents to prevent extraction and/or re-utilization ... of the contents of that database." Is such protection rational and desirable? Should copyright holders be able to obtain protection in addition to what they already have obtained under existing copyright laws? The Grand Chamber noted that sui generis database rights were created "to promote the establishment of storage and processing systems for existing information and not the creation of materials capable of being collected subsequently in a database." Do you agree?

4.   Article 11 of the European Community Database Directive allows European Union members to deny protection to databases produced in other countries that fail to offer comparable protection. Such a reciprocal requirement had led the United States Congress to consider legislative proposals for stronger database protection as part of an effort to maintain the competitive advantage of United States database producers. From the standpoint of international development, are reciprocal requirements desirable? Are such requirements consistent with the national treatment requirements mandated by the Berne and Paris Conventions and the TRIPS Agreement?

5.   Today, the United States has yet to offer sui generis protection to databases, although original, creative databases remain protected under copyright law. Likewise, although an international database treaty was proposed in the 1996 WIPO diplomatic conference, offering database protection for a term of twenty-five years, such a treaty has yet to be adopted. In retrospect, what accounts for the failure to provide *sui generis* protection at both the domestic and multilateral levels? How important are the *Feist* decision and the constitutional originality requirement as barriers to such protection in the United States?

6. In 2005, the European Commission released its first report on the European Community Database Directive. COMM'N OF THE EUROPEAN COMMUNITIES, FIRST EVALUATION OF DIRECTIVE 96/9/EC ON THE LEGAL PROTECTION OF DATABASES (2005). According to the report, there were 4085 EU-based database "entries" in 2001, the time when most of the first fifteen European Union member states had implemented the Directive into national laws. The number of "entries," however, declined three years later by close to a quarter to 3095. Although the Directive aimed to create a level-playing field between American and European database industries, "the European share decreased from 33% to 24% [between 2002 and 2004] while the US share increased from 62% to 72%. The ratio of European/US database production, which was nearly 1:2 in 1996, has become 1:3 in 2004." Given the limited benefits and potential harms, should the European Community Database Directive be repealed? Why or why not?

7. In *British Horseracing Board*, the Grand Chamber, a full bench of 13 judges, distinguished between "creating" and "obtaining" data. It also declared that the *sui generis* database right "concerns only acts of extraction and re-utilisation [of database contents, but does not] ... cover consultation of a database." Is it easy to draw a line between "creating" and "obtaining" data? What about "extracting and re-utilising" database contents on the one hand and "consulting" on the other? Are these distinctions workable? Why did the Grand Chamber make such distinctions?

B. MORAL RIGHTS

United States copyright law is work-centered, as compared to author- or producer-centered. It protects primarily the authors' *economic* rights, as compared to *personality* or *moral* rights. Section 106 of the Copyright Act, for example, protects the rights of authors to reproduce, distribute, adapt, publicly display, publicly perform, and digitally transmit creative works. Although the subsequently-added § 106A offers moral rights protection to works of visual art, such protection is very limited—and inadequate by the standards of most advocates of moral rights (even though *additional* protections may be found outside the copyright regime, as Roberta Kwall discusses in an excerpt below).

Unlike United States copyright law, the copyright laws of European countries, especially those on the continent, are generally author-centered. Hence the term "author's right" in lieu of "copyright": *droit d'auteur* in France, *Urheberrecht* in Germany, *diritto d'autore* in Italy, *chosakuken* in Japan, and *derecho de autor* in Spain. In addition to economic rights, these countries offer substantial protection for a rich variety of moral rights (*droit moral*).

The right of attribution (*droit de paternité*) is the right to claim authorship of the protected work. The right of integrity (*droit au respect de l'oeuvre*) is the right to prevent the distortion, mutilation, or other modification of the work in a manner prejudicial to the author's honor or reputation. The right of disclosure (*droit de divulgation*) is the right to determine when the work is ready for public dissemination and in what form the work will be disseminated. The right of withdrawal (*droit de retrait*) is the right to withdraw the work from public dissemination. The right of resale royalties (*droit de suite*) allows creative artists to share in the proceeds from the resale of their works for a limited period of time.

Today, many European commentators continue to question whether the United States is in full compliance with the moral rights obligations under the Berne Convention.

Berne Convention for the Protection of Literary and Artistic Works

Sept. 9, 1886, *revised at Paris* July 24, 1971

828 U.N.T.S. 221

Article 6*bis*

(1) Independently of the author's economic rights, and even after the transfer of the said rights, the author shall have the right to claim authorship of the work and to object to any distortion, mutilation or other modification of, or other derogatory action in relation to, the said work, which would be prejudicial to his honor or reputation.

(2) The rights granted to the author in accordance with the preceding paragraph shall, after his death, be maintained, at least until the expiry of the economic rights, and shall be exercisable by the persons or institutions authorized by the legislation of the country where protection is claimed. However, those countries whose legislation, at the moment of their ratification of or accession to this Act, does not provide for the protection after the death of the author of all the rights set out in the preceding paragraph may provide that some of these rights may, after his death, cease to be maintained.

(3) The means of redress for safeguarding the rights granted by this Article shall be governed by the legislation of the country where protection is claimed.

Code de la Propriété Intellectuelle [Intellectual Property Code] (France)

Title II
Authors' Rights

Art. L. 121–1.

An author shall enjoy the right to respect for his name, his authorship and his work.

This right shall attach to his person.

It shall be perpetual, inalienable and imprescriptible. It may be transmitted *mortis causa* to the heirs of the author.

Exercise may be conferred on another person under the provisions of a will.

Art. L. 121–2.

The author alone shall have the right to divulge his work. He shall determine the method of disclosure and shall fix the conditions thereof, subject to Article L. 132–24.

After his death, the right to disclose his posthumous works shall be exercised during their lifetime by the executor or executors designated by the author. If there are none, or after their death, and unless the author has willed otherwise, this right shall be exercised in the following order: by the descendants, by the spouse against whom there exists no final judgment of separation and who has not remarried, by the heirs other than descendants, who inherit all or part of the estate and by the universal legatees or donees of the totality of the future assets.

This right may be exercised even after expiry of the exclusive right of exploitation set out in Article L. 123–1.

Art. L. 121–3.

In the event of manifest abuse in the exercise or non-exercise of the right of disclosure by the deceased author's representatives referred to in Article L. 121–2, the first instance court may order any appropriate measure. The same shall apply in the event of a dispute between such representatives, if there is no known successor in title, no heir or no spouse entitled to inherit.

Such matters may be referred to the courts by the Minister responsible for culture.

Art. L. 121–4.

Notwithstanding assignment of his right of exploitation, the author shall enjoy a right to reconsider or of withdrawal, even after publication of his work, with respect to the assignee. However, he may only exercise that right on the condition that he indemnify the assignee beforehand for any prejudice the reconsideration or withdrawal may cause him. If the author decides to have his work published after having exercised his right to reconsider or of withdrawal, he shall be required to offer his rights of exploitation in the first instance to the assignee he originally chose and under the conditions originally determined.

Art. L. 121–5.

An audiovisual work shall be deemed completed when the final version has been established by common accord between the director or, possibly, the joint authors, on the one hand, and the producer, on the other.

Destruction of the master copy of such version shall be prohibited.

Any change made to that version by adding, deleting or modifying any element thereof shall require the agreement of the persons referred to in the first paragraph above.

Any transfer of an audiovisual work to another kind of medium with a view to a different mode of exploitation shall require prior consultation with the director.

The authors' own rights, as defined in Article L. 121–1, may be exercised by those authors only in respect of the completed audiovisual work.

Art. L. 121–6.

If one of the authors refuses to complete his contribution to an audiovisual work or is unable to complete such contribution due to circumstances beyond his control, he shall not be entitled to oppose use of that part of his contribution already in existence for the purpose of completing the work. He shall be deemed the author of such contribution and shall enjoy the rights deriving therefrom.

Art. L. 121–7.

Except for any stipulation more favorable to the author, such author may not:

1°. oppose modification of the software by the assignee of the rights referred to in item 2 of Article L. 122–6 where such modification does not prejudice either his honor or his reputation;

2°. exercise his right to reconsider or of withdrawal.

Art. L. 121–8.

The author alone shall have the right to make a collection of his articles and speeches and to publish them or to authorize their publication in such form.

With regard to all works published in such way in a newspaper or periodical, the author shall maintain his right, unless otherwise stipulated, to have them reproduced or to exploit them in any form whatsoever, on condition that such reproduction or exploitation is not such as to compete with the newspaper or periodical concerned.

TURNER ENTERTAINMENT CO. v. HUSTON

Cour d'appel [CA] [regional court of appeal] Versailles, civ. ch., Dec. 19, 1994 (Fr.)
Translated in ENT. L. REP., Mar. 1995, at 3

I

The cinematographic work entitled "ASPHALT JUNGLE" [*Quand la Ville Dort*] was produced in 1950 in the UNITED STATES by the METRO GOLDWYN MAYER (MGM) company, a division of LOEW's Inc. The film was shot in black and white by the late John HUSTON, a movie director of American nationality, at the time bound by a contract of employment to LOEW's Inc. and co-author of the screenplay with Ben MADDOW, bound to the same company by a contract as a salaried writer.

On 2nd May 1950, LOEW's Inc. obtained from the U.S. COPYRIGHT OFFICE a certificate of registration of its rights to the film. This registration was duly renewed in 1977. On 26th September 1986 the benefit of this registration was transferred to the TURNER ENTERTAINMENT Co. by virtue of a merger with MGM, including transfer of the ownership of MGM's movie library and connected rights.

The TURNER company had the movie colorized, an operation which on 20th June 1988 resulted in registration of a copyright application, and it enabled the Fifth French Television Channel (LA CINQ) to announce that it would broadcast this colorized version at 8:30 p.m. on 26th June 1988.

The broadcast was objected to by John HUSTON's heirs, Angelica, Daniel and Walter HUSTON, who were subsequently joined by Mr Ben MADDOW, the Societe des Auteurs et Compositeurs Dramatiques (SACD), the Societe des Realisateurs de Films (SRF), the Syndicat Frangais des Artistes Interpretes (SFA), the Federation Europeenne des Relisateurs de l'Audiovisuel (FERA), the Syndicat Frangais des Realisateurs de Television CGT and the Syndicat National des Techniciens de la Production Cinematographique et de Television. They opposed the broadcast because they deemed it a violation of the author's moral right, aggravated in their opinion by the fact that John HUSTON had opposed colorization of his works during his life. . . .

III

[T]he judges in first instance correctly stressed the "very different conceptions" of U.S. and French laws, the first focusing exclusively on the protection of economic rights without referring to the creative act underlying the inalienable moral right recognized by French law, viz. Section 6 of the Law of 11th March 1957, at the time applicable, which provides that "the author enjoys the right to respect for his name, his status, his work—this right is attached to his person—it is perpetual, inalienable and imprescribable—it is transmitted after death to the author's heirs".

John HUSTON and Ben MADDOW, of whom it is not disputed that the first is the co-author of the screenplay and the director of the film entitled "ASPHALT JUNGLE" and the second the co-author of the same film, as already referred to under (I–1), are in fact its authors, having created it, and whereas they are therefore, in the meaning of the aforesaid law, vested with the corresponding moral right, which is part of public law and therefore mandatorily protected.

Section 1 of Law No 64–689 of 8th July 1964 on the application of the principle of reciprocity with respect to copyright provides as follows:

> "Subject to the provisions of the international conventions to which FRANCE is a party, in the event that it is noted, after consultation of the Minister of Foreign Affairs, that a State does not provide adequate and effective protection for works disclosed for the first time in FRANCE, irrespective of the form thereof, works disclosed for the first time in the territory of the said State shall not benefit from the copyright protection recognized by French law. However, the integrity or authorship of such works may not be violated. In the case provided for in paragraph 1 heretofore, royalties shall be paid to organizations of general interest designated by decree."

The defect in protection thus likely to affect the foreign work on the conditions governing reciprocity, as laid out in paragraph 1, can only concern its economic aspects, i.e. the patrimonial rights attached thereto, in that it is limited by the general mandatory rule providing for respect of an author's moral right as proclaimed without reservation in paragraph 2.

It follows that the moral rights attached to the person of the creators of the work entitled "ASPHALT JUNGLE" could not be transferred and, therefore, the judges in first instance correctly ruled that Messrs and Mrs HUSTON and Ben MADDOW were entitled to claim recognition and protection thereof in FRANCE.

However, the TURNER company, which it is not disputed is the holder of the author's economic rights, maintains that these rights include the right to adapt the work and therefore to colorize the film entitled "ASPHALT JUNGLE", arguing that it cannot be maintained that this denatures the work; Me PIERREL, ex-officio, follows the same argument, submitting that the colorized version of the film is merely an adaptation of the original black-and-white version which is left intact and is therefore not affected.

However, "colorization" is a technique based on the use of computer and laser and it makes it possible, after transferring the original black-and-white tape onto a videographic media, to give color to a film which did not originally have color; the application of this process is in no event to be considered an adaptation, defined as "an original work both in its expression and in its composition", even if it borrows formal elements from the pre-existing work; colorization, far from meeting these criteria, in fact merely consists in modifying the work by adding an element thus far not part of the creator's aesthetic conception.

The judges in first instance in the present case have precisely pointed out that the aesthetic conception which earned John HU-STON his great fame is based on the interplay of black and white, which enabled him to create an atmosphere according to which he directed the actor and selected the backdrops; moreover, he expressed himself clearly about his film entitled "The Maltese Falcon" when stating, "I wanted to shoot it in black and white like a sculptor chooses to work in clay, to pour his work in bronze, to sculpt in marble".

In 1950, while color film technique was already widespread and another option was available, the film entitled "ASPHALT JUNGLE" was shot in black and white, following a deliberate aesthetic choice, according to a process which its authors considered best suited to the character of the work.

Therefore, the film's colorization without authorization and control by the authors or their heirs amounted to violation of the creative activity of its makers, even if it should satisfy the expectations of a certain public for commercially obvious reasons; the use of this process without the agreement of Messrs and Mrs HUSTON and Ben MADDOW infringed the moral right of the authors as mandatorily protected under French law; Messrs and Mrs HUSTON and Ben MADDOW have therefore good grounds to petition the court for reparation of their prejudice at the hands of the TURNER company, and they will therefore be allotted FRF 400,000 by way of damages and costs for the damage done; moreover, the judges in first instance correctly recognized their right to demand that LA CINQ SA be forbidden to broadcast the modified version of the film entitled "ASPHALT JUNGLE".

Lior Jacob Strahilevitz
The Right to Destroy
114 Yale L.J. 781 (2005)

Does a creator have more leeway to destroy a piece of property than an ordinary owner who acquires the property via purchase, inheritance, or gift? Joseph Sax says yes, at least in the case of works of art, because an "artist should be entitled to decide how the world will remember him or her." I agree with his bottom line, though I will elaborate on the justifications for this conclusion.

Creators often attempt to destroy their property.... Franz Kafka famously decided to have his unpublished manuscripts, letters, and diaries destroyed while he was in a sanitarium, dying of tuberculosis. To that end, he wrote his executor and friend, Max Brod, two separate notes directing him to burn, unread, all of Kafka's writings immediately. In addition to these notes, Kafka verbally directed Brod to destroy his written works. Included in the materials Kafka asked Brod to destroy were the only copies of his two then-unpublished masterpieces, *The Castle* and *The Trial*. Brod "did not honor his friend's last wish." Instead, he edited and published Kafka's novels, short stories, diaries, and other writings.

Kafka's dying wishes of artistic destruction were not unusual. The author Jacqueline Susann similarly directed her executor to burn her diary upon her passing. The diary had been valued at $3.8 million. Virgil evidently wanted the *Aeneid* burned upon his death, but he appears to have changed his mind after friends convinced him that Augustus would never allow such destruction. In 1954, at the age of twenty-four, an obscure artist decided to destroy all the paintings he had previously executed, as a way of "beginning afresh with a blank canvas." Within a few years, that artist, Jasper Johns, would produce a world-famous painting of the American flag and become one of the most talked-about artists of his era. More recently, Brett Weston, a well-known photographer, publicly incinerated a lifetime's worth of valuable negatives to commemorate his eightieth birthday.

Suppose the Kafka case, or something like it, had been litigated. Let us imagine a modern-day American Kafka, who[m] we'll call *K*, and a will that is being probated. Say the will contains unambiguous instructions for Brod to destroy all copies of *K*'s unwritten work. And yet Brod approaches the court seeking direction. Brod argues that the texts have great literary and commercial value and that to destroy them would constitute an unconscionable waste. What should a court do? Richard Posner states that these types of cases arise commonly and that courts typically would strike the direction to destroy the papers on public policy grounds. Assume our hypothetical court embraces this approach and directs Brod to publish the valuable K works, with the proceeds to be distributed among K's named beneficiaries. Is this the right result? I submit that the K papers and manuscripts should be destroyed, on the basis of any of four rationales.

First, we might reiterate the *ex ante* argument. A society that does not allow authors to have their draft works destroyed post-humously could have less literary product than a society that requires the preservation of all literary works not destroyed during the author's life. Protecting authors' rights to destroy should encourage high-risk, high-reward projects, and might prevent writers from worrying that they should not commit words to paper unless they have complete visions of the narrative structures for their work. Indeed, the society that respects the dead author's wish for his unfinished writings to be burned avoids putting the ailing artist in the terrible position of having to burn unfinished works that might be completed if he recovers. In the past, great artists have erred on the side of destruction out of fear that their unfinished works would tarnish their reputations.

Second, we might accept an economic rationale. K is in the best position to determine which of his works should form his artistic legacy. K has an economic interest (via his concern for the welfare of his beneficiaries) in assuring that the value of his published works is not diminished by the conceivably inferior quality of the unpublished works. After all, the law does not force Hugo Boss to ship its irregular or substandard clothing to discount sellers. Rather, it lets Hugo Boss opt for a reputation as a maker of high-status, invariably high-quality garments. By the same token, the court should defer to K's judgment about what actions will maximize the value of his estate. Because K's heirs would have the same economic interest in the value of his collective works, they should have the same opportunity to destroy works that might diminish his reputation.

Third and relatedly, ... [b]y destroying his unfinished works, K may wish to send a message to the public that he is not the type of artist who will tolerate, let alone publish, inferior works. A dramatic destruction of K's unfinished works certainly would garner the public's attention. Brod's publicized destruction of the work that had taken so much of K's time perhaps would rekindle public interest in those few works that K thought were worthy of publication.

Finally, there is another expressive component to K's destruction.... If a court decides to bar Brod from destroying K's unpublished works, it is forcing the departed K to speak when he would have preferred to remain silent. From a First Amendment perspective, a judicial remedy barring the destruction of literary documents would be problematic if it occurred during K's life. This may be particularly problematic in the context of a controversial or envelope-pushing work. K may have concluded that he only was willing to publish his novel if he could be around to defend it against the inevitable but unpredictable literary criticism that its publication would provoke.

K's death probably would obviate the possibility of a constitutional violation, but the state's action of forcing a dead person to share his private written words still seems to run afoul of the principles underlying the First Amendment right to remain silent. The line of First Amendment cases barring compelled speech sounds in the individual-autonomy-oriented conception of speech. Permitting someone to bar the publication of his own unspoken words enhances expressive liberty without destroying the expression of someone who wished to be heard. From this perspective, destruction of an expressive work by its creator is very different from destruction of a creative work by anyone else.

There are, in short, strong reasons to defer to the destructive wishes of those who have created cultural property, particularly when that property has not been published or publicly displayed. As long as the creator possesses testamentary capacity, deferring to destructive wishes in a will is appropriate.

Roberta Rosenthal Kwall
Copyright and the Moral Right: Is an American Marriage Possible?
38 VAND. L. REV. 1 (1985)

Despite the well-entrenched, if not perfectly uniform, position that the moral right enjoys in many European and Third World nations, creators in the United States are unable to benefit from express applications of the doctrine. Standing alone, this fact is neither a tribute to nor an indictment of our legal system. The critical inquiry is whether our failure to embrace the doctrine has resulted in inadequate protections for the important interests at stake. The overwhelming number of commentators who have studied this question have concluded that the scope of protection in America for the personal rights of creators is insufficient. The criticism is not surprising given that patchwork measures rarely approximate the degree of protection afforded by a cohesive legal theory whose exclusive objective is the specific protection of precise interests.

The principal doctrines that American courts have relied upon to protect a creator's moral rights include unfair competition, breach of contract, defamation, and invasion of privacy. The increasingly liberal applications of unfair competition law generally and section 43(a) of the Lanham Act in particular have popularized these doctrines as vehicles for redressing alleged violations of interests protected elsewhere by the right of integrity and paternity.

Courts rely upon express contractual provisions for granting relief to creators for violations of their integrity interests. In addition, many courts articulate a willingness to interpret ambiguous contracts to vindicate a creator's interests. In an extremely favorable decision for creators, *Gilliam v. American Broadcasting Companies, Inc.*, the Second Circuit held that extensive unauthorized editing of a work protected by common law copyright constitutes copyright infringement at least in the absence of a governing contractual provision. In general, however, if the contract in question does not address modification rights, American courts will protect a creator only against excessive mutilation of his work. American creators thus fare less successfully in modification challenges than their counterparts in moral right countries. As discussed earlier, foreign courts that maintain an inalienable moral right will uphold contractual provisions allowing reasonable alterations of a creator's work in certain contexts, but they will refrain from holding that a creator tacitly has waived his right of integrity by signing an agreement silent on modification rights.

The law of defamation offers creators an avenue for relief if their works are disseminated to the public in such a manner as to injure their professional reputations. The injury might take the form of the publication of a mutilated version of the creator's work under the creator's name, or a false attribution of authorship with respect to a work of poor quality with which the creator was not associated. The key to any successful defamation action, however, is the creator's showing that the unauthorized acts exposed him to contempt or public ridicule, thus injuring his professional standing. Alternatively, a creator whose works have been published without his authorization or who is the victim of a false attribution may seek to redress his injuries by suing for invasion of privacy.

Although the substitute theories discussed in this section afford creators varying levels of protection for their moral rights, American creators typically are at a relative disadvantage compared to creators in moral right countries. The major difficulty facing American creators is the additional burden of molding moral rights claims into other recognized causes of action. Given that all of the substitute theories are supported by a theoretical basis different from that of the moral right doctrine, a successful claim may require elements of proof which are not applicable directly to a moral rights claim. The moral right doctrine is concerned with the creator's personality rights and society's interest in preserving the integrity of its culture. These interests are not the exclusive, or even the primary, focus of any of the substitute theories, all of which developed in response to completely different social concerns. Unfair competition law, as evidenced by its traditional elements of competition, passing off of one's goods or services as those of another, and likelihood of confusion, seeks to protect economic rights and, to a lesser extent, to prevent consumer deception. Similar societal concerns underlie section 43(a) of the Lanham Act, through which Congress intended to vindicate a producer's economic interests by proscribing false representations. Given the significantly different objectives behind the moral right doctrine, on the one hand, and unfair competition law and section 43(a) of the Lanham Act on the other, any protection that a creator may receive for his personality rights under either of these substitute theories merely is fortuitous.

Defamation and invasion of privacy doctrines are of limited utility in protecting a creator's moral rights. The personality rights safeguarded by the moral right doctrine encompass more than protection for a creator's professional reputation or relief for injured feelings. In addition, courts that invoke either defamation or privacy theories frequently adhere to technical rules and requirements that narrow the application of these doctrines in situations concerning moral rights.

Even contract law, which is the purported basis for decision in many cases concerning the integrity and paternity components of the moral right doctrine, cannot function as an adequate substitute. In addition to the limitations presented by the privity requirement and the judiciary's general reluctance to afford extensive protections for creators absent express contractual provisions, relatively unknown creators face a disparity of bargaining power that frequently results in a loss of valuable protections.

Shostakovich v. Twentieth Century–Fox Film Corp. illustrates the unhappy plight of creators who cannot fit their moral rights cause of action into any of the alternate theories discussed above. In *Shostakovich* several prominent Russian composers sought injunctive relief against the defendant's use of their music in a film that, in the plaintiffs' view, had an anti-Soviet theme. In addition to the use of plaintiffs' music, which was in the public domain, the defendant used the plaintiffs' names on the credit lines. The *Shostakovich* plaintiffs based their right to relief on four grounds: (1) New York's statutory right of privacy; (2) defamation; (3) the deliberate infliction of an injury without just cause; and (4) violation of moral rights. With respect to the privacy claim, the court observed that "lack of copyright protection has long been held to permit others to use the names of authors in copying, publishing or compiling their works." As for the defamation claim, the court reasoned that the music's public domain status precluded any implication that the plaintiffs had approved of or endorsed the film, and thus the court refused to sustain plaintiffs' claim for libel. The court treated the plaintiffs' claim for the infliction of wilfull injury in conjunction with their moral rights claim. Although the court paid lip service to the moral right doctrine by noting that "conceivably under the doctrine of Moral Right the court could in a proper case, prevent the use of a composition or work, in the public domain, in such manner as would be violative of the author's rights," the court nevertheless declined the opportunity to vindicate the plaintiffs' interests. In refusing to grant plaintiffs their requested relief, the court emphasized that the plaintiffs made no allegations of distortion and no "clear showing of the infliction of a wilfull injury." Yet, an injury resulting from an inappropriate contextual use of a creator's work is actionable under the moral right doctrine, as evidenced by the French decision granting the plaintiffs in *Shostakovich* their requested relief. A reading of the American *Shostakovich* opinion suggests, however, that the court's discomfort with the moral right doctrine and the difficulty of its application provided the primary impetus for denying the plaintiffs' moral rights claims.

An even more fundamental drawback resulting from the judiciary's reliance on alternate theories rather than a cohesive framework to vindicate moral rights interests is the danger that the competing interests will not receive appropriate attention. Although the moral right doctrine seeks to protect the interests of creators and the public in general, entrepreneurs such as publishers, motion picture producers, broadcasters, and record manufacturers have valid interests that may be opposed diametrically to the right's existence and application. The appropriate balancing of competing interests in a given case depends not only upon the type of creation at issue but also upon its intended use. The adoption of a comprehensive moral right doctrine would provide the necessary framework within which these interests could be balanced effectively.

Although no comprehensive protection for a creator's moral rights currently exists in the United States, California and New York recently have enacted statutes affording visual artists protection for certain aspects of their moral rights. The California Art Preservation Act, which became effective on January 1, 1980, prohibits the intentional "physical defacement, mutilation, alteration or destruction of a work of fine art" by any person except the creating artist who owns and possesses the work. An artist may waive these protections, but only by "an instrument in writing expressly so providing which is signed by the artist." The Act contains a three year statute of limitations that runs from the occurrence of the act in question, and the artist's rights may be exercised by his heir, legatee, or personal representative for fifty years after his death. Remedies under the Act include injunctive relief, actual damages, punitive damages, reasonable attorneys' and expert witness fees, and any other relief that a court may deem appropriate. The statute's protection against destruction is particularly interesting given the reluctance of foreign jurisprudence to extend similarly the right of integrity. Nevertheless, the Act embodies a significant limitation with respect to protecting creators' integrity interests in that it is applicable only to works of "fine art" which have not been prepared under contract for commercial use by the purchaser. Moreover, the destructive act complained of must be intentional.

The New York statute, the Artists' Authorship Rights Act, is similar to the California Art Preservation Act. Under the New York law, effective January 1, 1984, no person other than the artist or someone acting under his authority can display publicly or publish a work of fine art or a reproduction thereof "in an altered, defaced, mutilated or modified form if the work is displayed, published or reproduced as being the work of the artist . . . and damage to the artist's reputation is reasonably likely to result therefrom." The New York statute guarantees the artist the right to compel recognition for his work of fine art as well as the right to disclaim authorship, and provides that a "[j]ust and valid reason for disclaiming authorship shall include that the work of fine art has been altered, defaced, mutilated or modified other than by the artist, without the artist's consent, and damage to the artist's reputation is reasonably likely to result or has resulted therefrom." Any artist who is aggrieved under the statute has a cause of action for legal and injunctive relief. Certain limitations are contained in the statute, however, including a qualified exemption for works prepared for advertising or trade use and the statute's narrowed applicability "only to works of fine art knowingly displayed in a place accessible to the public, published or reproduced" in New York state.

Although both the California and New York statutes represent a positive step for the protection of some moral rights for some creators, much more extensive legislation is needed in the United States so that creators of all categories can obtain a broader range of protections.

Notes and Questions

1. Cinematographic works provide some of the most challenging situations as far as the protection of moral rights is concerned. In the United States, where moral rights protection is limited, the work made

for hire arrangement usually vests the rights in movie producers—in part due to concerns over inconsistency and financial uncertainty caused by residual rights. In jurisdictions where stronger protection of moral rights is available, however, rights may be vested in many participants in a creative project. In France, for example, "[the] authorship of a cinematographic work vested in the co-authors (of the script, adaptation, dialogue, music and the director), although the Law introduced a legal presumption of assignment to the producer of the right to exploitation of the work." GILLIAN DAVIES, COPYRIGHT AND THE PUBLIC INTEREST 154 (2002). Other civil law countries in Europe have laws that either specify "a statutory list of authors of a film" or require courts to "determine who should count as an author on the basis of their creative contribution to its making." MICHAEL SPENCE, INTELLECTUAL PROPERTY 99 (2007).

2. Most European countries do not consider the movie producer a co-author of a cinematographic work. Instead of author's rights, the producer is given neighboring rights (rights *neighboring* to author's rights). In countries where moral rights can be waived, assigned, or devised, the producer usually ends up with a voluntary assignment by all co-authors of the right to exploitation of the cinematographic work. Such assignment is, indeed, presumed in France. Given such presumption and the widespread industry practice, is the protection of moral rights in film merely symbolic? Are there substantive reasons for maintaining such protection? Do you prefer this arrangement to the work made for hire arrangement commonly used by the United States entertainment industry?

3. *Huston* provides an instructive example of the choice of law issues discussed in Chapter 1.B. If United States law governed this particular case, Turner Entertainment would have been an institutional author pursuant to the work made for hire arrangement in United States copyright law. By contrast, if French law were applicable, as the court found in this case, Huston and Maddow would have retained their moral rights even though they assigned their economic rights to Turner. Given the importance of these distinctions, the choice of law issues were among the key issues addressed early on in the case.

4. The Visual Artists Rights Act of 1990 (VARA), 17 U.S.C. § 106A (2006), was enacted shortly after the United States joined the Berne Convention in 1988. (The Convention took effect March 1, 1989.) Professor Kwall's article, however, was written before the enactment of this statute. In the article, she discussed the various substitute theories that could be used to protect the authors' moral interests in their works? Do you agree with Professor Kwall that those theories put American authors "at a relative disadvantage compared to creators in moral right countries"? Is there evidence that American authors, before VARA, produced fewer or lower-quality works than authors from nations with strong moral rights protection? Has VARA put American authors at a level-playing field now? If not, what are its strengths and weaknesses?

5. One of the more controversial rights in the set of moral rights is the right to destroy, which is subsumed under the right of withdrawal. (This right is distinct from the right to prevent destruction subsumed under the right of integrity and covered by VARA for "work[s] of recognized stature.") Both Joseph Sax and Lior Strahilevitz argue that the protection of the authors' right to destroy is needed to encourage high-risk, high-reward projects. Do you agree? If Max Brod followed Franz Kafka's instruction to destroy all of his unpublished works upon his death, this world would never have read two of Kafka's highly influential masterpieces, *The Castle* and *The Trial*. Would society be worse off? Should there be a limit on when authors can destroy their works (just like what authors have to do before they withdraw their works from the public)?

6. There are significant similarities between moral rights and international human rights. For example, in the report accompanying the 1793 French revolutionary law, Le Chapelier declared: "The most sacred, the most legitimate, the most unassailable, and ... the most personal of all properties is the work which is the fruit of a writer's thoughts." Jane C. Ginsburg, *A Tale of Two Copyrights: Literary Property in Revolutionary France and America*, 64 TUL. L. REV. 991, 1007 (1990). Likewise, Article 27(2) of the Universal Declaration of Human Rights states: "Everyone has the right to the protection of the moral and material interests resulting from any scientific, literary or artistic production of which he [or she] is the author." Universal Declaration of Human Rights art. 27(2), G.A. Res. 217A, U.N. GAOR, 3d Sess., 1st plen. mtg., U.N. Doc A/810 (Dec. 10, 1948). Given the similar roots of these two sets of rights, is it fair to say that moral rights have been recognized as human rights?

7. Most recently, Amy Adler argued that "moral rights laws endanger art in the name of protecting it" and that the right of integrity "fails to recognize the profound artistic importance of modifying, even destroying, works of art, and of freeing art from the control of the artist." Amy M. Adler, *Against Moral Rights*, 97 CAL. L. REV. 263 (2009). According to her, "moral rights are premised on the precise conception of 'art' that artists have been rebelling against for the last forty years." To illustrate, she described Robert Rauschenberg's "Erased de Kooning Drawing":

> In 1953, Rauschenberg took a drawing by Willem de Kooning and spent a month erasing it. The resulting work is a "sheet of paper bearing the faint, ghostly shadow of its former markings." Entitling the work "Erased de Kooning Drawing/Robert Rauschenberg/1953," Rauschenberg exhibited the erasure as his own art. Rauschenberg wrote: "I wanted to create a work of art by [erasing].... Using my own work wasn't satisfactory.... I realized that it had to be something by someone who everybody agreed was great, and the most logical person for that was de Kooning."

Here is an example of how art can emerge from the near destruction of a previous piece. The Rauschenberg work depends on the fact that he violated not a reproduction of a work but an original, and not just any original, but an original by Willem de Kooning. To fully grasp the radical quality of Rauschenberg's work, one must remember the place of de Kooning in 1950s America. At that time, abstract expressionism so dominated American art (and our artistic place in the world) that de Kooning and his compatriots had come to be viewed as heroic and almost godlike. In that climate, erasing a drawing by de Kooning was a shocking, sacrilegious act. It captured, perhaps better than anything else Rauschenberg did, his scandalous assault on a particular conception of "art." For the generation of artists after de Kooning the question was: how would it be possible to make art in the wake of the godlike artists who came before them? Rauschenberg's answer was that new art might be about its own failure to achieve greatness, its impotent rebellion against the heroic past. Rauschenberg began to make art that, in the words of Douglas Crimp, was about "its own destruction."

Do you agree with Professor Adler? Would moral rights protection privilege certain conceptions of art? Didn't Justice Holmes remind us in *Bleistein v. Donaldson Lithographing Co.* that "[i]t would be a dangerous undertaking for persons trained only to the law to constitute themselves final judges of the worth of pictorial illustrations"? 188 U.S. 239, 251 (1903).

8. There are significant tensions—or maybe even conflicts—between the protection of moral rights and the enjoyment and exercise of the right to free expression (including the right to create parodies and satires). Nevertheless, even in jurisdictions with strong moral rights protection, the right to parody may exist as an exception to those rights. Article 122–5(4) of the Code de la Propriété Intellectuelle, for example, provides explicitly that "[o]nce a work has been disclosed, the author may not prohibit ... parody, pastiche and caricature, observing the rules of the genre." Given the coexistence of these two sets of rights, how can one reduce the tension between them?

9. Although the Berne Convention covers the protection of moral rights and has been incorporated by reference into the TRIPS Agreement, the Agreement states explicitly that disputes over a lack of protection of moral rights would not be subject to the mandatory dispute resolution process under the WTO. Are there rational reasons for excluding moral rights protection from such a process? Given the exclusion, can authors obtain stronger protection of their moral rights at the multilateral level?

C. LIMITATIONS AND EXCEPTIONS TO COPYRIGHT: FAIR USE/FAIR DEALING

In the copyright system, limitations and exceptions are as important as the grant of rights. Although the latter is rather uniform, the former diverges significantly throughout the world. While United States copyright law includes a broad and all-encompassing fair use standard, in addition to other limitations and exceptions stipulated in the copyright statute, "fair dealing" in other countries remains rather limited. Some countries and commentators, indeed, have questioned whether the United States fair use standard is consistent with the minimum standards required by the Berne Convention and the TRIPS Agreement, which includes a three-step test to help strike a balance between exclusive protection and public access needs.

Even more problematic for many developing countries, copyright protection has been strengthened considerably in the past few decades by virtue of new international, regional, and bilateral standards. Meanwhile, the limitations and exceptions that correspond to those new protections have not been added. Thus, many of the existing limitations and exceptions in United States copyright law are unavailable abroad, and the copyright systems of many developing countries remain unresponsive to their local needs, interests, and goals. In recent years, developing countries, commentators, and nongovernmental organizations have actively pushed for greater limitations and exceptions in the international copyright system. Such limitations and exceptions have also become part of the WIPO copyright agenda.

Berne Convention for the Protection of Literary and Artistic Works

Sept. 9, 1886, *revised at Paris* July 24, 1971

828 U.N.T.S. 221

Article 9

(2) It shall be a matter for legislation in the countries of the Union to permit the reproduction of such works in certain special cases, provided that such reproduction does not conflict with a normal exploitation of the work and does not unreasonably prejudice the legitimate interests of the author.

Agreement on Trade–Related Aspects of Intellectual Property Rights

Apr. 15, 1994
Marrakesh Agreement Establishing the World Trade Organization,
Annex 1C, Legal Instruments—Results of the Uruguay
Round, 33 I.L.M. 1197 (1994)

Article 13
Limitations and Exceptions

Members shall confine limitations or exceptions to exclusive rights to certain special cases which do not conflict with a normal exploitation of the work and do not unreasonably prejudice the legitimate interests of the right holder.

Panel Report
United States—Section 110(5) of the U.S. Copyright Act

WT/DS/160/R (June 15, 2000)

The European Communities alleges that the exemptions provided in subparagraphs (A) and (B) of Section 110(5) of the US Copyright Act are in violation of the United States' obligations under the TRIPS Agreement. In particular, it alleges that these US measures are incompatible with Article 9.1 of the TRIPS Agreement together with Articles 11(1)(ii) and 11*bis*(1)(iii) of the Berne Convention (1971) and that they cannot be justified under any express or implied exception or limitation permissible under the Berne Convention (1971) or the TRIPS Agreement. In the view of the EC, these measures cause prejudice to the legitimate rights of copyright owners, thus nullifying and impairing the rights of the European Communities.

The European Communities requests the Panel to find that the United States has violated its obligations under Article 9.1 of the TRIPS Agreement together with Articles 11*bis*(1)(iii) and 11(1)(ii) of the Berne Convention (1971) and to recommend that the United States bring its domestic legislation into conformity with its obligations under the TRIPS Agreement.

The United States contends that Section 110(5) of the US Copyright Act is fully consistent with its obligations under the TRIPS Agreement. The Agreement, incorporating the substantive provisions of the Berne Convention (1971), allows Members to place minor limitations on the exclusive rights of copyright owners. Article 13 of the TRIPS Agreement provides the standard by which to judge the appropriateness of such limitations or exceptions. The exemptions embodied in Section 110(5) fall within the Article 13 standard.

The United States requests the Panel to find that both subparagraphs (A) and (B) of Section 110(5) of the US Copyright Act meet the standard of Article 13 of the TRIPS Agreement and the substantive obligations of the Berne Convention (1971). Accordingly, the United States requests the Panel to dismiss the claims of the European Communities in this dispute. . . .

Article 13 of the TRIPS Agreement requires that limitations and exceptions to exclusive rights (1) be confined to certain special cases, (2) do not conflict with a normal exploitation of the work, and (3) do not unreasonably prejudice the legitimate interests of the right holder. The principle of effective treaty interpretation requires us to give a distinct meaning to each of the three conditions and to avoid a reading that could reduce any of the conditions to "redundancy or inutility". The three conditions apply on a cumulative basis, each being a separate and independent requirement that must be satisfied. Failure to comply with any one of the three conditions results in the Article 13 exception being disallowed. Both parties agree on the cumulative nature of the three conditions. The Panel shares their view. It may be noted at the outset that Article 13 cannot have more than a narrow or limited operation. Its tenor, consistent as it is with the provisions of Article 9(2) of the Berne Convention (1971), discloses that it was not intended to provide for exceptions or limitations except for those of a limited nature. The narrow sphere of its operation will emerge from our discussion and application of its provisions in the paragraphs which follow. . . .

"Certain special cases"

The ordinary meaning of "certain" is "known and particularised, but not explicitly identified", "determined, fixed, not variable; definitive, precise, exact". In other words, this term means that, under the first condition, an exception or limitation in national legislation must be clearly defined. However, there is no need to identify explicitly each and every possible situation to which the exception could apply, provided that the scope of the exception is known and particularised. This guarantees a sufficient degree of legal certainty.

We also have to give full effect to the ordinary meaning of the second word of the first condition. The term "special" connotes "having an individual or limited application or purpose", "containing details; precise, specific", "exceptional in quality or degree; unusual; out of the ordinary" or "distinctive in some way". This term means that more is needed than a clear definition in order to meet the standard of the first condition. In addition, an exception or limitation must be limited in its field of application or exceptional in its scope. In other words, an exception or limitation should be narrow in quantitative as well as a qualitative sense. This suggests a narrow scope as well as an exceptional or distinctive objective. To put this aspect of the first condition into the context of the second condition ("no conflict with a normal exploitation"), an exception or limitation should be the opposite of a non-special, i.e., a normal case.

The ordinary meaning of the term "case" refers to an "occurrence", "circumstance" or "event" or "fact". For example, in the context of the dispute at hand, the "case" could be described in terms of beneficiaries of the exceptions, equipment used, types of works or by other factors.

As regards the parties' arguments on whether the public policy purpose of an exception is relevant, we believe that the term "certain special cases" should not lightly be equated with "special purpose". It is difficult to reconcile the wording of Article 13 with the proposition that an exception or limitation must be justified in terms of a legitimate public policy purpose in order to fulfill the first condition of the Article. We also recall in this respect that in interpreting other WTO rules, such as the national treatment clauses of the GATT and the GATS, the Appellate Body has rejected interpretative tests which were based on the subjective aim or objective pursued by national legislation.

In our view, the first condition of Article 13 requires that a limitation or exception in national legislation should be clearly defined and should be narrow in its scope and reach. On the other hand, a limitation or exception may be compatible with the first condition even if it pursues a special purpose whose underlying legitimacy in a normative sense cannot be discerned. The wording of Article 13's first condition does not imply passing a judgment on the legitimacy of the exceptions in dispute. However, public policy purposes stated by law-makers when enacting a limitation or exception may be useful from a factual perspective for making inferences about the scope of a limitation or exception or the clarity of its definition. . . .

"Not conflict with a normal exploitation of the work"

The ordinary meaning of the term "exploit" connotes "making use of" or "utilising for one's own ends". We believe that "exploitation" of musical works thus refers to the activity by which copyright owners employ the exclusive rights conferred on them to extract economic value from their rights to those works.

We note that the ordinary meaning of the term "normal" can be defined as "constituting or conforming to a type or standard; regular, usual, typical, ordinary, conventional. . . ." In our opinion, these definitions appear to reflect two connotations: the first one appears to be of an empirical nature, i.e., what is regular, usual, typical or ordinary. The other one reflects a somewhat more normative, if not dynamic, approach, i.e., conforming to a type or standard. We do not feel compelled to pass a judgment on which one of these connotations could be more relevant. Based on Article 31 of the Vienna Convention [on the Law of Treaties], we will attempt to develop a harmonious interpretation which gives meaning and effect to both connotations of "normal".

If "normal" exploitation were equated with full use of all exclusive rights conferred by copyrights, the exception clause of Article 13 would be left devoid of meaning. Therefore, "normal" exploitation clearly means something less than full use of an exclusive right. . . . We believe that an exception or limitation to an exclusive right in domestic legislation rises to the level of a conflict with a normal exploitation of the work (i.e., the copyright or rather the whole bundle of exclusive rights conferred by the ownership of the copyright), if uses, that in principle are covered by that right but exempted under the exception or limitation, enter into economic competition with the ways that right holders normally extract economic value from that right to the work (i.e., the copyright) and thereby deprive them of significant or tangible commercial gains. . . .

"Not unreasonably prejudice the legitimate interests of the right holder"

We note that the analysis of the third condition of Article 13 of the TRIPS Agreement implies several steps. First, one has to define what are the "interests" of right holders at stake and which attributes make them "legitimate". Then, it is necessary to develop an interpretation of the term "prejudice" and what amount of it reaches a level that should be considered "unreasonable".

The ordinary meaning of the term "interests" may encompass a legal right or title to a property or to use or benefit of a property (including intellectual property). It may also refer to a concern about a potential detriment or advantage, and more generally to something that is of some importance to a natural or legal person. Accordingly, the notion of "interests" is not necessarily limited to actual or potential economic advantage or detriment.

The term "legitimate" has the meanings of

"(a) conformable to, sanctioned or authorized by, law or principle; lawful; justifiable; proper;

(b) normal, regular, conformable to a recognized standard type."

Thus, the term relates to lawfulness from a legal positivist perspective, but it has also the connotation of legitimacy from a more normative perspective, in the context of calling for the protection of interests that are justifiable in the light of the objectives that underlie the protection of exclusive rights.

We note that the ordinary meaning of "prejudice" connotes damage, harm or injury. "Not unreasonable" connotes a slightly stricter threshold than "reasonable". The latter term means "proportionate", "within the limits of reason, not greatly less or more than might be thought likely or appropriate", or "of a fair, average or considerable amount or size".

Given that the parties do not question the "legitimacy" of the interest of right holders to exercise their rights for economic gain, the crucial question becomes which degree or level of "prejudice" may be considered as "unreasonable". Before dealing with the question of what amount or which kind of prejudice reaches a level beyond reasonable, we need to find a way to measure or quantify legitimate interests.

In our view, one—albeit incomplete and thus conservative— way of looking at legitimate interests is the economic value of the exclusive rights conferred by copyright on their holders. It is possible to estimate in economic terms the value of exercising, e.g., by licensing, such rights. That is not to say that legitimate interests are necessarily limited to this economic value.

Ruth Okediji
Toward an International Fair Use Doctrine
39 Colum. J. Transnat'l L. 75 (2000)

The compatibility of the fair use doctrine with the United States' obligations under the Berne Convention was not formally questioned or disputed at the time of U.S. accession. It was strongly evident throughout the debates over accession that the international community, including the World Intellectual Property Organization, was willing to accept less than full compliance in exchange for the increased importance that U.S. accession would bring to the Berne Convention. Since accession to the Berne Convention, however, the copyright climate in the Unites States has undergone a dramatic transformation. The copyright industry has demanded and received greater rights for owners and stronger protection for copyrighted works. This maximalist trend manifested concretely in the initiation of negotiations for heightened universal norms of intellectual property protection established by the TRIPS Agreement and enforceable under the auspices of the new institutional apparatus for global trade, the WTO. Domestic implementation of subsequent copyright treaties, such as the WIPO Copyright Treaty and the WIPO Performances and Phonograms Treaty, continued to reflect this aggrandizement of owners' rights. Thus, today, the fair use doctrine may be directly challenged by foreign trade partners as inconsistent with United States' obligations under international copyright treaties and indirectly by domestic interests which align with foreign trade partners to utilize international fora to alter the design of domestic copyright policy.

With regard to foreign challenges, several trading partners requested clarification of the fair use doctrine within the framework of the TRIPS Council Review of Legislation. Copyright policy in the United States has traditionally recognized a qualitatively broader scope of limitations and exceptions to authors' rights as the means through which the Constitutional goal of "progress of science and useful arts" is accomplished. Although countries such as the United Kingdom and Canada have "fair dealing" and "fair use" provisions in their copyright legislation, these provisions differ significantly in scope and purpose from the American fair use doctrine. Hence, the European Community, Australia and New Zealand respectively asked the United States to justify how the exceptions to the reproduction right afforded under copyright law, including the fair use doctrine, are consistent with Article 9(2) of the Berne Convention and Article 13 of TRIPS. Specifically, the European Community asked the United States to explain "how the fair use doctrine, as it has been broadly applied and interpreted by U.S. courts, particularly in connection with a 'parody' that diminishes the value of a work, is consistent with TRIPS Article 13, given the obligation to 'confine limitations or exceptions to exclusive rights to certain special cases which do not conflict with a normal exploitation of the work and do not unreasonably prejudice the legitimate interests of the right holder.'" Australia posed a question regarding the consistency of fair use with Article 9(2) of the Berne Convention and Article 13 of TRIPS in light of *Sega Enterprises Ltd. v. Accolade, Inc.* and *Princeton University Press v. Michigan Document Services Inc.*

The U.S. government's response maintained that the fair use doctrine is consistent with its obligations under the Berne and TRIPS Agreements. It argued that the fair use doctrine "embodies essentially the same goals as Article 13 of TRIPS, and is applied and interpreted in a way *entirely congruent* with the standards set forth in that Article." According to the response, fair use permits "limited and reasonable uses without permission or payment" and cites quotation in a book review of portions of the book being reviewed as the "classic" example of fair use. The government's response then enumerated the four fair use factors and stated that "the fourth factor, which specifically focuses on the impact on potential market exploitation of the work, is the *most* important."

There are at least three potential arguments to support the supposition that the fair use doctrine violates Article 9(2) of the Berne Convention and, de facto, Article 13 of the TRIPS Agreement. First, the *indeterminacy* of the fair use doctrine violates the Berne Convention. Second, the *breadth* of the fair use doctrine violates the Berne Convention standard for permissible exceptions to authors' rights. Third, with particular reference to the TRIPS Agreement, the fair use doctrine may be challenged as a *nullification and impairment* of the expected benefits that trading partners reasonably should expect under the TRIPS Agreement. None of these arguments, however, is likely to foster international challenge of the doctrine for reasons I outline following my analysis of each argument. I begin with an evaluation of the U.S. government's response to the Review of Legislation.

An evaluation of the substance of the government's response leads unfortunately, but understandably, to the conclusion that the reply was a less than accurate depiction of the fair use doctrine and how it operates in domestic courts. With regard to the argument of indeterminacy it is misleading to assert categorically that a U.S. court will find a particular use "unfair." The historical development and application of the fair use doctrine demonstrates that the only certainty involved in construing fair use is *uncertainty* in how a court will ultimately rule. As Congress noted in its House Report on the 1976 Act, fair use is a doctrine with "no real definition," but a "set of criteria, which though in no case definitive or determinative, provides some gauge for balancing the equities." The application of fair use is wholly a case-by-case determination. While it is possible to predict trends given certain fact patterns, the unpredictability of the outcome is part of what makes fair use a "troublesome" doctrine. In addition, while the Supreme Court has stated that the market impact is an important aspect of a fair use analysis, the most recent pronouncement from the Supreme Court regarding fair use makes it clear that a negative impact on the market is *not* conclusive as to whether the use is unfair. Thus, the statements that "in applying the fair use doctrine, the courts have consistently refused to excuse uses that go too far and interfere with the copyright owner's normal market for the work" and "those uses that have been permitted have generally involved productive and noncommercial uses of limited amounts of material from the copyrighted work" are patently inconsistent with the tenor of the Supreme Court in *Campbell v. Acuff–Rose* and other case law. Furthermore, some courts have permitted commercial uses of significant parts of the copyrighted work. As Justice Souter explained in *Campbell*, "the more transformative the new work, the less will be the significance of other factors, like commercialism, that may weigh against a finding of fair use." Accordingly, in a fairly recent decision, the U.S. Court of Appeals for the Ninth Circuit held that the copying of software in order to create a compatible product for sale did not lead to a presumption of unfairness, contrary to the District Court's opinion. Instead, the Ninth Circuit, quoting *Campbell*, held that the fact that copying was for a commercial purpose was only a "separate factor that tends to weigh against a finding of fair use." The Court held ultimately that the use in question was protected by fair use. In sum, the government's representations presented a more rosy picture of Berne Convention compatibility than is in fact the case.

The breadth of the fair use doctrine also raises a question regarding Berne compatibility. The fair use doctrine is broadly applicable to all uses of a copyrighted work; indeed, the breadth of the doctrine is rooted in its equitable nature. Courts are vested with the discretion to determine when a particular use may violate the equitable principles that undergird the doctrine, but fair use is not limited to a narrow set of cases or particular circumstances. It is true that some uses tend to fall more squarely within the parameters of fair use, such as criticisms or book reviews, but in the majority of cases the question of fair use is extremely fact specific and the vast body of case law on this matter reveals a wide spectrum of judicial opinions. Factors such as the particular circuit in which the case is heard, the relative copyright expertise of the court and the courts' own persuasion about copyright policy tend to provide more likely measurements of what may or may not be held to be a fair use. Thus, in *Sony Computer Entertainment, Inc. v. Connectix Corp.*, the Court held that the competition that would be engendered by the introduction of the defendant's competing computer game is a legitimate use and "an attempt to monopolize the market by making it impossible for others to compete runs counter to the statutory purpose of promoting creative expression...." Conversely, in *Texaco v. American Geophysical Union*, where multiple copies of journal articles were made for the purposes of research, the court held that the availability of a mass licensing mechanism precluded the possibility of a fair use defense for defendant Texaco. The fair use doctrine is not limited to a particular right; an alleged infringement of any of the enumerated copyright rights may give rise to a fair use defense. Congress was explicit, when incorporating the fair use doctrine into the Copyright Act, that what was being codified was the common law doctrine— with all its breadth and indeterminacy.

The third argument for violation of the Berne/TRIPS treaties, which is likely to be controversial as well as analytically complex, is the claim that the indeterminacy and breadth of the fair use doctrine constitute a nullification or impairment of the benefits of the TRIPS Agreement. The concept of nullification and impairment refers to the denial of benefits reasonably expected, even if not explicitly stated, under the Agreement. It is a means by which parties to a treaty may be held accountable for deviating from a norm to which they made no express commitment. Nullification and Impairment (NI) is substantially similar to the implied obligation of good faith in common law contracts. In this regard NI is both a rule of construction and a substantive obligation on the part of states to act in a manner that preserves the benefit of the bargain made under the agreement. While NI appears to hold a promise for trading partners who wish to challenge the fair use doctrine, an examination of the trade cases that have invoked this principle suggests that the political costs of such a claim will be high indeed and the likelihood of success minimal. First, the concept of NI is highly problematic because it invades space that sovereign states may have deliberately (even if not expressly) reserved to themselves under a theory of retained sovereignty. Further, it purports to challenge the sovereign prerogative to define the terms under which that state chose to accede to a particular treaty and its application may, in fact, result in an expansion of those terms. The highly political nature of a charge of NI has led the WTO to treat such claims very cautiously. In a recent trade dispute involving a complaint about access to the Japanese film market brought by the United States, the United States alleged that certain Japanese governmental measures effectively excluded U.S. film makers from the Japanese market. The United States claimed both a GATT violation as well as a NI claim. On the NI claim, the Panel found that since the United States was aware of the measures it complained of at the time the tariff concessions were made, it could not claim that it had any "legitimate" expectations that were frustrated by Japan's regulations. The Panel stated that NI is an "exceptional remedy" and the burden of proving a violation rests on the complaining party. The silence of the international community about the fair use doctrine and the fact that the member states of the WTO have been aware of the fair use doctrine suggests, at least in this brief evaluation, that a NI claim on the grounds of the fair use doctrine is fraught with difficulty and not likely to be considered meritorious by a WTO Panel.

Other than the questions posed during the TRIPS Council Review of Legislation, there has been a deafening silence over the incompatibility of the fair use doctrine with the Berne Convention, despite the historical evidence available that points to the limited scope of Article 9(2). Ironically, the rules of treaty interpretation in the Vienna Convention, as construed by some scholars, discourage resort to *travaux preparatories*—that is, materials used in the development and negotiation of an agreement—as a guide to interpreting the treaty in question. In this view, the negotiating history of Article 9(2) of the Berne Convention would not be a legitimate source to rely on for the purposes of determining its precise scope. If this is the case, merely construing the ordinary meaning of the text might arguably lead to a determination that the fair use doctrine is consistent with Article 9(2), particularly since it gives discretion to national legislation to determine exceptions to the right of reproduction. This result is particularly plausible given that the fair use factors are weighed in a balance by the courts and are not simply a *carte blanche* excuse to violate copyright. Recently, for example, courts have given even more weight to the economic impact of the potential fair use. If an international tribunal simply compared these recent results in the application of the fair use doctrine with the rules of treaty interpretation and the language of Article 9(2), it might be more likely to yield a ruling in favor of the doctrine's compatibility with the Berne Convention.

Ironically, however, the U.S. approach to treaty interpretation favors examination of documents external to the treaty to aid in the interpretation of the treaty. This position is reflected in Section 325 of the *Restatement (Third) of Foreign Relations.* Comment (g) to Section 325 states in part:

> The Convention's inhospitality to *travaux* is not wholly consistent with the attitude of the International Court of Justice and not at all that of United States courts.... Courts in the United States are generally more willing than those of other states to look outside the instrument to determine its meaning.

In most cases, the United States' approach to interpretation may lead to the same result as an international tribunal. But as a matter of process, this may be inconsistent with the international law of treaties. Thus, in evaluating the approach called for by the *Restatement*, an international tribunal might find the United States' interpretation erroneous and any action consistent with this interpretation that would yield a result contrary to a strict text-based interpretation would be held to be a violation of the treaty. But that is not likely to be the case with regard to the fair use problem because U.S. reliance on the negotiations leading up to Article 9(2) should ineluctably lead to the conclusion that the fair use doctrine is inconsistent with the Berne Convention, thus producing the same result that commentators to Article 9(2) have suggested is the appropriate scope of exceptions permitted under the Berne Convention.

Hong Kong Copyright Ordinance

(1997) Cap. 528 (H.K.)

Section 38
Research and private study

(1) Fair dealing with a work for the purposes of research or private study does not infringe any copyright in the work or, in the case of a published edition, in the typographical arrangement.

(2) Copying by a person other than the researcher or student himself is not fair dealing if—

(a) in the case of a librarian, or a person acting on behalf of a librarian, he does anything which regulations under section 49 would not permit to be done under section 47 or 48 (articles or parts of published works: restriction on multiple copies of same material); or

(b) in any other case, the person doing the copying knows or has reason to believe that it will result in copies of substantially the same material being provided to more than one person at substantially the same time and for substantially the same purpose.

(3) In determining whether any dealing with a work is fair dealing under subsection (1), the court shall take into account all the circumstances of the case and, in particular—

(a) the purpose and nature of the dealing, including whether the dealing is for a non-profit-making purpose and whether the dealing is of a commercial nature;

(b) the nature of the work;

(c) the amount and substantiality of the portion dealt with in relation to the work as a whole; and

(d) the effect of the dealing on the potential market for or value of the work.

Section 39
Criticism, review and news reporting

(1) Fair dealing with a work for the purpose of criticism or review, of that or another work or of a performance of a work, if it is accompanied by a sufficient acknowledgement, does not infringe any copyright in the work or, in the case of a published edition, in the typographical arrangement.

(2) Fair dealing with a work for the purpose of reporting current events, if (subject to subsection (3)) it is accompanied by a

sufficient acknowledgement, does not infringe any copyright in the work.

(3) No acknowledgement is required in connection with the reporting of current events by means of a sound recording, film, broadcast or cable programme.

Section 41A
Fair dealing for purposes of giving or receiving instruction

(1) Fair dealing with a work by or on behalf of a teacher or by a pupil for the purposes of giving or receiving instruction in a specified course of study provided by an educational establishment does not infringe the copyright in the work or, in the case of a published edition, in the typographical arrangement.

(2) [identical to Section 38(3)]

(3) Where any dealing with a work involves the inclusion of any passage or excerpt from a published literary or dramatic work in an anthology—

(a) if the inclusion is not accompanied by a sufficient acknowledgement, the dealing is not fair dealing under subsection (1); and

(b) if the inclusion is accompanied by a sufficient acknowledgement, subsection (2) applies in determining whether the dealing is fair dealing under subsection (1).

(4) Where any dealing with a work involves the making of a recording of a broadcast or cable programme or a copy of such a recording—

(a) if an acknowledgement of authorship or other creative effort contained in the work recorded is not incorporated in the recording, the dealing is not fair dealing under subsection (1); and

(b) if an acknowledgement of authorship or other creative effort contained in the work recorded is incorporated in the recording, subsection (2) applies in determining whether the dealing is fair dealing under subsection (1).

Notes and Questions

1. As shown in the Hong Kong Copyright Ordinance, not all jurisdictions provide a broad and flexible fair use privilege similar to § 107 of the United States Copyright Act. The excepted provisions, for example, made it clear that fair dealing is available only for particular purposes under specified conditions. If copyright law standards continue to undergo harmonization, should other countries expand their limitations and exceptions to copyright by adopting our fair use stan-

dard? Or should we curtail our fair use privilege in the name of international harmonization?

2. In *Campbell v. Acuff–Rose Music, Inc.*, 510 U.S. 569, 579 (1994), the United States Supreme Court has underscored "the fair use doctrine's guarantee of breathing space" in the copyright system, suggesting that the fair use privilege is necessitated by the First Amendment to the United States Constitution. If the fair use privilege relies heavily on the existence of the First Amendment, would it be correct to suggest that exceptions and limitations to copyright in other countries depend on their local conditions, cultural contexts, and historical traditions? If so, wouldn't it be futile to harmonize the different exceptions and limitations around the world?

3. Based on the differences over limitations and exceptions in copyright law, can you describe the different ways the copyright system can be designed? For example, some commentators argue that the broad grants provided in United States copyright law necessitate flexible exceptions, while more narrow grants in European laws make the development of more rigid exceptions acceptable. Do you agree? As an illustration of this argument, the European Community Information Society Directive includes detailed exceptions for publicly accessible libraries, educational establishments, museums, archives, broadcasting organizations, noncommercial social organizations (such as hospitals and prisons). European Parliament and Council Directive 01/29, On the Harmonisation of Certain Aspects of Copyright and Related Rights in the Information Society, 2001 O.J. (L 167) 10. That directive also makes exceptions for uses that benefit the disabled, for public security purposes and for performance or reporting of administrative, parliamentary or judicial proceedings.

4. Harmonization of limitations and exceptions is no easy task. When the European Community sought to harmonize the copyright laws of its member states as applied to the Internet—or, in European parlance, the Information Society—the harmonization directive includes more than twenty *optional* limitations and exceptions. Unfortunately, such a "laundry list" has not led to greater harmonization among European Union member states. As Bernt Hugenholtz lamented:

> What makes the Directive a total failure, in terms of harmonisation, is that the exemptions allowed under Article 5 are optional, not mandatory (except for 5.1). Member States are not obliged to implement the entire list, but may pick and choose at will. It is expected that most Member States will prefer to keep intact their national laws as much as possible. At best, some countries will add one or two exemptions from the list, now bearing the E.C.'s seal of approval. So much for approximation!

P.B. Hugenholtz, *Why the Copyright Directive Is Unimportant, and Possibly Invalid*, 22 EUR. INTELL. PROP. REV. 499, 501 (2000). If you were to harmonize copyright laws within the European Community, what would you do?

5. Since the beginning of their operations, the WTO panels and the Appellate Body have embraced the Vienna Convention on the Law of Treaties as part of the customary rules of interpretation. Article 31(1) of the Vienna Convention provides: "A treaty shall be interpreted in good faith in accordance with the ordinary meaning to be given to the terms of the treaty in their context and in the light of its object and purpose." Vienna Convention on the Law of Treaties, *entered into force* Jan. 27, 1980, 8 I.L.M. 679 (1969). Do you agree with the WTO panel's interpretation of the three-step test in *United States—Section 110(5) of the U.S. Copyright Act*?

6. Professor Okediji argues that the fair use privilege in United States copyright law is likely to satisfy the three-step test under the TRIPS Agreement. After reading the WTO panel decision, do you agree with her?

7. *United States—Section 110(5) of the U.S. Copyright Act* provides a very interesting example showing how the United States may violate the TRIPS Agreement just like its developing trading partners. In that case, the WTO panel found that the business exemption in United States Copyright law, which enabled selected restaurants and small establishments to play copyrighted music without compensating copyright holders, was inconsistent with the Berne Convention as incorporated into the TRIPS Agreement. Notwithstanding this adversary ruling, the United States did not amend § 110(5)(B) of its copyright law. If the United States can decline to amend its law, can other countries follow suit? If so, what is the point of having a mandatory dispute settlement process in the first place?

D. TECHNOLOGICAL PROTECTION MEASURES

The latest development in the copyright area is the provision of legal measures to support extra-judicial technological mechanisms that are used to protect copyrighted works. Such development has been rather controversial, especially in the developing world. Although there is a general consensus about the need to update copyright laws in light of changes in the digital environment, there remains *no* consensus concerning whether the existing copyright system is inadequate to respond to new challenges created by digital technology and the information revolution. Even those who find the current system inadequate disagree over how much *additional* protection is needed. While additional protection no doubt would benefit *some* authors and their supporting industries, the costs to users, consumers, and the public at large can be quite high. Thus, policymakers continue to struggle in their efforts to strike the appropriate balance between additional protection of authors and taking advantage of the many new opportunities created by the Internet and new media technologies.

WIPO Copyright Treaty

Adopted Dec. 20, 1996
S. Treaty Doc. No. 105–17, at 1 (1997)

Article 11
Obligations concerning Technological Measures

Contracting Parties shall provide adequate legal protection and effective legal remedies against the circumvention of effective technological measures that are used by authors in connection with the exercise of their rights under this Treaty or the Berne Convention and that restrict acts, in respect of their works, which are not authorized by the authors concerned or permitted by law.

Canadian Copyright Act

R.S.C., ch. C–34, § 42(1) (1985)

Every person who knowingly

(a) makes for sale or rental an infringing copy of a work or other subject-matter in which copyright subsists,

(b) sells or rents out, or by way of trade exposes or offers for sale or rental, an infringing copy of a work or other subject-matter in which copyright subsists,

(c) distributes infringing copies of a work or other subject-matter in which copyright subsists, either for the purpose of trade or to such an extent as to affect prejudicially the owner of the copyright,

(d) by way of trade exhibits in public an infringing copy of a work or other subject-matter in which copyright subsists, or

(e) imports for sale or rental into Canada any infringing copy of a work or other subject-matter in which copyright subsists

is guilty of an offence and liable

(f) on summary conviction, to a fine not exceeding twenty-five thousand dollars or to imprisonment for a term not exceeding six months or to both, or

(g) on conviction on indictment, to a fine not exceeding one million dollars or to imprisonment for a term not exceeding five years or to both.

Ian R. Kerr, Alana Maurushat & Christian S. Tacit
**Technical Protection Measures:
Tilting at Copyright's Windmill**

34 Ottawa L. Rev. 7 (2002)

[The WIPO Copyright Treaty and the WIPO Performances and Phonograms Treaty] do not mandate whether implemented legislation must include civil or criminal sanctions in order to meet the "effective remedies" requirement.... [T]his affords substantial leeway as to how WIPO obligations may be fulfilled. Canada could therefore choose to limit its sanctions to civil remedies of the sort traditionally available to copyright litigants, such as injunctive relief, compensatory damages, punitive damages, or statutory damages. Alternatively, Canada could introduce quasi-criminal provisions to the *Copyright Act* through an anti-circumvention or anti-device measure. Another option would be to amend the relevant *Criminal Code* provisions, making circumvention a computer crime. A combination of any of the above remedies is also a possibility. Some possibilities make more sense for anti-circumvention measures, while other possibilities make more sense for anti-device measures.

One of the chief conceptual difficulties in devising a scheme of effective remedies is the fact that the act of circumventing a TPM [technological protection measure] is usually distinct from the act of infringing the copyright it seeks to protect.

In the context of civil sanctions, it is unclear what the appropriate remedy should be for circumventions unrelated to infringement since it is unclear whether any damages would be suffered. Presumably, some form of statutory damages would therefore be made available. It is unclear what goals such a sanction would achieve other than serving as a specific or general deterrent. Given that the entire impetus of the relevant provisions of *WCT* and *WPPT* is to provide effective remedies to copyright owners whose TPMs have been undermined (at least it is in the civil context), it is unclear the extent to which non-remedial sanctions are appropriate. In any event, such a remedy is an unlikely choice given that we will suggest that anti-circumvention measures cannot be justified unless they are tied to infringement. Where the circumvention is tied to infringement, a different kind of conceptual problem arises. Given that the victim of a circumvention that results in infringement is *already* entitled to remedies pursuant to copyright law and, in many instances, under the law of contract (pursuant to a licence), what need is there for an additional sanction?

It has been suggested that sanctions be directed at the level of commercial rather than individual circumvention. This is a useful suggestion, not only from a deep pockets perspective but also because it might reduce the likelihood of cases such as *Sklyarov,* the Russian computer scientist who was thrown into an American jail for nearly five months after he was charged with trafficking in, and offering to the public, a software program that could circumvent technological protections on works subject to copyright when he arrived in the U.S. to deliver an article at a conference.

In the Canadian context, it would likewise be possible to introduce a quasi-criminal provision. Such a provision could bear similarity to section 42 of the *Copyright Act.* Alternatively, it could parallel the anti-circumvention provisions contained in sections 9 and 10 of the *Radiocommunication Act.* Under this approach, the unauthorized trafficking in circumvention devices would be a criminal offence. Again, as a matter of policy, prosecutions could occur at the commercial level and not at the level of individual use of devices by individuals.

A circumvention and anti-device provision could also be promulgated through the *Criminal Code* by amending the computer crime provisions. For example, an amendment could be made to the provisions on "unauthorized use of a computer," broadening the scope of this provision from "computer service" and "computer system" and extending it to include tampering with TPMs. In the *Consultation Paper on Digital Copyright Issues,* it was suggested that, "in certain cases with commercial motivations, where the scale of circumvention has consequences for the copyright sectors as a whole, there should be appropriate criminal sanctions." While it may be desirable to prevent the circumvention of TPMs where there are significant commercial implications, what would be an appropriate threshold for "commercial motivation" and "consequences for copyright sectors as a whole"? These are broad and vague statements that may not withstand constitutional scrutiny.

Criminal and quasi-criminal provisions raise a number of other particular concerns. For example, what level of *mens rea* would be required? The "knowingly" standard found in section 42 of the *Copyright Act* seems like an appropriate point of departure. But what exactly must be known? For an anti-circumvention provision, is the required *mens rea* simply a knowledge requirement that X "knowingly circumvents a TPM"? Or is it a specific intent offence, that X "knowingly circumvents a TPM for the purpose of an infringing use . . ."? Of these possibilities, it is suggested that the latter is preferred as it ties the circumvention to infringement and offers a clear defence for scientific researchers as well as those permitted to gain access to the work under copyright law exceptions.

What about for an anti-device provision? Is the relevant offence the manufacture, trade (etc.) of a device, the purpose of which is to circumvent a TPM? Or is it the manufacture, trade (etc.) of a device, the purpose of which is to infringe copyright through the circumvention of a TPM? The problem with the former approach is that it is not tied to infringement. The problem with the latter approach is that legitimate manufacturers and distributors selling products with substantial non-infringing uses might be caught by such a provision if the TPM can also be used for infringing purposes. Even worse, illegitimate manufacturers and distributors might not be caught by such a provision if they are able to demonstrate that their products can be used for non-infringing purposes.... [A] stethoscope can be used to monitor a heart in crisis or to crack a safe. Software devices can also serve dual or multi-purposes.

If the purpose of a criminal provision is to deter members of society from infringing copyright, will a criminal prohibition against circumvention or trafficking in circumvention devices achieve this end? When one considers the recent Napster controversy and the continuing proliferation of satellite black boxes, the very idea of relying on criminal offences to achieve a deterrent effect for doing something that so many members of society do not believe is wrong raises difficulties, including a decrease in public respect for the law and an increase in the rate at which the law is transgressed.

One further consideration is the impact that criminal sanctions may have on the development of innovative technology. The potential stigma of a criminal charge may act to discourage capital flow from innovative technology and may deter new and important forms of computer programming, such as the development of open-source software. It could also prevent high quality researchers from coming to Canada.

All of the above considerations lead to the suggestion that criminal sanctions ought to be avoided. Although they have the salutary effect of requiring more onerous proof of an intent to infringe and ought therefore to result in fewer legal actions, ... such provisions are subject to misuse, often resulting in a chilling effect on various important forms of social participation.

Policy makers should take into account that whatever measures are chosen, they should be mindful of the possible differences between what such policy measures purport to achieve and what they will *actually* achieve.

Peter K. Yu
Anticircumvention and Anti-anticircumvention
84 DENV. U. L. REV. 13 (2006)

[T]he DMCA [Digital Millennium Copyright Act] was designed specifically to deal with the threat created by digital technologies under conditions specific to the United States, including the stage of its economic development, the structure of its content and communications industries, the state of available technology, the overall market conditions, and the average living standards of local consumers. Because these conditions are unlikely to be present in less developed countries, the DMCA serves as an inappropriate model for the implementation of the WIPO Internet Treaties. In fact, the U.K. Commission on Intellectual Property Rights has advised against the adoption of similar legislation by less developed countries. As the Commission stated in its final report:

> We believe developing countries would probably be unwise to endorse the WIPO Copyright Treaty, unless they have very specific reasons for doing so, and should retain their freedom to legislate on technological measures. It follows that developing countries, or indeed other developed countries, should not follow the example of the DMCA in forbidding all circumvention of technological protection. In particular, we take the view that legislation such as the DMCA shifts the balance too far in favour of producers of copyright material at the expense of the historic rights of users. Its replication globally could be very harmful to the interests of developing countries in accessing information and knowledge they require for their development.

It is important to remember that the DMCA is not the only way, but one of the many possible ways, to implement the WIPO Internet Treaties. As Ian Kerr, Alana Maurushat, and Christian Tacit noted:

> it is clear that there is no singular correct approach to interpreting articles 11 [of the WCT] and 18 [of the WPPT]. The WCT and WPPT provide WIPO Members with large degrees of latitude as to how a particular state might choose to fulfill its obligations with respect to the relevant provisions. Consequently, there is considerable flexibility as to how [each country] might implement these provisions, should the Government elect to ratify the two WIPO Treaties.

Thus, countries can comply with the treaties without ever introducing an anticircumvention regime. In the context of the United

States, for example, Pamela Samuelson contended that "the DMCA was largely unnecessary to implement the WIPO Copyright Treaty because U.S. law already complied with all but one minor provision of that treaty [concerning the protection of the integrity of rights management information]." Dan Burk cited the common law "doctrine of contributory infringement, which attributes copyright liability to providers of technical devices that lack a substantial noninfringing use." Indeed, in light of the substantial overlap between the treaty and then-existing U.S. law, "the Clinton Administration initially considered whether the WIPO Copyright Treaty might even be sent to the Senate for ratification 'clean' of implementing legislation."

Even if anticircumvention protection is needed, the DMCA may not serve as a good model. As Jessica Litman noted, "[a]ll the [WCT] required, and all that made policy sense, was to give copyright owners remedies against people who circumvented technological protection in aid of infringement and redress against others—including device makers and sellers—who deliberately facilitated circumvention for an infringing purpose." Likewise, Coenraad Visser reminded us that the treaty "is much more limited than the wording of the DMCA. It does not strike at manufacturing devices; it strikes only at the actual circumvention."

In fact, from Australia to Japan, countries have implemented the WIPO Internet Treaties differently. Likewise, [Article 6(4) of] the EC Information Society Directive, which sought to implement the treaties, differs from the DMCA in providing an additional requirement that each member state

> take appropriate measures to ensure that rightholders make available to the beneficiary of [the specified] exception or limitation provided for in national law ... the means of benefiting from that exception or limitation, to the extent necessary to benefit from that exception or limitation and where that beneficiary has legal access to the protected work or subject-matter concerned.

Some commentators even suggested that the treaties can be implemented by adopting legislation outside the copyright system (and the greater copyright system that includes paracopyright laws). Ian Kerr and others, for example, noted that the protection of technological measures "could be dealt with in other kinds of legislation, such as criminal law or competition law."

Moreover, although the digital revolution affects both developed and less developed countries, these countries face different challenges and obtain different benefits from the opportunities created by the Internet and new media technologies. While the Internet serves mainly as a communication medium or a commercial marketplace for the United States and other developed countries, it provides for many less developed countries an important leapfrogging tool to catch up with their more developed counterparts. To take advantage of this leapfrogging tool, less developed countries pushed aggressively for the recognition of the importance of access to information and knowledge in the recent World Summit on the Information Society. In that forum, and elsewhere, they have also questioned the compatibility of intellectual property protection with their development goals. Their position is understandable. As James Boyle noted in the early days of the Internet, "[t]he intellectual property regime could make or break the educational, political, scientific, and cultural promise of the Net." Thus, strong intellectual property protection not only may not be in the interest of less developed countries, but may take away their rare opportunities to catch up with their more developed counterparts.

To make matters worse, the DMCA is based on three assumptions that may be invalid in the less developed world. The first assumption concerns the claim that most works will exist in both DRM and non-DRM formats. If consumers are unhappy with the protected format, or if that format prevents users from enjoying noninfringing uses, they can always switch to an identical product in an unprotected format. In *United States v. Elcom Ltd.*, for example, the court reminded us that the DMCA "does not 'prevent access to matters in the public domain' or allow any publisher to remove from the public domain and acquire rights in any public domain work." Rather, it allows copyright holders to "gain[] a technological protection against copying that particular electronic version of the work."

While the *Elcom* court's assumption that copyrighted works are always available in both protected and unprotected formats is invalid even in developed countries, it is particularly problematic in the less developed world, which faces an acute shortage of copyrighted works. As the U.K. Commission on Intellectual Property Rights observed:

> In the tertiary sector, the evidence indicates that access to books and other materials for education and research remains a critical problem in many developing countries, particularly the poorest. Most developing countries remain heavily dependent on imported textbooks and reference books, as this sector is often not commercially feasible for struggling local publishers to enter. The prices of such books are beyond the means of most students.

Even worse, a copy-protected copy on the Internet sometimes may be the only available copy. Even materials that are in the public domain of developed countries may not be available in those countries.

Moreover, although the WIPO Internet Treaties, the DMCA, and similar anticircumvention laws do not extend to public domain materials, it is naive to assume that these materials are always freely available. Today, public domain works are increasingly bundled with copyrighted materials, such as copyrighted introduction or editorial comments. As a result, the bundled materials, including both the copyrighted and public domain portions, will be protected by technological measures supported by the anticircumvention regime. Because many less developed countries lack a choice of materials in both protected and unprotected formats, sophisticated DRM systems "may exclude access to these materials altogether and impose a heavy burden that will delay the participation of those countries in the global knowledge-based society."

The second assumption concerns the availability of decryption tools or technological expertise to perform the needed circumvention as allowed under the narrowly-crafted exceptions. Because of their inevitable dual-use nature and the continued merger of access-control and use-control technologies, decryption tools are unlikely to be widely available. The limited Internet connectivity in many of these countries has also reduced access to these tools, although such access will increase as connectivity improves.

Even if the needed decryption tools are available, it is very likely that these tools or related services will have to be imported into less developed countries until they can develop their own technological expertise. Less developed countries are therefore at the mercy of their developed counterparts. If circumvention technologies are banned in the exporting developed countries, less developed countries may not be able to obtain access to protected works even if they manage to obtain an exception in the international intellectual property agreements to prevent the decryption tools or services from being outlawed in their own countries.

To some extent, the plight of less developed countries in the circumvention area is similar to the access-to-medicines problems they currently experience. Lacking the technical capacity to develop or manufacture drugs, these countries often have to import pharmaceutical products from abroad—regardless of whether these products are on- or off-patent. While there is no doubt that the access-to-medicines problem has an immediate and arguably more severe impact, the access-to-circumvention-tools problem will touch on education and cultural development and will therefore have a more lasting impact.

To deal with the access-to-medicines problem, the WTO member states have adopted a proposal to amend the ... TRIPs

Agreement ... to allow member states with insufficient or no manufacturing capacity to import generic versions of on-patent pharmaceuticals. If DRM systems are widely deployed throughout the world and if they have prevented people in less developed countries from having access to basic educational and research materials, a similar exception may be needed to enlarge access to the needed circumvention tools or services. Indeed, many international intellectual property treaties already contain technology transfer and technical assistance provisions that can be easily extended to these tools. Article 67 of the TRIPs Agreement, for example, requires developed countries to provide technical and financial cooperation to less and least developed countries "on request and on mutually agreed terms and conditions."

The final assumption states that the DMCA only creates inconvenience. As the United States Court of Appeals for the Second Circuit declared in *Universal City Studios, Inc. v. Corley*, it "kn[e]w of no authority for the proposition that fair use, as protected by the Copyright Act, much less the Constitution, guarantees copying by the optimum method or in the identical format of the original." Likewise, in *United States v. Elcom Ltd.*, the court explained that fair use is still available even though "[t]he fair user may find it more difficult to engage in certain fair uses with regard to electronic books." These observations were similar to the position articulated by Jesse Feder when he was the Acting Associate Register for Policy and International Affairs of the United States Copyright Office: "[T]he ability to make a perfect digital reproduction of something is not something that is inherent in fair use. Fair use entails copying, but it does not have to be a perfect digital reproduction."

From the perspectives of the proponents, judges, and officials, the DMCA has adequately preserved the users' ability to obtain legitimate access through traditional analog means even though it may have reduced consumer convenience. Consumers may not be able to make copies "by the optimum method or in the identical format of the original." However, they can always do so by employing analog fixation devices and techniques—sometimes as simple as the use of pen and paper. As the Second Circuit noted in *Corley*, the DMCA continues to allow one

> to make a variety of traditional fair uses of DVD movies, such as commenting on their content, quoting excerpts from their screenplays, and even recording portions of the video images and sounds on film or tape by pointing a camera, a camcorder, or a microphone at a monitor as it displays the DVD movie.

What the court did not mention is that the use of these analog tools and techniques "will often be costly or impractical." As Alfred Yen pointed out, these alternatives sometimes require the purchase of analog equipment as well as the technical expertise to set up such equipment. The inferior results of analog reproduction also raise the question "[w]hy should the rights holders benefit from the new opportunities of DRM systems in order to protect their legitimate interests, while the beneficiaries of a copyright limitation have to fall back on an inferior and sometimes outdated version of the work in order to carry out their legitimate interests?"

Moreover, inconvenience in one nation may be inaccessibility in another. Due to limited resources and the lack of infrastructure development in many less developed countries, inconvenience can become such a heavy burden that would eliminate access entirely. As June Besek noted in the Kernochan Center report, "there is a continuum between 'inconvenient' and 'impossible.' There may well be circumstances in which the exercise of a privilege is so inconvenient as to be impossible, as a practical matter."

. . . [T]here is [also] no guarantee that the traditional analog means of noninfringing uses will always be available in the near future. "[S]ome copyright owners [already] have expressed a desire to use technology, perhaps backed by legal requirements, to 'plug the analog hole' and prevent such copying of copyrighted works." If the analog hole is plugged, or severely shrunk, anticircumvention legislation is more than a mere inconvenience. . . .

[Finally, a]n anticircumvention regime may create unintended consequences that would greatly hurt consumers in less developed countries. For example, it may require new supporting technology and equipment that may be nonexistent or highly unaffordable in less developed countries. Even in the developed world, consumer advocates have been worried that the introduction of copy-protected CDs, which may not be playable on older car stereos, personal computers, and CD players, may force consumers to buy new hardware they do not otherwise need or cannot afford. Indeed, when Sony released Celine Dion's album as an encrypted CD in 2002, consumer advocates called for record companies to properly label those CDs to avoid confusion and to allow consumers to choose away from those products. Two California consumers even filed a class action lawsuit against the major record labels.

While it is already problematic in developed countries to require consumers to purchase new devices that support the technological measures employed, it would be particularly disturbing if the anticircumvention regime required consumers in less developed countries to purchase new end devices that they could not find or afford. By definition, less developed countries have few resources, and people there have very limited disposable income. Some may even have a difficult time meeting such basic needs as clean drinking water, food, shelter, electricity, schools, and basic health care. While it is hard, though not impossible, to explain why people in such circumstances need copyrighted Hollywood movies or popular music, technological measures have also been used to restrict access to basic educational products and research materials. Thus, an anticircumvention regime that renders household products obsolete is likely to have a very significant impact on less developed countries—much greater than the impact on its developed counterparts.

Notes and Questions

1. Commentators have discussed both "technological protection measures" (TPMs) and "digital rights management" (DRMs) tools (DRMs). Are they just different terms used in different jurisdictions (for example, TPMs in Europe and Commonwealth countries and DRMs in the United States)? Or are there discernable differences? If so, what are their strengths and weaknesses?

2. The anticircumvention provision of the DMCA was designed to implement the WIPO Copyright Treaty. Read 17 U.S.C. § 1201 (2006) and compare it with Article 11 of the WIPO Copyright Treaty and Article 6(4) of the European Community Information Society Directive (mentioned in the excerpt). Can the treaty be implemented differently? Are there more desirable alternatives? What are the benefits and drawbacks of the current United States approach?

3. Should there be different anticircumvention regimes among developed and less developed countries? In the past, the latter have pushed for special and differential treatment. The Berne Convention, for example, includes an optional appendix that allows nationals in less developed countries to obtain compulsory licenses for reproduction and translation purposes? Should less developed countries demand similar treatments concerning the protection of technological protection measures?

4. Commentators in the United States and elsewhere have increasingly embraced the misuse doctrine, which provides a specific defense in situations where copyright holders use their rights in a way that restricts competition or violates some other important policy, such as free speech. In the context of technological protection measures, Dan Burk has suggested the application of the misuse doctrine to provide a new defense known as "anticircumvention misuse." Dan L. Burk, *Anti–Circumvention Misuse*, 50 UCLA L. Rev. 1095 (2003). For further discussion of the copyright misuse doctrine and other copyright abuses under Canadian and United States law, see John T. Cross & Peter K. Yu, *Competition Law and Copyright Misuse*, 56 Drake L. Rev. 427 (2008).

5. The Canadian copyright law—and, for that matter, copyright laws in other Commonwealth countries—focuses on the "infringing copy." This approach is quite different from the one taken in United States copyright law, which focuses on an act of infringement regardless of whether an infringing copy exists. What explains these differences? Would such differences be semantic only? Or would they affect the substantive protection of copyright holders? What would you consider to be "an infringing copy" on the Internet?

6. In the excerpt, James Boyle noted that "[t]he intellectual property regime could make or break the educational, political, scientific, and cultural promise of the Net." At the turn of this millennium, there have also been extensive discussions of the digital divide—the proverbial gap between the information haves and have-nots. *See* Peter K. Yu, *Bridging the Digital Divide: Equality in the Information Age*, 20 Cardozo Arts & Ent. L.J. 1 (2002). Today, commentators have generally expanded this divide to cover not just access to information technology, but also access to digital content. In light of this continuing gap and the immense potential of information technology, Professor Okediji argued that "[l]imitations on access to digital informational works . . . should be offset by a proportional increase in access to print works." Ruth L. Okediji, *Sustainable Access to Copyrighted Digital Information Works in Developing Countries*, *in* International Public Goods and Transfer of Technology Under a Globalized Intellectual Property Regime 142, 185 (Keith E. Maskus & Jerome H. Reichman eds., 2005). Do you agree with her? Should less developed countries have greater flexibility in the copyright system with respect to digital works?

Chapter 4

TRADEMARKS AND SIMILAR INDICIA

Trademarks raise a number of practical problems for mark holders engaged in global business. Those attempting to establish a mark worldwide during a multiyear expansion effort face a number of practical impediments. For example, can uses by others that arise in foreign jurisdictions prevent efforts to establish a brand's reputation internationally? To what degree should the mark belong to an entity that has not yet begun using a mark within the region? Can one obtain trademark rights for the same subject matter from one jurisdiction to another? Do some jurisdictions differ on the scope of protection for trademarks? Other complications arise for many word marks because they are inherently language-based forms of communication. Translation presents challenges for efforts to avoid consumer confusion, particularly where multiple languages may be spoken within a particular nation.

A. NONTRADITIONAL TRADEMARKS: SMELLS, COLOR, SOUNDS AND TASTES

In the United States the subject matter of trademarks is generally very broad. Nontraditional marks such as colors, smells, sounds and tastes can be registered and protected. However, in Europe, nontraditional marks may be denied registration if they are not able to be "represented graphically." *See* Council Directive 89/104, To Approximate the Laws of the Member States Relating to Trade Marks, art. 2, 1989 O.J. (L 40) 1; Council Regulation 40/94, On the Community Trade Mark, art. 4, 1994 O.J. (L 11) 1. Courts in Europe have further expressed concern with the ability of competitors to use certain nontraditional marks and the ability of those marks to be distinctive. They have denied registration of nontraditional marks on those bases. This section reviews several cases considering the graphic representation requirement and the registration of nontraditional marks.

SIECKMANN v. DEUTSCHES PATENT-UND MARKENAMT

European Court of Justice
Case C–273/00, 2002 E.C.R. I–11737

[T]he Bundespatentgericht (Federal Patents Court) referred to the Court for a preliminary ruling under Article 234 EC two questions on the interpretation of Article 2 of First Council Directive 89/104/EEC ... to approximate the laws of the Member States relating to trade marks....

[T]he Deutsches Patent- und Markenamt (German Patent and Trade Mark Office) [refused] to register [Sieckmann's] olfactory mark [in connection with services including advertising, education and food and drink]....

Article 2 of the Directive contains a list of examples of signs of which a trade mark may consist. It is worded as follows:

"A trade mark may consist of any sign capable of being represented graphically, particularly words, including personal names, designs, letters, numerals, the shape of goods or of their packaging, provided that such signs are capable of distinguishing the goods or services of one undertaking from those of other undertakings." ...

German Law on the Protection of Trade Marks and other Identification Marks ... transposed the Directive into German law....

The purpose of Article 2 of the Directive must be interpreted as meaning that a trade mark may consist of a sign which is not in itself capable of being perceived visually, provided that it can be represented graphically. That provision states that a trade mark may consist of 'particularly words, including personal names, designs, letters, numerals, the shape of goods or of their packaging ...'. Admittedly, it mentions only signs which are capable of being perceived visually, are two-dimensional or three-dimensional and can thus be represented by means of letters or written characters or by a picture. However, as is clear from the language of both Article 2 of the Directive and the seventh recital in the preamble thereto, which refers to a 'list [of] examples' of signs which may constitute a trade mark, that list is not exhaustive. Consequently, that provision, although it does not mention signs which are not in themselves capable of being perceived visually, such as odours, does not, however, expressly exclude them.

That graphic representation must enable the sign to be represented visually, particularly by means of images, lines or characters, so that it can be precisely identified. . . .

First, the function of the graphic representability requirement is, in particular, to define the mark itself in order to determine the precise subject of the protection afforded by the registered mark to its proprietor. . . .

On the one hand, the competent authorities must know with clarity and precision the nature of the signs of which a mark consists in order to be able to fulfill their obligations in relation to the prior examination of registration applications and to the publication and maintenance of an appropriate and precise register of trade marks.

On the other hand, economic operators must, with clarity and precision, be able to find out about registrations or applications for registration made by their current or potential competitors and thus to receive relevant information about the rights of third parties.

If the users of that register are to be able to determine the precise nature of a mark on the basis of its registration, its graphic representation in the register must be self-contained, easily accessible and intelligible.

Furthermore, in order to fulfill its role as a registered trade mark a sign must always be perceived unambiguously and in the same way so that the mark is guaranteed as an indication of origin. In the light of the duration of a mark's registration and the fact that, as the Directive provides, it can be renewed for varying periods, the representation must be durable.

Finally, the object of the representation is specifically to avoid any element of subjectivity in the process of identifying and perceiving the sign. Consequently, the means of graphic representation must be unequivocal and objective.

. . . [T]he answer to the first question must be that Article 2 of the Directive must be interpreted as meaning that a trade mark may consist of a sign which is not in itself capable of being perceived visually, provided that it can be represented graphically, particularly by means of images, lines or characters, and that the representation is clear, precise, self-contained, easily accessible, intelligible, durable and objective.

By its second question, the referring court seeks essentially to ascertain whether Article 2 of the Directive must be interpreted as meaning that, in respect of an olfactory sign . . . the requirements of graphic representability are satisfied by a chemical formula, by a description in written words, by the deposit of an odour sample or by a combination of those elements. . . .

In respect of the representation of the odour by a description, Mr Sieckmann points out that olfactory marks already exist in the European Union and the United States and that, in the main proceedings, the olfactory sign which was the subject of the registration application is based on 'a balsamically fruity scent with a slight hint of cinnamon', which corresponds to the classification of the perfume industry in the European Union.

As regards the representation of the mark to be protected by the deposit of a sample of it, Mr Sieckmann claims . . . that mark may be obtained from local laboratory suppliers or from manufacturers and distributors of fine organic chemicals. . . .

The Austrian and United Kingdom Governments and the Commission submit that . . . the mere indication of the chemical formula as the graphic representation of an odour does not make it possible to identify the odour with certainty, because of different factors which influence the manner in which it can actually be perceived, such as concentration, quantity, temperature or the substance bearing the odour. Furthermore, those elements preclude the possibility of representing odours by means of olfactory samples.

The United Kingdom Government contends, in particular, that the chemical formula does not represent the odour of the chemical itself. Upon reading a chemical formula few people will understand what product it represents and, even if they do, they may well not understand what the product smells like. . . .

As to the possibility of describing an odour in words, the Commission submits that such a description . . . can be interpreted in a subjective way, that is, differently by different people.

The United Kingdom Government considers that it is possible that a description in words of an odour could graphically represent it, for the purposes of Article 2 of the Directive. The circumstances in which such a representation would be acceptable are likely to be rare, mainly because it would be difficult to make such a description sufficiently clear and precise properly to represent the sign in question.

As regards the deposit of an odour sample, the Austrian Government and the Commission submit that an odour changes over time because of volatilisation or other phenomena and that a deposit can therefore not produce a lasting olfactory impression capable of constituting a graphic representation. . . .

As regards a chemical formula, ... few people would recognise in such a formula the odour in question. Such a formula is not sufficiently intelligible. In addition, ... a chemical formula does not represent the odour of a substance, but the substance as such, and nor is it sufficiently clear and precise....

In respect of the description of an odour, although it is graphic, it is not sufficiently clear, precise and objective.

As to the deposit of an odour sample, it does not constitute a graphic representation for the purposes of Article 2 of the Directive. Moreover, an odour sample is not sufficiently stable or durable.

If, in respect of an olfactory sign, a chemical formula, a description in words or the deposit of an odour sample are not capable of satisfying, in themselves, the requirements of graphic representability, nor is a combination of those elements able to satisfy such requirements, in particular those relating to clarity and precision.

... [T]he answer to the second question must be that, in respect of an olfactory sign, the requirements of graphic representability are not satisfied by a chemical formula, by a description in written words, by the deposit of an odour sample or by a combination of those elements.

Notes and Questions

1.   What does *Sieckmann* require for a nontraditional mark to be registrable as a trademark? What specifically must be provided for odor to satisfy the graphic representation requirement?

2.   Is *Sieckmann* concerned with "odor depletion" or "odor confusion"? Does *Sieckmann* include a limitation similar to the "aesthetic functionality" doctrine in United States trademark law?

3.   Article 15(1) of the TRIPS Agreement provides:

Any sign, or any combination of signs, capable of distinguishing the goods or services of one undertaking from those of other undertakings, shall be capable of constituting a trademark. Such signs, in particular words including personal names, letters, numerals, figurative elements and combinations of colours as well as any combination of such signs, shall be eligible for registration as trademarks. Where signs are not inherently capable of distinguishing the relevant goods or services, Members may make registrability depend on distinctiveness acquired through use. Members may require, as a condition of registration, that signs be visually perceptible.

Is the *Sieckmann* interpretation of the graphic representation requirement consistent with Article 15(1)?

ELI LILLY & CO.'S APPLICATION

Second Board of Appeal, Office of Harmonization for the Internal Market
[2004] E.T.M.R. 4

By an application filed on 7 January 2000 the appellant seeks to register THE TASTE OF ARTIFICIAL STRAWBERRY FLAVOUR as a gustatory trade mark for [pharmaceutical products]. The appellant offered a description of the mark in the following terms: 'The mark consists of the taste of artificial strawberry flavour.'

By letter of 21 February 2000 the examiner informed the appellant that the mark was not eligible for registration because it did not comply with Article 7(1)(a) and (b) of Council Regulation (EC) 40/94 of 20 December 1993 on the Community trade mark ('CTMR'). The examiner argued as follows:

— The mark is not capable of being represented graphically. The vague description 'artificial strawberry flavour' does not allow for comprehension of the actual taste being referred to; since a strawberry taste may be simulated in many different ways with variable results. The mark is too indefinite in nature and scope to perform the function of distinguishing the goods or services of one undertaking from those of other undertakings. It is therefore not eligible for registration under Article 7(1)(a) CTMR. . . .

Article 7 CTMR provides . . . :

'1.   The following shall not be registered:

(a) signs which do not conform to the requirements of Article 4;

(b) trade marks which are devoid of any distinctive character. . . .'

The Board notes that at the time when the examiner waived the objection under Article 7(1)(a) CTMR in conjunction with Article 4 CTMR the Court of Justice had not yet given its judgment in Case C–273/00 *Sieckmann*. In that judgment the Court held that in respect of an olfactory sign the requirement of graphic representability is not satisfied by a description in written words. Logically the same would appear to apply to gustatory signs. In any event it is not necessary to rule on that issue since the objection based on Article 7(1)(b) CTMR is well founded.

The underlying purpose of Article 7(1)(b) to (e) CTMR is to prevent signs which any trader may legitimately wish to use from being reserved to the exclusive use of a single undertaking by means of registration as a trade mark. That has been confirmed by the Court of Justice in *Libertel*. . . . In that judgment the Court held that there is a public interest in not unduly restricting the availability of colours for other traders who offer for sale goods or services of the same type as those in respect of which registration is sought. The same reasoning appears to apply to tastes.

Any manufacturer of products such as pharmaceutical preparations is entitled to add the flavour of artificial strawberries to those products for the purpose of disguising any unpleasant taste that they might otherwise have or simply for the purpose of making them pleasant to taste. If the appellant were given an exclusive right to use such a 'sign' under Article 9 CTMR, that would interfere unduly with the freedom of the appellant's competitors.

Even if the anti-competitive effects of registration of the TASTE OF ARTIFICIAL STRAWBERRIES as a trade mark are disregarded, it is in any event clear that such a taste cannot distinguish the pharmaceutical preparations of one undertaking from those of another. A feature that any manufacturer of such goods is entitled to use cannot distinguish the goods of one manufacturer from those of competing undertakings. Moreover, the taste is unlikely to be perceived by consumers as a trade mark; they are far more likely to assume that it is intended to disguise the unpleasant taste of the product.

Notes and Questions

1.   Does the court appear to be concerned with "aesthetic functionality" and/or "utilitarian functionality"? Does the court provide much guidance with application of the test to determine if a "trademark use would unduly interfere with the freedom of the appellant's competitors"? If so, what type of guidance?

2.   In Case C–283/01, *Shield Mark BV v. Joost Kist h.o.d.n. Memex*, 2003 E.C.R. I–14313, the European Court of Justice ("ECJ") determined that sounds may satisfy the graphic representation requirement, but only in a very specific way:

> [I]n the case of a sound sign, [the *Seickmann*] requirements are not satisfied when the sign is represented graphically by means of a description using the written language, such as an indication that the sign consists of the notes going to make up a musical work, or the indication that it is the cry of an animal, or by means of a simple onomatopoeia, without more, or by means of a sequence of musical notes, without more. On the other hand, those requirements are satisfied where the sign is represented by a stave divided into measures and showing, in particular, a clef, musical notes and rests whose form indicates the relative value and, where necessary, accidentals.

3.   Why can a sound satisfy the graphic representation requirement with "a stave divided into measures and showing, in particular, a

clef, [and] musical notes," but not odors with a chemical formula? Can a sound, such as an animal noise or a motorcycle engine sound, satisfy the graphic representation requirement? *See* Jennifer Davis, *Between a Sign and a Brand: Mapping the Boundaries of a Registered Trade Mark in European Union Trademark Law*, *in* TRADEMARKS AND BRANDS: AN INTERDISCIPLINARY CRITIQUE 73 (Lionel Bently, Jennifer Davis & Jane C. Ginsburg eds., 2008).

4. What could satisfy the graphic representation requirement for taste?

5. In Case C–104/01, *Libertel Groep BV v. Benelux–Merkenbureau*, 2003 E.C.R. I–3793, the ECJ specified how color could be represented to satisfy the graphical representation requirement and other concerns:

> A colour *per se*, not spatially delimited, may, in respect of certain goods and services, have a distinctive character ... provided that ... it may be represented graphically ... using an internationally recognised identification code....
>
> The fact that registration as a trade mark of a colour *per se* is sought for a large number of goods or services, or for a specific product or service or for a specific group of goods or services, is relevant, together with all the other circumstances of the particular case, to assessing both the distinctive character of the colour in respect of which registration is sought, and whether its registration would run counter to the general interest in not unduly limiting the availability of colours for the other operators who offer for sale goods or services of the same type as those in respect of which registration is sought.

Can color be registered without a demonstration of acquired distinctiveness under Article 2 of First Council Directive 89/104/EEC, quoted in *Sieckmann*? Does the second paragraph quoted above set forth an equivalent to the "aesthetic functionality doctrine" in United States trademark law?

6. Campbell Thompson and Bill Ladas discuss the state of trademark law in Australia concerning the protectability of color:

> Colour is registrable under the Australian Trade Marks Act 1995 ("ATMA"), just as it is in the European Economic Area ("EEA"). But such registrations under the ATMA are a relatively rare beast: as at October 15, 2006, there were only about 75 Australian registered trade marks in total for colour alone, only about 30 of which covered a single colour....
>
> Moreover, single colour registrations in Australia are typically very narrow in scope. Protection is not normally obtained for a mere abstract colour in relation to designated goods or services, but instead the trade mark monopoly is limited in scope to specific uses of a colour on particular objects, as depicted in drawings included in the application. Thus Veuve Clicquot's exclusive trade marks rights in the colour orange

for champagne or sparkling wine are limited to its use as the colour of a label....

On September 4, 2006 a Full Court of the Federal Court handed down *Woolworths*.... [T]he court refused two BP applications for "colour green" trade marks. The decision ... reinforces the accepted view in Australia that abstract colour applications are not capable of distinguishing goods or services. It seems clear that the Australian approach of defining various monopolies for colour trade marks differs from the EEA's after *Libertel*, which gave its imprimatur to the registration of single colours in the abstract.

Campbell Thompson & Bill Ladas, *How Green Is My Trade Mark?: Woolworths v. BP*, 29 EUR. INTELL. PROP. REV. 29, 29–30 (2007). In Case C–49/02, *Heidelberger Bauchemie GmbH*, 2004 E.C.R. I–6129, the ECJ determined that an abstract combination of colors could be registrable. *See id.* ("[C]olours or combinations of colours ... claimed in the abstract, without contours, and in shades which are named in words by reference to a colour sample and specified according to an internationally recognised colour classification system may constitute a trade mark [if] ... the application for registration includes a systematic arrangement associating the colours concerned in a predetermined and uniform way."). Which view has the United States adopted? (Or "Which view is preferable?")

B. IMMORAL AND AGAINST PUBLIC POLICY

In the United Kingdom, Ireland, and continental Europe, marks that are contrary to morality and public policy are not registrable. *See* Council Directive 89/104 arts. 3.1(f), (g); Council Regulation 40/94 arts. 7.1(f), (g); Trade Marks Act, 1994, § 3(3) (U.K.). The United States Lanham Act incorporates similar policy concerns, such as the prohibition against registering scandalous or immoral marks. The concept of what is considered contrary to morality and public policy varies from country to country and evolves over time. This variability can make it difficult to predict what a given nation might consider immoral or against public policy. Moreover, there are interesting issues as to whether marks that would offend a minority group within a country would be contrary to the morality and public policy of that nation as a whole.

In the United States, marks that are scandalous or immoral are judged from the perspective a substantial composite of the general public, whereas disparaging marks are evaluated from a substantial number of the particular group allegedly disparaged. In Europe, the question is complicated by the Community trade mark ("CTM") system. Is a purported Community trade mark not registrable because it is contrary to morality and public policy in a single nation? Is it still enforceable? The following materials examine some of these issues and discuss how New Zealand's approach toward claims by minority groups that a mark is contrary to morality or public policy differs from that of the United States.

APPLICATION OF KENNETH (TRADING AS SCREW YOU)

Office of Harmonization for the Internal Market, 1st Bd. App.
[2007] E.T.M.R. 7

[T]he examiner [rejected registration of SCREW YOU as a Community trade mark (CTM) in connection with Class 9, sunglasses; Class 10, condoms, contraceptives, breast pumps, artificial breasts, sex toys; Class 25, clothing; Class 28, sporting apparatus, and Class 33, alcoholic beverages] pursuant to Art. 7(1)(f) of Council Regulation no.40/94 [because] the word "screw" was ... a coarse slang term equivalent to the word "fuck" and the expression SCREW YOU was a profane expression used to insult a person....

[T]he appellant informed the Board that SCREW YOU had been registered in the United Kingdom on 28 April 2006 for the following goods:

Class 10—Condoms.

Class 32—Beers....

Reasons

... Article 7(1)(f) CTMR prohibits the registration of "trade marks which are contrary to public policy or to accepted principles of morality". By virtue of Art. 7(2) CTMR, the grounds of non-registrability set out in Art. 7(1) do not have to exist throughout the European Union; it is sufficient if they "obtain in only part of the Community".... The registration of SCREW YOU as a trade mark for certain goods in the United Kingdom is therefore a relevant consideration but it is not decisive....

The question whether a trade mark can be registered under Art. 7(1)(f) is separate from the question whether it can be used. No provision of the CTMR ... says that a trade mark which has been refused registration under Art. 7(1)(f) cannot be used; that is essentially a matter for national law. Conversely, when the Office decides to accept a trade mark that is in dubious taste, the mere fact that it has been registered as a CTM does not mean that its use cannot be prohibited in the Member States....

The right to freedom of expression embodied in Art. 10 [of the European Convention for the Protection of Human Rights and Fundamental Freedoms, which should also be considered] includes commercial expression and is subject to limitation only for specific purposes, which include the prevention of disorder and the protection of morals. . . .

[T]he Office must apply the standards of a reasonable person with normal levels of sensitivity and tolerance. The Office should not refuse to register a trade mark which is only likely to offend a small minority of exceptionally puritanical citizens. Similarly, it should not allow a trade mark on the register simply because it would not offend the equally small minority at the other end of the spectrum who find even gross obscenity acceptable. . . . It is also necessary to consider the context in which the mark is likely to be encountered, assuming normal use of the mark in connection with the goods and services covered by the application. . . .

The mark applied for

The question is, just how vulgar, insulting and profane is the expression SCREW YOU in the English language? Both as a verb and as a noun, the word "screw" has entirely innocent meanings. It is, however, one of a number of coarse terms used in the English language to refer to copulation. The *New Shorter Oxford English Dictionary* lists the verb "screw" as a synonym of "fuck" and describes the expression as "coarse slang". . . .

The appellant has argued that SCREW YOU is less offensive and insulting than the term "fuck you", which is undoubtedly true, despite the fact that both terms convey the same abusive message and employ the same sexual connotation. It is also fair to say that society has altered to the point where public swearing and cursing is now generally more acceptable than it was 20 or 30 years ago. Certain expressions that would never have been intentionally broadcast on prime-time British television a few decades ago are now considered permissible and . . . the term SCREW YOU [was used] on the popular early evening British television soap "EastEnders" and on the American animated show "The Simpsons" when broadcast in the United Kingdom.

It is significant, however, that as a matter of public policy, freedom of artistic expression is regarded as a higher priority than freedom of commercial expression and consequently it is more fiercely protected. The use of profanities in the name of art and literature is circumscribed with great reluctance in democratic and open societies. The same is true in relation to expressing opinions. A militant atheist may write an article for public consumption ridiculing religion, for example, and the State will not intervene. But a trade mark mocking, or exploiting the name of, the founder of a major world religion might nonetheless be kept off the register. . . .

Therefore, the fact that the term SCREW YOU is occasionally heard spoken on British television programmes at family viewing times is not decisive when assessing the level of offence it may cause the public or determining whether the degree of displeasure felt by the public would be greater when repeatedly exposed to the term through advertisements. . . .

It is probable that a substantial number of citizens with a normal level of sensitivity and tolerance would be upset by regular commercial exposure to the term. This is especially so for parents with young children and for the elderly, who may well have grown up regarding such expressions as deeply unpleasant, not to say disgusting. . . .

The goods applied for

The goods listed in the application under Classes 9, 25, 28 and 33 are ordinary items marketed in outlets used by the general public. The use of the trade mark SCREW YOU in relation to such goods would inevitably cause a significant section of that public to be upset and affronted. The Board therefore upholds the examiner's objection in relation to those goods. . . .

In relation to artificial breasts and breast pumps of a type that is normally sold exclusively in sex shops, the Board considers that the relevant consuming public is unlikely to be perturbed by the use of the term SCREW YOU as a trade mark. The same reasoning applies to "sex toys (vibrators, dolls)", which are likely to be found only in sex shops or on websites specialising in sex products. A person who enters a sex shop or visits a website devoted to sex products is, by definition, unlikely to be offended by a trade mark which contains crude, sexually charged language.

Notes and Questions

1. In the United States, various versions of SCREW YOU have been applied for by the applicant in the *Kenneth* decision and others at the U.S. Patent and Trademark Office. *See* U.S. Trademark Serial Number 78874735 (pending application for SCREW YOU in classes including fruit juice, carbonated beverages, fruit smoothies and moisturizing cream as well as condoms); U.S. Trademark Serial Number 78699134 (pending application for SCREW YOU in classes including boots, shirts, socks, and sandals); and U.S. Trademark Serial Number 77247278 (pending application for SCREW U in classes including providing a television show on home improvement"). The status of these applications is not resolved as of this writing.

2. Why do you think that the CTM registration for SCREW YOU in some classes has been denied and affirmed, but the registration for SCREW YOU was allowed in the United Kingdom for certain items? What

is the standard applied in determining whether a CTM should be denied registration as contrary to public policy or accepted principles of morality? How does it differ from the U.S. standard for determining whether a mark is scandalous or immoral?

SPORTING KICKS LTD'S APPLICATION

United Kingdom Trade Marks Registry
[2007] E.T.M.R. 10

Sporting Kicks Ltd ... applied to register [a] ... trade mark in ... Classes 25 and 26:

Class 25—Clothing, footwear, headgear.

Class 26—Lace, embroidery, pins, needles, buttons, hooks, pin badges, badges....

[A] trade mark examiner [rejected registration of] "Inter City Firm" [because i]ts use is contrary to public policy [pursuant to Section 3(3)(a)] as it would be seen to promote football hooliganism"....

Section 3(3)(a) of the Act reads as follows:

"A trade mark shall not be registered if it is—

(a) contrary to public policy or to accepted principles of morality"....

The mark of the application is, on the face of it, innocuous. It includes the words "inter city" and a commonly recognised symbol, and may convey the impression that it is something to do with the railways. However, this is not the case. The Inter City Firm is a name which was chosen by a group of hooligans and in a review of a book by Cass Pennant, *Congratulations You Have Just Met the ICF*, ... the following is stated:

> "The Inter City Firm were the most notorious firm of football hooligans this country has ever seen. They were hard, terrifyingly vicious, brilliantly organised, tremendously feared and highly fashionable"....

I am of the view that its registration and use for clothing and badges, etc., is likely to lead to an increase in football violence by individuals or gangs. For instance, a football fan from Chelsea seeing a rival fan from West Ham wearing a shirt bearing the applicant's mark could easily be goaded or provoked into violence. In this sense it is a "badge of antagonism". In fact the use of the mark on the goods at issue is liable to be seen by the public as a badge of allegiance to, or membership of, a criminal gang.

[Sporting Kick's] contended that hooliganism associated with the Inter City Firm is now non-existent and the mark is considered to be a retro sign. It is difficult to prove one way or another whether the Inter City Firm is a gang which is presently in existence. . . .

[U]nder Annex A, the Wikipedia website (dated 2004) lists the Inter City Firm under "Active Hooligan Groups". In 2001, on the "Spiked Life" website, there is a report referring to an article in *The Sun* newspaper (dated 13 July 1998) which says ". . . Beckham and his family had been targeted by the notorious Inter City Firm (ICF)—Britain's most feared hooligans". . . .

Therefore, in conclusion of my consideration of the objection under s. 3(3)(a), it is my opinion that registration of the mark would be contrary to public policy. Such a sign falls within a category of marks that may be described as "anti-social branding". Furthermore, the mark comprises a display which is potentially threatening to others and likely to cause alarm or distress. Given renewed interest in groups such as the Inter City Firm it is against public policy to register a mark which might be interpreted as glorifying or promoting their exploits.

Notes and Questions

1.   What does the court mean by "anti-social branding"?

2.   In Japan, gang names are refused registration as scandalous or "contrary to public policy or accepted principles of morality." *See* JAPAN PATENT OFFICE, TRADEMARK EXAMINATION MANUAL § 42.19 (2001) ("Handling of Marks Related to Gangs (Gang Marks etc.)").

3.   Should religious symbols or names of religious figures be denied registrability as scandalous or "contrary to public policy or accepted principles of morality"? Does it matter what goods are sold in connection with the purported mark? What would constitute a "religion"? *See Basic Trademark SA's application*, [2006] E.T.M.R. 24 (2005) (Trade Marks Registry (U.K.)) (upholding rejection of trademark application for mark JESUS because it would be offensive to significant number of British citizens, and thus immoral and/or contrary to public order); *Japan Tobacco Inc v. Administrator–General*, [1992] 38 F.L.R. 20 (Fiji) (upholding rejection of trademark application for a mark that included an image of a dove with a branch in its beak with the words PEACE used in connection with tobacco products as immoral); *cf.* U.S. Trademark Registration Number 3396393 (SHAKE YOUR BUDDHA in class including T-shirts allowed by Trademark Office); U.S. Trademark Registration Number 3135983 (BUDDHA-BAR in class including optical goods). *But cf.* In re *Hines*, 32 U.S.P.Q. 2d (BNA) 1376 (T.T.A.B. 1994) (BUDDHA BEACHWEAR with design in class including clothing is disparaging).

4.   In the United States, would the mark HELLS ANGELS be refused registration or protection under a scandalous, immoral or disparaging

standard? *See* U.S. Trademark Registration Number 333883 (HELLS AN-GELS in classes including T-shirts, belt buckles and books).

5. In Canada, the mark "Miss Nude Universe" used in connec-tion with T-shirts, blouses and slacks, and the operation of a beauty pageant was not held "scandalous, obscene, or immoral." *See Miss Universe v. Bohna*, [1991] 36 C.P.R. (3d) 76 ("By itself the word 'nude' is a perfectively adjective and I am not satisfied that the public at large would view it in this context as taking on a 'scandalous, obscene, or immoral' character").

6. In the United Kingdom, if the purported scandalous mark is also arguably a slogan with a political message or connotation, trade-mark protection may cover that mark when used in connection with T-shirts. *See Scranage's Trade Mark Application*, [2008] E.T.M.R. 43 (Trade Marks Registry (U.K.)) (reversing denial of registration of mark THERE AIN'T NO F IN JUSTICE which contains double entendre of F IN instead of "effing" used in connection with T-shirts and caps as contrary to accepted principles of morality).

7. If the purported mark appears to denigrate a particular coun-try as producing inferior goods, should the mark be unregistrable because it is "contrary to accepted principles of morality"? *See Alvito Holdings Ltd's Application*, [2008] E.T.M.R. 28 (OHIM (4th Bd. App.)) (affirming on other grounds decision by examiner that the slogan NOT MADE IN CHINA was not registrable as contrary to accepted principles of morality because it inferred that goods made in China were inferior to those made outside of China, and was counterproductive to good trade relations between China and Europe).

8. Do you think the mark BIN LADEN used in connection with sporting goods would be against public policy for use in Europe and the United States? *See Application of Kenneth*, [2007] E.T.M.R. 7 (OHIM (Grand Bd.)) ("Few would question that signs which appear to glorify terrorism or offend the victims of terrorism should not be registered."). The United States Patent and Trademark Office has received trade-mark applications for KILL OSAMA BIN LADEN and OSAMA BIN LADEN. *See* U.S. Trademark Serial Number 76695183 (KILL OSAMA BIN LADEN in class including video games); U.S. Trademark Serial Number 77086418 (OSAMA BIN LADEN in class including hats and shirts).

* * *

One interesting issue concerns the protection of the rights of indigenous peoples from having their images or symbols registered as trademarks. In New Zealand, the legislation concerning the scandalous exclusion specifically precludes registration of marks that would likely offend a substantial number of the public, includ-ing the Maori people. The following article examines that provision.

Bryan Thompson
New Zealand Tackles the Maori Issue

MANAGING INTELL. PROP., Feb. 2002, at 48

A new Trade Marks Bill has been introduced to the New Zealand Parliament, to replace the 1953 Trade Marks Act. One of the most controversial provisions is a specific prohibition against registration of trade marks likely to offend a significant section of the community. . . .

Maori concerns

A key aspect of legislation of New Zealand is consideration of the 1840 Treaty of Waitangi, whereby Britain acquired sovereignty over New Zealand from the Maori people, who first arrived in New Zealand about 1000 years ago. The [New Zealand] government . . . formed a Maori Trade Marks Focus Group to consider Maori concerns about the inherent conflict between protection of trade marks as required by the TRIPS Agreement, and the right that the Maori people claimed to control use of their language and insignia as trade marks.

In 1997 the Maori Trade Marks Focus Group produced a document entitled *Maori and Trade Marks—A Discussion Paper*. This expressed concern about the proposed wording "significant section of the community". Its main concern was that the term "significant" should be defined so that it is not limited to a large number. The group wished the Maori people to have the opportunity to object to the registration of trade marks which were offensive to smaller groups of Maori—*whanau, hapu,* and *iwi*—what Europeans might describe as extended families, clans or tribes. . . .

[T]he 2001 Trade Marks Bill

Prohibition on marks

The new prohibition on registration of offensive trade marks is contained in section 17(1)(b)(ii) of the Trade Marks Bill. This provides as follows:

"The Commissioner must not do any of the following things: . . .

(b) register a trade mark or part of a trade mark if— . . .
(ii) the Commissioner considers that, on reasonable grounds, its use or registration would be likely to offend a significant section of the community, including Maori."

Clause 177 of the Bill provides that the commissioner must appoint an advisory committee and clause 178 provides: "The function of an advisory committee is to advise the Commissioner whether the proposed use or registration of a trade mark that is, or appears to be, derivative of Maori imagery or text is, or is likely to be, offensive to Maori." ...

In the principle the wording ["likely to offend a significant section of the community"] is an excellent solution. It appears more amenable to a multicultural society such as New Zealand than the phrase "contrary to public policy or to accepted principles of morality" as in the UK, Singapore and other overseas legislation. It focuses on "offensiveness", yet is limited to only those marks which offend a significant section of the community. Determining what is a significant section of the community may create difficulties in individual cases. However, this seems less difficult to determine than what is "contrary to public policy" or contrary to "accepted principles of morality." ...

Siding with the Committee

It is a political reality in New Zealand that careful consideration must be given to Maori sensitivities. This means it is possible that a politically-conscious commissioner of trade marks might be reluctant to differ from a view expressed by the advisory committee. There is therefore a genuine concern among the New Zealand business community that the commissioner's role is determining whether or not a trade mark is going to offend the Maori people may be hijacked by a statutorily mandated advisory committee, the membership of which is not defined, except that it is appointed and discharged by the commissioner.

The danger is that if there is an objection by the advisory committee, some form of consent process might become the de facto solution, with all the problems that would entail. For example, there might be considerable difficulty in determining who really had the right to give such consent. . . .

New Zealanders from Elsewhere

The term "significant section of the community" is not limited to racial or ethnic groups. There are many other different cultural and religious groups in New Zealand, for example Christians, Jews, Hindus and Muslims, among others. This clause could be used to prevent registration of any trade mark the use or registration of which would be likely to offend any of these ethnic, cultural or religious groups, not just those of Maori or European origin. . . .

Notes and Questions

1. Section 17(1)(c) of the New Zealand Trademark Act of 2002 contains the language "likely to offend a significant section of the

community, including Maori." How should the Commissioner determine the membership of the Maori advisory committee? Will membership in the Maori advisory committee favor one group over another? Should other minority groups in New Zealand also have committees? Is reliance on committees preferable to the Unites States approach that frequently considers survey evidence submitted by the parties?

2. What kind of evidence do you think the Commissioner would rely upon to determine if a mark is "likely to offend a significant section of the community," such as the Chinese community within New Zealand?

3. One dispute concerning usage of the Maori language involved the Lego company:

> The world renowned Lego company used certain Maori names to identify its BIONICLE toys. The characters included Toa, Whenua and the evil beast Makuta, who inhabit the imaginary island of Mata Nui. Some of the names Lego used had, and continue to have, a particular cultural and religious significance. Some Maori complained to Lego about its use of the names, stating that the uses trivialized and inappropriately used Maori culture. Those Maori emphasized that had Lego consulted them, some names could have been used that were not culturally inappropriate and would have been just as effective in evoking the imagery that Lego sought.... It would seem that after some negotiation Lego undertook to cease using some Maori words.

Susy Frankel, *Trademarks and Traditional Knowledge and Cultural Intellectual Property*, *in* TRADEMARK LAW AND THEORY: A HANDBOOK OF CONTEMPORARY RESEARCH 439 (Graeme B. Dinwoodie & Mark D. Janis, eds., 2008).

4. Words in the Maori language have been registered as trademarks, and some members of the Maori tribe may consider their registration beneficial:

> In New Zealand, where Maori words and symbols can be found in many registered trademarks, *Te Waka Toi* (the Maori Arts Board of Creative New Zealand), in consultation with Maori artists, likewise registered a "Maori made mark" and two companion marks—a "mainly Maori mark" and a "Maori co-production mark." These marks are used to promote and sell authentic, quality Maori arts and crafts, and also to authenticate exhibitions and performances of Maori artists by Maori artists. The creation of these marks is a direct response to the bourgeoning tourism trade to New Zealand, which often involves the sale of cheap and culturally offensive objects imitating Maori art, such as plastic tiki.

Coenraad Visser, *Culture, Traditional Knowledge, and Trademarks: A View from the South, in* TRADEMARK LAW AND THEORY: A HANDBOOK OF CONTEMPORARY RESEARCH, *supra*, at 476.

C. INFRINGEMENT AND USE

This section reviews recent cases generally concerning trademark infringement and use. This issue is critically important because it defines in part the scope of protection a trademark may possess and in some cases whether protection may exist in the first instance. Most countries apply a series of factors similar to the so-called *"Polaroid"* or *"Sleekcraft"* factors to determine whether there is a likelihood of confusion as the touchstone test to determine trademark infringement.

Like United States courts, European courts are struggling with the doctrine of trademark use. The ECJ and the Court of Appeal cases involving the football club Arsenal have recognized that a claim of trademark infringement may exist based on an arguably non-trademark use after sale of the product. However, there is a question as to whether similar use in the Internet context is sufficient for trademark infringement. The High Court of Justice of England and Wales addressed infringement in the context of meta-tag and banner use, but left more questions than answers.

Currently, the law is in flux worldwide. Is trademark use a threshold question? Is it part of the infringement analysis? Or is it especially relevant to a defense? The ECJ recently received several questions concerning infringing use and Google's Adwords program from French courts, a German court and the Dutch Supreme Court. One commentator has noted that there are almost 40 decisions concerning sponsored links in France alone. Posting of Frédéric Glaize to Class 46 Blog, http://class46.eu/2008/08/official-translation-of-questions.html (Aug. 6, 2008, 09:30). A recent decision in Israel, *Matim Li Fashion Chain for Large Sizes Ltd v. Crazy Line Ltd* (included below) recently confronted the question of infringement and the purchase of keywords.

ARSENAL FOOTBALL CLUB v. REED
European Court of Justice
Case C–206/01, 2002 E.C.R. I–10273

[T]he High Court of Justice of England and Wales, Chancery Division, referred to the Court for a preliminary ruling ... two questions on the interpretation of Article 5(1)(a) of the First Council Directive ... to approximate the laws of the Member States relating to trade marks....

Article 5(1) of the Directive [which section 10(1) of the Trade Marks Act tracks] provides:

'The registered trade mark shall confer on the proprietor exclusive rights therein. The proprietor shall be entitled to prevent all third parties not having his consent from using in the course of trade:

(a) any sign which is identical with the trade mark in relation to goods or services which are identical with those for which the trade mark is registered;

(b) any sign where, because of its identity with, or similarity to, the trade mark and the identity or similarity of the goods or services covered by the trade mark and the sign, there exists a likelihood of confusion on the part of the public, which includes the likelihood of association between the sign and the trade mark.' ...

Article 6(1) of the Directive reads as follows:

'The trade mark shall not entitle the proprietor to prohibit a third party from using, in the course of trade,

(a) his own name or address;

(b) indications concerning the kind, quality, quantity, intended purpose, value, geographical origin, the time of production of goods or of rendering of the service, or other characteristics of goods or services;

(c) the trade mark where it is necessary to indicate the intended purpose of a product or service, in particular as accessories or spare parts;

provided he uses them in accordance with honest practices in industrial or commercial matters.' ...

Arsenal FC is a well-known football club in the English Premier League. It is nicknamed the 'Gunners' and has for a long time been associated with two emblems, a cannon device and a shield device.

In 1989 Arsenal FC had ... the words 'Arsenal' and 'Arsenal Gunners' and the cannon and shield emblems registered as trade marks for a class of goods comprising articles of outer clothing, articles of sports clothing and footwear. Arsenal FC designs and supplies its own products or has them made and supplied by its network of approved resellers....

Since 1970 Mr Reed has sold football souvenirs and memorabilia, almost all marked with signs referring to Arsenal FC, from several stalls located outside the grounds of Arsenal FC's stadium....

[O]n that stall there was a large sign with the following text:

'The word or logo(s) on the goods offered for sale, are used solely to adorn the product and does not imply or indicate any affiliation or relationship with the manufacturers or distributors of any other product, only goods with official Arsenal merchandise tags are official Arsenal merchandise.' ...

As to Arsenal FC's claim concerning infringement of its trade marks, based on section 10(1) and (2)(b) of the Trade Marks Act 1994, the High Court rejected their argument that the use by Mr Reed of the signs registered as trade marks was perceived by those to whom they were addressed as a badge of origin, so that the use was a 'trade mark use'.

According to the High Court, the signs affixed to Mr Reed's goods were in fact perceived by the public as 'badges of support, loyalty or affiliation'. . . .

[T]he ... argument, namely that only trade mark use is covered, comes up against a difficulty connected with the wording of the Directive and the Trade Marks Act 1994, which both define infringement as the use of a 'sign', not of a 'trade mark'. . . .

[T]he essential function of a trade mark is to guarantee the identity of origin of the marked goods or services to the consumer or end user by enabling him, without any possibility of confusion, to distinguish the goods or services from others which have another origin. For the trade mark to be able to fulfil its essential role in the system of undistorted competition which the Treaty seeks to establish and maintain, it must offer a guarantee that all the goods or services bearing it have been manufactured or supplied under the control of a single undertaking which is responsible for their quality. . . .

It follows that the exclusive right under Article 5(1)(a) of the Directive was conferred in order to enable the trade mark proprietor to protect his specific interests as proprietor, that is, to ensure that the trade mark can fulfil its functions. . . .

The proprietor may not prohibit the use of a sign identical to the trade mark for goods identical to those for which the mark is registered if that use cannot affect his own interests as proprietor of the mark, having regard to its functions. Thus certain uses for purely descriptive purposes are excluded from the scope of Article 5(1) of the Directive because they do not affect any of the interests which that provision aims to protect, and do not therefore fall within the concept of use within the meaning of that provision. . . . In the present case, the use of the sign takes place in the context of sales to consumers and is obviously not intended for purely descriptive purposes relating to the characteristics of the product offered. . . .

Having regard to the presentation of the word 'Arsenal' on the goods at issue in the main proceedings and the other secondary markings on them, the use of that sign is such as to create the impression that there is a material link in the course of trade between the goods concerned and the trade mark proprietor.

That conclusion is not affected by the presence on Mr Reed's stall of the notice stating that the goods at issue in the main proceedings are not official Arsenal FC products.... [T]here is a clear possibility in the present case that some consumers, in particular if they come across the goods after they have been sold by Mr Reed and taken away from the stall where the notice appears, may interpret the sign as designating Arsenal FC as the undertaking of origin of the goods.

Moreover, in the present case, there is also no guarantee ... that all the goods designated by the trade mark have been manufactured or supplied under the control of a single undertaking which is responsible for their quality....

In those circumstances, the use of a sign which is identical to the trade mark at issue in the main proceedings is liable to jeopardise the guarantee of origin which constitutes the essential function of the mark....

In the light of the foregoing, the answer to the national court's questions must be that, in a situation which is not covered by Article 6(1) of the Directive, where a third party uses in the course of trade a sign which is identical to a validly registered trade mark on goods which are identical to those for which it is registered, the trade mark proprietor is entitled, in circumstances such as those in the present case, to rely on Article 5(1)(a) of the Directive to prevent that use. It is immaterial that, in the context of that use, the sign is perceived as a badge of support for or loyalty or affiliation to the trade mark proprietor.

Notes and Questions

1. In Case C–228/03, *Gillette Company v. LA–Laboratories Ltd Oy.*, 2005 E.C.R. I–2337, the ECJ determined:

The condition of 'honest use' within the meaning of Article 6(1)(c) of Directive 89/104, constitutes in substance the expression of a duty to act fairly in relation to the legitimate interests of the trade mark owner.

The use of the trade mark will not be in accordance with honest practices in industrial and commercial matters if, for example: [1] it is done in such a manner as to give the impression that there is a commercial connection between the third party and the trade mark owner; [2] it affects the value of the trade mark by taking unfair advantage of its distinctive character or repute; [3] it entails the discrediting or denigration of that mark; [4] or where the third party presents its product as an imitation or replica of the product bearing the trade mark of which it is not the owner.

The fact that a third party uses a trade mark of which it is not the owner in order to indicate the intended purpose of the product which it markets does not necessarily mean that it is presenting it as being of the same quality as, or having equivalent properties to, those of the product bearing the trade mark. Whether there has been such presentation depends on the facts of the case, and it is for the referring court to determine whether it has taken place by reference to the circumstances.

Are these rulings consistent with the ECJ *Arsenal* decision? Did Mr. Reed have a defense under the U.K. legislation implementing section 6(1) of the European Community Trademark Directive? Why or why not?

2.   Does the Lanham Act include a provision similar to Article 5(1)(a) of the Directive? How was Article 5(1)(a) relevant to the ECJ *Arsenal* decision?

3.   In *Arsenal*, the ECJ refers to the fact that the infringement provision of section 5(1) of the Directive refers to use of a "sign" as opposed to use as a "trademark" as an infringement. How does the language of the Directive differ from the infringement provisions of a registered mark in the Lanham Act?

4.   After the ECJ *Arsenal* decision, the case was sent back to the High Court of Justice of England and Wales. The judge in that case determined that the use of the "Arsenal" mark by Reed was not a trademark use by the alleged infringer and there was no infringement. *See Arsenal Football Club v. Matthew Reed*, [2002] EWHC (Ch) 2695. The case was then appealed to the Court of Appeal. The Court of Appeal found for Arsenal and stated:

It is important to note that the ECJ is not concerned with whether the use complained about is trade mark use. The consideration is whether the third party's use affects or is likely to affect the functions of the trade mark. An instance of where that will occur is given, namely where a competitor wishes to take unfair advantage of the reputation of the trade mark by selling products illegally bearing the mark. That would happen whether or not the third party's use was trade mark use or whether there was confusion.

Arsenal Football Club v. Matthew Reed, [2003] EWCA (Civ) 696 (Court of Appeal).

5.   Do the U.K. courts and the ECJ appear to accept a theory of likelihood of confusion based on "post-sale" confusion? Note that

Article 4(1)(b) of the European Community Trademark Directive defines infringement as "a likelihood of confusion on the part of the public, which includes the likelihood of association with the earlier trade mark." What is a "likelihood of association"? How different is the likelihood of association from the likelihood of confusion? Was likelihood of association an issue under the *Arsenal* facts?

REED EXECUTIVE v. REED BUSINESS INFORMATION LTD.

Court of Appeal of England and Wales
[2004] EWCA (Civ) 159

The appellants are Reed Business Information Ltd., Reed Elsevier (UK) Ltd. and totaljobs.com Ltd.... [collectively "RBI"].

For many years RBI have published a big range (about 50) of magazines and journals....

[R]espondents ["Reed Employment" started] in 1960 when Mr Alec Reed rented his first shop in Hounslow. He advertised for secretarial and clerical workers.... The business expanded geographically and in the kinds of job-seeker and employer for whom it catered. When RBI commenced the activities complained of (September 1999) the respondents had long been a nationwide business covering a wide spectrum of types of jobs....

Reed Employment registered ["Reed" for employment services] in 1986, shortly after registration of marks for services became possible in this country....

In ... early 1996 it was advertising job vacancies on its website, www.reed.co.uk....

RBI ... create[d] a special dedicated jobs-related website, totaljobs.com....

Art 5(1)(b) ... involves a global assessment of the likelihood of confusion as to origin of the goods or services concerned. This involves an assessment of the distinctiveness of the mark, and involves the assessment of many factors familiar in passing-off cases....

Those who wish to have their banner advertisements pop-up in this unasked for fashion have to pay for it, paying the appropriate search-engine company. Banners can be totally random or tied to particular search terms. Here RBI paid Yahoo for a totaljobs banner linked to the search terms "recruitment", and "job." They were given a free extra of their own name. Yahoo chose "reed" rather than "reed elsevier". The consequence is that a Yahoo search done under any of these terms was apt to cause the totaljobs banner to appear. If it did, the user could click-through to the totaljobs website.

The Judge held that when the banner was triggered by the word "Reed" there was infringement, although loss could not be proved merely because the banner appeared. . . .

I am unable to agree with this. The banner itself referred only to totaljobs—there was no visible appearance of the word Reed at all. Whether the use as a reserved word can fairly be regarded as "use in the course of trade" or not (as to which I express no opinion), I cannot see that causing the unarguably inoffensive-in-itself banner to appear on a search under the name "Reed" or "Reed jobs" can amount to an Art. 5.1(b) infringement. The web-using member of the public knows that all sorts of banners appear when he or she does a search and they are or may be triggered by something in the search. He or she also knows that searches produce fuzzy results—results with much rubbish thrown in. The idea that a search under the name Reed would make anyone think there was a trade connection between a totaljobs banner making no reference to the word "Reed" and Reed Employment is fanciful. No likelihood of confusion was established.

That is not to say, of course, that if anyone actually clicked through (and few did) and found an infringing use, there could not be infringement. Whether there was or not would depend solely on the site content, not the banner.

If this had been an Art. 5.1(a) case then the position might have been different. For then there would have been no require-ment to prove a likelihood of confusion. The question would appear to turn on whether the use of the word "Reed" by Yahoo at the instance of RBI properly amounted to a "use in the course of trade". It may be that an invisible use of this sort is not use at all for the purposes of this trade mark legislation—the computers who "read" sets of letters merely "look for" patterns of 0s and 1s—there is no meaning being conveyed to anyone—no "sign." . . .

Search engines have elaborate indexing systems which can take account not only of visible matter in a website but also matter which never appears visibly—so called "metatags". The conse-quence is that whenever a user conducts a search which includes a word in a metatag, the search results will include that site along with all other sites which use that matter, either in visible or hidden form. That is why, when you conduct a search, some of the results appear to have nothing to do with your search term. Sometimes the metadata is translated into visible text in a search engine results page, for instance in a phrase "totaljobs is the new recruitment service from Reed Business Information."

The order in which search results appear is a matter for the particular search engine's secret system. Naturally website owners play the game of trying to get their site to appear high up in any search....

[The Judge] held that RBI's metatag use was passing off and an infringement. The totaljobs site, in various versions, had the words "Reed Business Information" as a metatag. Evidence was led as to what happened if a search under the phrase "Reed jobs" was made. In all cases where totaljobs was listed, it came below the Reed Employment site in the search results (which, as is usual, included many other results, irrelevant to both sides). Obviously anyone looking for Reed Employment would find them rather than totaljobs. I am unable to see how there could be passing off. No-one is likely to be misled—there is no misrepresentation. This is equally so whether the search engine itself rendered visible the metatag or not....

Assuming metatag use counts as use of a trade mark, there is simply no confusion here. I confess to not following the Judge's reasoning on the point. He said that the "ultimate purpose [of the metatag] is to use the sign to suggest a connection which does not exist." But purpose is irrelevant to trade mark infringement and causing a site to appear in a search result, without more, does not suggest any connection with anyone else....

Again I would wish to reserve my opinion in relation to Art. 5.1(a). There are several difficult questions: (a) First, does metatag use count as use of a trade mark at all? In this context it must be remembered that use is important not only for infringement but also for saving a mark from non-use. In the latter context it would at least be odd that a wholly invisible use could defeat a non-use attack. Mr Hobbs suggested that metatag use should be treated in the same way as uses of a trade mark which ultimately are read by people, such as uses on a DVD. But in those cases the ultimate function of a trade mark is achieved—an indication to someone of trade origin. Uses read only by computers may not count—they never convey a message to anyone. (b) If metatag use does count as use, is there infringement if the marks and goods or services are identical? This is important: one way of competing with another is to use his trade mark in your metatag—so that a search for him will also produce you in the search results. Some might think this unfair—but others that this is good competition provided that no-one is misled. (c) If metatag use can fall within the infringement provisions of Art 5, can the defences under Art. 6.1(a) apply, for instance the own name defence? The Judge thought they could not because the use was invisible. That makes little sense—why should visibility be irrelevant to Art. 5.1 (both limbs) but relevant to Art. 6.1? Mr Hobbs felt unable to support the Judge in this regard, accepting (again as a member of the realist school) all defences were in principle available to metatag use. However, as I say, I do not have to consider this further.

Accordingly I hold that there was no infringement by the use of the "Reed Business Information" metatags.

Notes and Questions

1. Why do you suppose that this case was not asserted under U.K. legislation implementing Article 5(1)(a) of the European Community Trademark Directive?

2. Is use of a registered trademark on a website as a metatag an infringing use after *Reed*? Does intent of the user of the metatag matter? What about "initial interest" confusion? Should that doctrine apply to trademarks used as metatags? How would Article 6(1) of the Directive apply to metatags? Are metatags still used by search engines to produce search results?

MATIM LI FASHION CHAIN FOR LARGE SIZES LTD. v. CRAZY LINE LTD.

Tel Aviv District Court
(unreported July 31, 2006) (Isr.), *available at* 38 INT'L
REV. INTELL. PROP. & COMP. L. 238 (2007)*

MAGEN ALTUVIA, J.

The dispute at bar concerns the use of Petitioners' registered trademarks through the Google internet website, whether such use constitutes a violation of rights. . . .

Factual Background

The Google internet website, a well-known and perhaps the leading search engine on the internet, among others things, provides a paid service to those who wish to advertise at the margins or at the top of the webpage which is mostly used to display internet search results. . . . Both Petitioners and Respondent 1 run retail chains for women's fashion. . . . Petitioners claim to have developed a unique line of fashionable large size apparel for women and fashionable pregnancy clothing identified by the brand [Hebrew for "fits me"] or "ml". . . .

It appears that both Petitioners and Respondent 1 target, at least partially, the same group of consumers. . . .

The Claims of the Parties

Petitioners operate a website in which much thought and money has been invested, and it serves as a marketing channel in

---

* Zohar Efroni provided the unofficial
English translation of this opinion.

itself for the chain and its products, while providing useful information to interested individuals (www.matimli.co.il). Petitioners purport that all Respondents are aware of their activity mentioned above, and that Respondents 1 and 2 have been advised by Petitioners to cease from making the described use of the trademarks as keywords, which triggers the advertisements of Respondent 1 on the Google website, although users are actually attempting to locate the website of Petitioner or other information concerning it. Petitioners claim that the advertisement of Respondent 1 appears as the first search result, in bold print. Such practice of using the trademarks constitutes bad-faith infringing advertising, as the reputation associated with the trademarks is well known to Respondents, which is the reason for feeding the search engine with the said trademarks as keywords. . . .

Discussion

The Google search engine is a useful tool for locating information on the internet. Without such tools, the enormous amount of information posted on the internet would be much less available and accessible. The search engine enables the location of information by using search words, retrieving information that is partly relevant, and very often largely irrelevant, to the needs of the user. Any user of an internet search engine is well aware of this fact, or learns it quickly from his own experience after conducting one or two searches. . . .

In the absence of the commercial dimension of advertising, a significant portion of the motivation to operate and develop search engines would vanish. In this context and in connection to the growing trend to directing advertising and marketing efforts at potential consumers, Google, similar to other search engines, has developed Google AdWords. . . . The advertisements could be said to be "hung" in the designated advertising zone on the Google results page. The reasonable user of the Google search function (and similar search engines) certainly knows that he should expect to see various modes of advertising, e.g. banners that occasionally capture portions of the screen before being removed, pop-up windows that sometimes require software applications in order to block them, and so on. . . .

Against this backdrop, it is clear why Respondent 1 rightfully wishes to advertise its website, just like Petitioners. The internet, including search engines, is an advertising forum similar to other advertising media. There is no flaw in a method of advertising that focuses on a certain segment of the market that has shown an initial interest in a certain area. The ability to identify and capture market segments is a marketing/advertising strategy and a part of healthy commercial competition, provided that it is conducted in conformity with general law and is fair and reasonable, i.e. by respecting the right of privacy and legally protected rights of competitors. The principle of freedom of occupation, as well as the values of free competition, provides the conceptual and legal rationale to justify such strategies. In addition, the public right of information, as a dimension of the constitutional tenet of human dignity and freedom, should be considered.

We can analogize the situation to that of a shoe-shop owner (called K) who wants to hang advertising posters of his shop on the walls of an escalator or at the exit of the parking lot of a shopping center on the way to shoe-shop owner M ... use of the space on the wall by K for competing advertising actually makes use of the information that M's customers belong to a market segment that is interested in buying shoes. Moreover, this particular public may be aware of the reputation of this shop or the other in the shoe business. What is the ground for preventing such advertising in a market that values free competition and praises the freedom to choose and practice an occupation? Would hanging an advertisement of K's business near to M's shop, or even opening a shoe business in close proximity, violate M's trademark rights? Would it be reasonable to argue that such advertising, which lacks any mentioning of M's trademark, is likely to confuse consumers into thinking that K's products are in fact M's products or that such advertising dilutes the reputation of M? Is there any false description involved? Is it an unreasonable prevention of access or impairment that could amount to finding a tort of unfair competition or deception? ... It seems that the answers to all these questions should be in the negative....

The same also holds true with regard to the virtual "shopping mall" in Google. Everyone knows that the advertisement purchased by Respondent 1 appears in the area designated to sponsored links. The advertisement itself, as well as the website and the link leading to the website, does not make any reference to the words and letters that are arguably protected as trademarks. The only use by Respondent 1 of the combination of words and letters is in the context of keywords. This does not amount to infringement, even according to the view that would not always mandate consumer deception or confusion as a basis for trademark infringement.

Even if I cannot adopt the view that "use between computers" falls categorically outside the scope of "use" within the meaning of trademark law, and even if sponsored links may be considered as conferring some advantage on Respondent 1, in the balance of interests between the need for intellectual property protection, on the one hand, and the need to foster competition and availability of information to the public, on the other hand, the latter weighs more heavily in favor of finding no illicit advantage that would amount to trademark infringement. It seems that the controlling approach to trademark infringement requires an element of consumer deception or confusion. In the case at bar, Petitioners did not show that any of the Respondents, inasmuch as they make use of the trademarks, create confusion or a likelihood of confusion about whether the products of one were the products of the other, or whether one is benefiting from the reputation of the other, even assuming that both parties target the same market. This seems to be the spearhead of the issue that may arise between the parties and, therefore, I find that the use as described above does not amount to infringement of Petitioners' trademarks.

Notes and Questions

1.   Do you think the court assumes too much about the knowledge of "average" Internet users? Do you think the result should be different if the trademark purchased as a keyword is used in the sponsored link and/or in the paragraph with the sponsored link? Do you believe the analogy between Internet advertising and physical signage is apt?

2.   Numerous cases in France have held that the purchase of keywords by a competitor can be an infringement and that Google is also liable for use of its Adwords program and keyword suggestion tool. *See* Tribunal de grande instance [T.G.I.] [ordinary court of original jurisdiction] Nanterre, 2e Ch., Aug. 3, 2004 (Fr.) (Viaticum & Luteciel v. Google France); Tribunal de grande instance [T.G.I.] [ordinary court of original jurisdiction] Paris, Dec. 8, 2005 (Fr.) (Kertel v. Google France); and Tribunal de grande instance [T.G.I.] [ordinary court of original jurisdiction] Nanterre, Dec. 14, 2005 (Fr.) (Eurochallenges v. Google France). For possible explanations for this disparity with other jurisdictions, see Charlotte J. Romano, *Comparative Advertising in the United States and France*, 25 Nw. J. INT'L L. & BUS. 371, 374, 409 (2005) (noting that France considers trademark rights as property rights and generally disfavors comparative advertising more than the United States); *see also* Anheuser–Busch, Inc. v. Portugal, No. 73049/01 (Eur. Ct. H.R. Jan. 11, 2007) (Grand Chamber) (holding that Article 1 of Protocol No. 1 to the European Convention of Human Rights, which protects the right "to the peaceful enjoyment of [one's] possessions," covers both registered marks and trademark applications of a multinational corporation).

3.   The trademark blog Class 46 released a copy of the official translations of the questions sent to the ECJ by three French courts:

Questions referred

Must Article 5(1)(a) and (b) of First Council Directive 89/104/EEC of 21 December 1988 to approximate the laws of the Member States relating to trade marks and Article 9(1)(a) and (b) of Council Regulation (EC) No 40/94 of 20 December 1993 on the Community trade mark be interpreted as meaning that a provider of a paid referencing service who makes available to advertisers keywords reproducing or imitating registered trade marks and arranges by the referencing agreement to create and favourably display, on the basis of those keywords, advertising links to sites offering infringing goods is using those trade marks in a manner which their proprietor is entitled to prevent? . . .

In the event that such use does not constitute a use which may be prevented by the trade mark proprietor under the directive or the regulation, may the provider of the paid referencing service be regarded as providing an information society service consisting of the storage of information provided by the recipient of the service, within the meaning of Article 14 of Directive 2000/31 of 8 June 2000, so that that provider cannot incur liability until it has been notified by the trade mark proprietor of the unlawful use of the sign by the advertiser?

Posting of Frédéric Glaize to Class 46 Blog, http://class46.eu/2008/08/official-translation-of-questions.html (Aug. 6, 2008, 09:30).

D.   FOREIGN EQUIVALENTS

1.   ESTABLISHING LOCAL PROTECTION IN A GLOBAL ECONOMY

Marks incorporating foreign words or phrases present special considerations. Consider whether a federal registration for "Blue Ribbon" should bar a later registration for the term "Cordon Bleu" for use on similar products. On their face, the phrases sound and look very different. Nonetheless, the literal meaning of "Cordon Bleu" and "Blue Ribbon" is the same after the former is translated into English. Should a court consider this fact when assessing the availability of protection or the likelihood of confusion? Further, should it matter that the phrase "Cordon Bleu" has already entered the American vernacular as referring to excellence in cooking?

The doctrine of foreign equivalents permits consideration of translations of foreign words. For example, the Trademark Trial and Appeals Board denied a registration for "Buenos Dias" in connection with soap based on a prior registration for "Good Morning" latherless shaving cream. In support, the Board noted that Good Morning soap had been sold in packaging that included Spanish words and phrases, and that Spanish speakers "would be likely to translate 'Buenos Dias' into its 'Good Morning' English equivalent and mistakenly believe that the 'Buenos Dias' product was a product emanating from" the registrant who owned the Good Morning mark. In re *American Safety Razor*, 2 U.S.P.Q. 2d (BNA)

1459 (T.T.A.B. 1987); *see also* In re *Maclin–Zimmer–McGill Tobac-co Co.*, 262 F. 635 (C.A.D.C. 1920) (refusing registration for application for "El Gallo," based on a prior registration for the English equivalent term "Rooster" where both were directed to use with tobacco products).

Although these examples derive from the United States, the doctrine has been applied in some foreign courts. As one example, the Greek Administrative Trademark Committee considered an opposition to register a mark ΤΡΕΑΟΣ ΤΑΥΡΟΣ FULL ENERGY DRINK, in red lettering along with a picture of a bull, against a blue and silver background. The mark was associated with non-alcoholic beverages. The Committee agreed with the opponent, the Austrian company Red Bull GmbH, who markets an energy drink under the mark "Red Bull" with similar packaging. This determination was based on the finding that the mark's overall impression was likely to cause confusion. As one source describes, the Committee observed, "the English translation of the Greek word ΤΑΥΡΟ, which was used in the opposed mark, is 'bull,' and that said word was the dominating feature of the word portion of the opposed mark." *The Thirteenth Annual International Review of Trademark Jurisprudence*, 96 TRADEMARK REP. 267 (2006) (summarizing Decision No. 8165/2005 of the Greek Administrative Trademark Committee).

When reading the following two decisions from Canada, consider the problems confronting those seeking to protect their marks against foreign equivalents under the applicable standards.

KRAZY GLUE INC. v. GROUP CYANOMEX S.A. DE C.V.

Federal Court of Canada (Trial Division)
45 C.P.R. (3d) 161 (1992) (Can.)

McGILLIS, J.

The Appellant opposed the application of the Respondent to register KOLA LOKA as a trade-mark on the basis that it was confusing with KRAZY GLUE, a trade-mark registered to the Appellant. The Chairman of the Trademarks Opposition Board rejected the opposition and the Appellant now appeals from that decision pursuant to section 56 of the Trade-marks Act.

In 1984, the Respondent, which is a company in the Republic of Mexico, filed an application to register the trade-mark KOLA LOKA based on its proposed use in Canada in association with adhesives for solid objects. The application was advertised for opposition purposes in the *Trade-marks Journal*. In late 1984, the Appellant, which owns the registered trade-marks KRAZY GLUE and KRAZY LOCK, filed a Statement of Opposition with the Registrar of Trade-marks. It opposed the registration of KOLA LOKA on the grounds that the proposed trade-mark was not registrable as it was confusing with the trade-marks of the Appellant and not distinctive. With respect to distinctiveness, the proposed trade-mark was basically a Spanish equivalent of the well known trade-mark KRAZY GLUE and, since a substantial proportion of the Canadian population understands or speaks Spanish, there was a substantial likelihood that confusion would result . . . .

KRAZY GLUE is a distinctive, well-known trade-mark entitled to a wide scope of protection in Canada. Furthermore, KRAZY GLUE was used as a trade-mark in Canada for some time prior to the date of the filing by KOLA LOKA for registration. The wares associated with KRAZY GLUE and KOLA LOKA are identical and would travel through the same channels of trade. However, there is no resemblance whatsoever between KRAZY GLUE and KOLA LOKA either in appearance or sound.

. . . [T]he main issue to be determined on this appeal is the degree of resemblance in the ideas suggested by the two trade-marks. Even accepting the evidence of the Appellant that "kola loka" is the phonetic equivalent of "cola loca" which means "crazy glue" in Spanish, it would be necessary for the average consumer, having a vague or imperfect recollection of the registered trade-mark KRAZY GLUE, to be capable of making this translation from Spanish to English in order to be confused by the ideas suggested by KRAZY GLUE and KOLA LOKA. However, I have found as a fact that only a minimal proportion of the Canadian population speaks Spanish as a mother tongue or understands Spanish sufficiently to be capable of making the translation. I therefore conclude, on the basis of the facts established by the evidence, that the average consumer, having a vague or imperfect recollection of the registered trade-mark KRAZY GLUE, would find no degree of resemblance whatsoever in the ideas suggested by KOLA LOKA and KRAZY GLUE. Furthermore, I would have reached the same conclusion even if the evidence tendered on appeal had established the existence of Spanish communities in Toronto and Quebec City. The mere fact that ethnic enclaves exist in two urban centres in the country would not be sufficient to displace the well established average consumer test. Rather, such a fact, if established on the evidence, would constitute only an additional element to be considered in addressing the central question of the likelihood of confusion . . . .

The Appellant further submitted that it would be useful in the context of the facts of this case to consider the doctrine of foreign equivalents as applied in the United States of America. The doctrine of foreign equivalents in the United States of America essentially provides that foreign words or terms may not be registered as a trade-mark if the English language equivalent has been previously registered for products which might reasonably be assumed to come from the same source. This doctrine is not based on any statutory provision, but rather is merely a principle to be applied in determining the registrability of a trade-mark. I see no basis for importing this American doctrine.

CHEUNG KONG (HOLDINGS) LIMITED v. LIVING REALTY INC.

Federal Court of Canada (Trial Division)
[2000] 2 F.C. 501 (Can.)

EVANS J.

The respondent Living Realty Inc. sought to register a trade-mark consisting of Chinese characters (the transliteration of which was Cheung Kong SA IP, which, in English, means Long River Real Business) for use in association with real estate and investment services, principally in Toronto and the surrounding areas. The application was opposed by the applicant Cheung Kong (Holdings) Limited, a Hong Kong corporation and registered owner of the Canadian trade mark "Cheung Kong" used in Canada by its Canadian subsidiary Cheung Kong Holdings (Canada) Limited in association with specified services, including real estate development and investment. . . .

The Trade-marks Opposition Board (the Registrar) dismissed the opposition. . . .

The Registrar . . . found that there was no reasonable likelihood of confusion between the marks, principally because there was no "resemblance between the trade-marks . . . in appearance or sound or in the ideas suggested by them". He held that the perception of a resemblance in the idea conveyed by a mark must be assessed from the perspective of the "average Canadian consumer", a hypothetical person who is not "familiar with the Chinese language". This was an appeal from the Registrar's decision. . . .

[T]he Registrar erred in considering the possibility of confusion from the perspective of the average Canadian, who does not understand Chinese characters, and therefore would not know that the first two characters in Living Realty's mark transliterated into "Cheung Kong", and meant "long river", and hence would not confuse it with the opponent's registered trade-mark. . . .

The facts herein suggested that a substantial number of consumers of Living Realty's services understand the meaning of the Chinese characters that comprise its proposed mark. First, Living Realty's business has been centred on the sale of real estate in Toronto, although it has also included properties in the surrounding area. Judicial notice was taken of the existence of a substantial Chinese community in Greater Toronto. Second, Living Realty targeted the Chinese community, although not to the exclusion of non-Chinese clients. It was therefore hard to maintain that a substantial number of actual consumers were not reasonably likely to confuse Living Realty's mark with Cheung Kong's as a result of the identical and distinctive nature of the idea conveyed by the marks, particularly given the similarities of the services offered by the parties.

Since the likelihood of confusion should be assessed from the perspective of the average person who is likely to consume the wares or services in question, if it could be inferred from the evidence that a significant proportion of the likely consumers of Living Realty's clients were familiar with Chinese characters, the Registrar should have taken this into consideration as part of the surrounding circumstances when determining whether there was a likelihood of confusion with Cheung Kong's mark. If the Registrar based his conclusion on the fact that the average Canadian cannot read Chinese characters, without regard to whether the evidence indicated that a significant number of the consumers of Living Realty's services were likely to be able to transliterate the first two characters of the proposed mark into Cheung Kong, or transliterate it into "long river," then he erred in law. . . .

It was possible to infer that a substantial number of Living Realty's clients were Chinese speakers who might be expected to associate the Chinese characters mark with the Cheung Kong mark.

The inherent distinctiveness of the marks to those able to read the marks of both parties, the overlapping nature of the services associated with the marks and the identical idea that they convey, namely "long river", were sufficient to preclude Living Realty from discharging its burden of proving, on the balance of probabilities, that there was no reasonable likelihood of confusion between the marks.

Notes and Questions

1. *Krazy Glue* and *Cheung Kong* were decided against the back-drop of § 6(5) of the Canadian Trade-marks Act, which provides the controlling standard for evaluating trademarks:

> In determining whether trade-marks or trade-names are con-fusing, the court or the Registrar, as the case may be, shall have regard to all the surrounding circumstances including
>
> (a) the inherent distinctiveness of the trade-marks or trade-names and the extent to which they have become known;

(b) the length of time the trade-marks or trade-names have been in use;

(c) the nature of the wares, services or business;

(d) the nature of the trade; and

(e) the degree of resemblance between the trade-marks or trade-names in appearance or sound or in the ideas suggested by them.

Which of these factors would have the most impact on the facts of the *Cheung Kong* case? In what manner, if any, would the last factor impact the result? How, if at all, would the outcome be affected if the doctrine of foreign equivalents had been applied, rather than the likelihood of confusion standard applied by *Cheung Kong*?

2.   In jurisdictions that apply the doctrine of foreign equivalents, should this principle be applied to all marks? Consider the following from the United States Patent and Trademark Office, advising that under United States standards "[t]he doctrine should be applied only when it is likely that the ordinary American purchaser would stop and translate the foreign word into its English equivalent." TRADEMARK MANUAL OF EXAMINING PROCEDURE § 1207.01(b)(vi). As one example, in *Palm Bay Imports, Inc. v. Veuve Clicquot Ponsardin Maison Fondee En 1772*, the Federal Circuit held that the mark "The Widow" did not create a likelihood of confusion with the mark "Veuve Clicquot." Although the court recognized that a large percentage of Americans speak French, the court found it "improbable that the average American purchaser would stop and translate 'Veuve' into "widow." Is this standard consistent with the treatment of "Buenos Dias" in the United States decision *American Safety Razor*, described *supra?* How about the Canadian *Krazy Glue* standard?

3.   In *Otokoyama Co., Ltd. v. Wine of Japan Import, Inc.*, 175 F.3d 266 (2d Cir. 1999), a United States court applied the doctrine of foreign equivalents to a Japanese mark that meant a certain type of "sake." *Otokoyama* explained that the genericide applies to marks in a foreign language, stating:

> This extension rests on the assumption that there are (or someday will be) customers in the United States who speak that foreign language. Because of the diversity of the population of the United States, coupled with temporary visitors, all of whom are part of the United States marketplace, commerce in the United States utilizes innumerable foreign languages. No merchant may obtain the exclusive right over a trademark designation if that exclusivity would prevent competitors from designating a product as what it is in the foreign language their customers know best. Courts and the USPTO apply this policy, known as the doctrine of "foreign equivalents."

One author has proposed that the doctrine of foreign equivalents "should only be applied when an appreciable number of ordinary

American purchasers of the particular goods or services in the United States, who speak English as well as the pertinent foreign language, will understand the meaning of the foreign-word mark at issue, and will actually translate that mark into its English equivalent." Elizabeth Rest, *Lost in Translation: A Critical Examination of Conflicting Decisions Applying the Doctrine of Foreign Equivalents*, 96 TRADEMARK REP. 1211, 1213 (2006). Which of these two approaches is preferable as a matter of trademark policy?

4. In *French Transit, Ltd. v. Modern Coupon Systems*, Inc., 818 F. Supp. 635 (S.D.N.Y. 1993), the court determined that the doctrine of foreign equivalents did not apply to the mark "Le Crystal Naturel" because the mark was a mix of English and foreign words. In doing so, the court relied on two Board decisions that had declined to apply the doctrine where the French articles "le" and "la" had been placed before English words. *See also* In re *Universal Package Corp.*, 222 U.S.P.Q. (BNA) 344 (T.T.A.B. 1984) ("Le Case" for jewelry boxes, reasoning that the addition of French gave consumers a different commercial impression than "The Case," as "[t]he French article imparts to the mark a French flavor"); In re *Johanna Farms Inc.*, 8 U.S.P.Q. 2d (BNA) 1408 (T.T.A.B. 1988) ("La Yogurt" for yogurt, where survey evidence and "consumer correspondence demonstrate that most users and purchasers of yogurt view 'La Yogurt' as identifying a brand and not a product category").

A number of courts do not fully articulate reasons to reject the application of the doctrine. For example, in *Toho Co., Ltd. v. William Morrow and Co.*, 33 F. Supp. 2d 1206, 1216 (C.D. Cal. 1998), the court rejected the argument that the mark "Godzilla" should be considered generic as the hybrid of Japanese words meaning "gorilla" and "whale," and stating only the mark was a "a fanciful, arbitrary word used to describe a fire-breathing, pre-historic, often-schizophrenic dinosaur."

2. TRANSLATION: ASCERTAINING MEANING FOR FOREIGN EQUIVALENTS

Where the doctrine of foreign equivalents applies, decision makers have examined a variety of information to determine a mark's meaning. Should the court limit translations to "official" sources such as a foreign dictionary? Or should the court consider slang or colloquial understandings?

In *Enrique Bernat F., S.A. v. Guadalajara, Inc.*, 210 F.3d 439 (5th Cir. 2000), the court considered the status of the mark "Chupa Chups," used for marketing lollipops, asserted against a defendant that marketed a lollipop under the mark "Chupa Gurts." On appeal from the entry of a preliminary injunction, the Fifth Circuit eschewed the district court's reliance on Spanish–English dictionary meanings of "chupa" as "to lick" or "to suck." Instead, *Enrique Bernat* ruled that the defendant's evidence of the term's colloquial meaning as a "lollipop" in certain Spanish-speaking countries should have been considered to determine the strength of the mark:

> Spanish-speakers from Mexico and parts of South America will understand "chupa" to be the generic designator of "lollipop." . . . Moreover, the policy of international comity has substantial weight in this situation. If we permit Chupa Chups to monopolize the term "chupa," we will impede other Mexican candy makers' ability to compete effectively in the U.S. lollipop market. Just as we do not expect Mexico to interfere with Tootsie's ability to market its product in Mexico by granting trademark protection in the word "pop" to another American confectioner, so we cannot justify debilitating Dulces Vero's attempts to market "Chupa Gurts" in the United States by sanctioning Chupa Chups' bid for trademark protection in the word "chupa."

Note that the relevant meaning of the phrase in *Enrique Bernat* is based on the understanding established within the foreign country, not the country in which the mark is asserted. *Pizzeria Uno Corp. v. Temple*, 747 F.2d 1522 (4th Cir. 1984), also adopted this approach. In that case, the court considered the validity of the term "Uno" (meaning "one" in Italian) used in association with a chain of "Pizzeria Uno" restaurants. Although the English translation of "one" colloquially means "the best" in the United States, the analysis emphasized that "Uno" had not been used for that connotation in either Latin or Italian.

E. FAMOUS AND WELL–KNOWN MARKS

1. ESTABLISHING AND ENFORCING RIGHTS WORLDWIDE

As discussed in depth in Chapter 1, intellectual property rights are generally considered territorial to a particular nation or region. This principle has some applicability in trademark law, although with less stringency than the other areas of intellectual property law. Nonetheless, borders have not yet become completely irrelevant and, in some instances, may still present some practical problems in establishing and enforcing trademarks worldwide. As an example, both the Federal and Fifth Circuits have held that a mark holder's use of a mark in commerce within Japan did not establish rights under United States trademark law. *See Person's Co., Ltd. v. Christman*, 900 F.2d 1565, 1569 (Fed. Cir. 1990); *Fuji Photo Film Co. v. Shinohara Shoji Kabushiki Kaisha*, 754 F.2d 591, 599 (5th Cir. 1985).

Trademark law's concern with encouraging mark holders to develop marks, and to protect consumers against confusion, extend beyond geographic borders. As one author observes:

In such a smaller but more intensely networked world, brand manufacturers are no longer confined to local markets. They function in an integrated global market place. Brand producers find themselves providing goods and services in bigger and bigger markets created by free trade pacts and the creation of single markets throughout the world. Brands such as COCA-COLA, MCDONALD'S, CARTIER, SMIRNOFF, ROLLS-ROYCE, FERRARI, KODAK, SONY, CNN and DHL have virtually become household names to the global citizen. Against the reality of this background, there is certainly no doubt in the minds of businessmen that the reputation and goodwill attached to their famous brands have become detached from national and local borders.

Frederick W. Mostert, *Well–Known and Famous Marks: Is Harmony Possible in the Global Village?*, 86 TRADEMARK REP. 103 (1996).

2. THE FAMOUS MARKS DOCTRINE

Some jurisdictions recognize broad protection for well-known marks. For example, in *McDonald's v. Joburgers Drive–Inn*, 1997 (1) SA 1 (1996) (S. Afr.), the fast-food chain McDonald's sought to enjoin trademark infringement by a South African company. The defendant had commenced selling fast food—including hamburgers—under the marks "McDonald" or "McDonald's" in South Africa after McDonald's had a global presence but before McDonald's had any restaurants in that country. McDonald's' entry into South Africa would have been difficult under the United States Comprehensive Anti–Apartheid Act, which was in force between 1986 and 1991.

In the trademark litigation against Joburgers, McDonald's relied on a South African statute that allowed an owner of a well-known trademark to restrain the use of a similar mark where such use was likely to cause confusion. The *Joburgers* court granted relief, finding that those consumers most likely to purchase the products were likely to be confused, stating:

The evidence adduced by McDonald's leads ... to the inference that its marks, and particularly the mark McDonald's, are well known amongst the more affluent people in the country. People who travel, watch television, and who read local and foreign publications, are likely to know about it. They would have seen McDonald's outlets in other countries, and seen or heard its advertisements there or its spillover here in foreign journals, television shows, etc. Although the extent of such spillover has not been quantified it must be substantial.

What justifies granting McDonald's relief when Joburgers was first to establish trademark rights? Does the fact that McDonald's had become known in South Africa justify enjoining local users from adopting the same mark? Does it matter that the defendant had issued a press release that stated "[t]he chain will serve McMuffins and Big Mac burgers. Restaurants will also be decorated with a large M device similar to two joined arches"? What impact might McDonald's' inability to use its well-known trade symbols in the South African market have on the Court's decision?

GRUPO GIGANTE SA DE CV v. DALLO & CO.

391 F.3d 1088 (9th Cir. 2004)

KLEINFELD, Circuit Judge.

This is a trademark case. The contest is between a large Mexican grocery chain that has long used the mark, but not in the United States, and a small American chain that was the first to use the mark in the United States, but did so, long after the Mexican chain began using it, in a locality where shoppers were familiar with the Mexican mark.

Grupo Gigante S.A. de C.V. ("Grupo Gigante") operates a large chain of grocery stores in Mexico, called "Gigante," meaning "Giant" in Spanish. Grupo Gigante first called a store "Gigante" in Mexico City in 1962. In 1963, Grupo Gigante registered the "Gigante" mark as a trade name in Mexico, and has kept its registration current ever since. The chain was quite successful, and it had expanded into Baja California, Mexico by 1987. By 1991, Grupo Gigante had almost 100 stores in Mexico, including six in Baja, all using the mark "Gigante." Two of the Baja stores were in Tijuana, a city on the U.S.–Mexican border, just south of San Diego.

As of August 1991, Grupo Gigante had not opened any stores in the United States. That month, Michael Dallo began operating a grocery store in San Diego, using the name "Gigante Market." In October 1996, Dallo and one of his brothers, Chris Dallo, opened a second store in San Diego, also under the name Gigante Market.

In 1995, which was after the opening of the Dallos' first store and before the opening of their second, Grupo Gigante began exploring the possibility of expanding into Southern California. It learned of the Dallos' Gigante Market in San Diego. Grupo Gigante decided against entering the California market at that time. It did nothing about the Dallos' store despite Grupo Gigante's knowledge that the Dallos were using "Gigante" in the store's name.

In 1998, Grupo Gigante decided that the time had come to enter the Southern California market. It arranged a meeting with Michael Dallo in June 1998 to discuss the Dallos' use of the name "Gigante." Grupo Gigante was unsuccessful at this meeting in its attempt to convince Dallo to stop using the "Gigante" mark. Also in June 1998, Grupo Gigante registered the "Gigante" mark with the state of California. The Dallos did likewise in July 1998. Neither has registered the mark federally.

About one year later, in May 1999, Grupo Gigante opened its first United States store. That store was followed by a second later that year, and then by a third in 2000. All three stores were in the Los Angeles area. All were called "Gigante," like Grupo Gigante's Mexican stores. In July 1999, after learning of the opening of Grupo Gigante's first United States store, the Dallos sent Grupo Gigante a cease-and-desist letter, making the same demand of Grupo Gigante that Grupo Gigante had made of them earlier: stop using the name Gigante. Grupo Gigante responded several days later by filing this lawsuit. Its claim was based on numerous federal and state theories, including trademark infringement under the Lanham Act. . . .

Under the principle of first in time equals first in right, priority ordinarily comes with earlier *use* of a mark in commerce. It is 'not enough to have invented the mark first or even to have registered it first.' If the first-in-time principle were all that mattered, this case would end there. It is undisputed that Grupo Gigante used the mark in commerce for decades before the Dallos did. But the facts of this case implicate another well-established principle of trademark law, the "territoriality principle." The territoriality principle, as stated in a treatise, says that "[p]riority of trademark rights in the United States depends solely upon priority of use in the United States, not on priority of use anywhere in the world." J. Thomas McCarthy, McCarthy on Trademarks and Unfair Competition § 29:2, at 29–6 (4th ed. 2002). Earlier use in another country usually just does not count. Although we have not had occasion to address this principle, it has been described by our sister circuits as "basic to trademark law," in large part because "trademark rights exist in each country solely according to that country's statutory scheme." Fuji Photo Film Co. v. Shinohara Shoji Kabushiki Kaisha, 754 F.2d 591, 599 (5th Cir. 1985); *see also* Person's Co., Ltd. v. Christman, 900 F.2d 1565, 1569 (Fed. Cir. 1990). While Grupo Gigante used the mark for decades before the Dallos used it, Grupo Gigante's use was in Mexico, not in the United States. Within the San Diego area, on the northern side of the border, the Dallos were the first users of the "Gigante" mark. Thus, according to the territoriality principle, the Dallos' rights to use the mark would trump Grupo Gigante's.

Grupo Gigante does not contest the existence of the territoriality principle. But like the first-in-time, first-in-right principle, it is not absolute. The exception, as Grupo Gigante presents it, is that when foreign use of a mark achieves a certain level of fame for that mark within the United States, the territoriality principle no longer serves to deny priority to the earlier foreign user. . . .

We hold that there is a famous mark exception to the territoriality principle. While the territoriality principle is a long-standing and important doctrine within trademark law, it cannot be absolute. An absolute territoriality rule without a famous-mark exception would promote consumer confusion and fraud. Commerce crosses borders. In this nation of immigrants, so do people. Trademark is, at its core, about protecting against consumer confusion and "palming off." There can be no justification for using trademark law to fool immigrants into thinking that they are buying from the store they liked back home. . . .

The district court held that the correct inquiry was to determine whether the mark had attained secondary meaning in the San Diego area. . . .

Under what has become known as the *Tea Rose–Rectanus* doctrine, priority of use in one geographic area within the United States does not necessarily suffice to establish priority in another area. . . . The point of this doctrine is that in the remote area, where no one is likely to know of the earlier user, it is unlikely that consumers would be confused by the second user's use of the mark. Secondary meaning comes into play in determining just how far each user's priority extends. . . .

Assume, for example, that Grupo Gigante had been using the mark in Arizona as well as in various parts of Mexico, and that it had met all the other requirements of having a protectable interest in the mark, including having established secondary meaning throughout Arizona. Under the *Tea Rose–Rectanus* doctrine, Grupo Gigante would have priority in San Diego, and thus be able to stop the Dallos' use of the mark, only if the secondary meaning from Grupo Gigante's use of the mark in Arizona extended to San Diego as well. If, on the other hand, the secondary meaning from Grupo Gigante's use were limited to Arizona, then the Dallos might be free to continue using the mark in San Diego. . . .

Under the district court's interpretation of the exception to the territoriality principle, the fact that Grupo Gigante's earlier use of the mark was entirely outside of the United States becomes irrelevant.

The problem with this is that treating international use differently is what the territoriality principle does. This interpretation of the exception would effectively eliminate the territoriality principle by eliminating any effect of international borders on protectability. . . .

The territoriality principle has a long history in the common law, and at least two circuits have described it as "basic to trademark law." *Fuji Photo*, 754 F.2d at 599; *Person's*, 900 F.2d at 1569. That status reflects the lack of a uniform trademark regime across international borders. Furthermore, we are arguably required by the Paris Convention, of which the United States is a signatory, to preserve the territoriality principle in some form. . . . [W]e reject Grupo Gigante's argument that we should define the well-known mark exception as merely an inquiry into whether the mark has achieved secondary meaning in the area where the foreign user wishes to assert protection. . . .

[S]econdary meaning is not enough.

In addition, where the mark has not before been used in the American market, the court must be satisfied, by a preponderance of the evidence, that a *substantial* percentage of consumers in the relevant American market is familiar with the foreign mark. The relevant American market is the geographic area where the defendant uses the alleged infringing mark. In making this determination, the court should consider such factors as the intentional copying of the mark by the defendant, and whether customers of the American firm are likely to think they are patronizing the same firm that uses the mark in another country. While these factors are not necessarily determinative, they are particularly relevant because they bear heavily on the risks of consumer confusion and fraud, which are the reasons for having a famous-mark exception.

Because the district court did not have the benefit of this additional test, we vacate and remand so that it may be applied.

Notes and Questions

1. *Grupo Gigante's* conclusion that well-known marks represent an exception to the territoriality principle is not uniformly accepted. In 2007, the Second Circuit rejected the Lanham Act's inclusion of a well-known marks exception, finding a lack of a statutory basis to support the doctrine. *ITC Ltd. v. Punchgini, Inc.*, 482 F.3d 135 (2d Cir. 2007). The appellate court explained, "[b]efore we construe the Lanham Act to include such a significant departure from the principle of territoriality, we will wait for Congress to express its intent more clearly." Although the *Punchgini* court recognized that "persuasive policy argument can be advanced in support of the famous marks doctrine," the court found that "any policy arguments in favor of the famous marks doctrine must be submitted to Congress for it to determine whether and under what circumstances to accord federal recognition to such an

exception to the basic principle of territoriality." Do you think *Grupo Gigante* or *Punchgini* provides the better rule? Why? Alternatively, should a court rely on the law of remedies and deny the mark holder's right as a matter of public interest?

2.   Assume that you wish to open a restaurant in Los Angeles that features international flavors. Under *Joburgers* and *Grupo Gigante*, would you consider a conflicting foreign mark a problem in adopting your chosen restaurant name? If your restaurant becomes popular and you open more locations, how does the famous marks doctrine impact your policing costs? Consider the following critique of the famous mark doctrine as implemented by the courts:

> These courts elevate concerns about domestic consumer confu-
> sion without consideration of other values underlying territori-
> ality. As demonstrated above, trademark law may adopt a
> territorial (or national) stance in order to pursue other objec-
> tives. By ignoring an increase in uncertainty and search costs,
> and by undermining the established international systems for
> registration of rights on a multinational basis, these courts
> have undervalued the importance of territoriality rooted in
> national political and economic structures.

Graeme B. Dinwoodie, *Trademarks and Territory: Detaching Trademark Law from the Nation–State*, 41 Hous. L. Rev. 885, 932 (2004).

3.   What is a "well-known" mark? WIPO has promulgated a Joint Recommendation Concerning Provisions on the Protection of Well–Known Marks, a non-binding document for members of the Paris Convention and WIPO. Joint Recommendation Concerning Provisions on the Protection of Well–Known Marks, WIPO Doc. A/34/13, at 3 (adopted Sept. 20 to 29, 1999). The document contains a list of factors to be considered in determining whether a mark is well-known:

> 1.   the degree of knowledge or recognition of the mark in the relevant sector of the public;
>
> 2.   the duration, extent and geographical area of any use of the mark;
>
> 3.   the duration, extent and geographical area of any promotion of the mark, including advertising or publicity and the presentation, at fairs or exhibitions, of the goods and/or services to which the mark applies;
>
> 4.   the duration and geographical area of any registrations, and/or any applications for registration, of the mark, to the extent that they reflect use or recognition of the mark;
>
> 5.   the record of successful enforcement of rights in the mark, in particular, the extent to which the mark was recognized as well known by competent authorities; and
>
> 6.   the value associated with the mark.

Article 3 of the Joint Recommendation states that member states "shall protect a well-known mark against conflicting marks, business identifiers and domain names, at least with effect from the time when the mark has become well known in the Member State." The Joint Recommendation specifically excludes whether "the mark has been used in, or that the mark has been registered or that an application for registration of the mark has been filed in or in respect of, the Member State" as a prerequisite to protection. Is this approach preferable to the one that taken by the *Grupo Gigante* court?

F. TRADEMARK DILUTION

Although it may be said that the boundaries of dilution law are uncertain under United States law, the situation becomes more complex on the international stage. Notwithstanding dilution's origins in Europe, even the European nations cannot agree on the full scope of the doctrine. Today, each nation's requirements vary widely from others. The following material provides an overview of some of the points of divergence.

VERIMARK (PTY) LTD. v. BMW AG

Supreme Court of Appeal of South Africa
[2007] S.C.A. 53 (S. Afr.)

HARMS ADP.

The well-known BMW logo is registered in different classes and those in contention are registered (a) in class 3 for, amongst others, cleaning and polishing preparations and vehicle polishes (the polish mark, TM 1987/05127); and (b) in class 12 for vehicles, automobiles and the like (the car mark, TM 1956/00818/1)....

Verimark is the market leader in the field of direct response television marketing in which demonstrative television commercials are used. Two of its many products are its Diamond Guard car care kit and Diamond Guard car polish. These have been widely advertised and sold since 1996. Throughout this period Verimark used vehicles of different makes, but more particularly BMW cars, to demonstrate the wonders of these products. In one particular television flight a BMW car is first treated with Diamond Guard and then an inflammable liquid is poured onto the hood of the car and set alight without causing any damage to the car's paintwork. In another instance an older and cheaper car is treated with Diamond Guard and it then metamorphoses into a shining BMW. The complaint of BMW is that its logo on the BMW car is clearly visible....

This brings me to BMW's case based on s 34(1)(c)—the anti-dilution provision—which provides (to the extent relevant) that the unauthorized use in the course of trade in relation to any goods of a mark identical to a registered trade mark, if the latter is well known in the Republic and the use of the mark would be likely to take unfair advantage of, or be detrimental to, the distinctive character or the repute of the registered trade mark amounts to trade mark infringement, notwithstanding the absence of confusion or deception.

It is common cause that the BMW logo is well known and that the issue is whether Verimark's use as described is likely to take 'unfair advantage' of the distinctive character or the repute of the BMW mark, in other words, whether there is the likelihood of dilution through an unfair blurring of BMW's logo, it being accepted that Verimark's use is not detrimental to nor does it tarnish BMW's logo.

Contrary to rather wide *dicta* in *Johnstone* stating the opposite, the position in our law is that this provision does not require trade mark use in the sense discussed as a pre-condition for liability. In other words, the provision "aims at more than safeguarding a product's 'badge of origin' or its 'source-denoting function'." It also protects the reputation, advertising value or selling power of a well known mark. But that does not mean that the fact that the mark has been used in a non trade mark sense is irrelevant; to the contrary, it may be very relevant to determine whether unfair advantage has been taken of or whether the use was detrimental to the mark.

... [T]he provision is not intended to enable the proprietor of a well-known registered mark to object as a matter of course to the use of a sign which may remind people of his mark; there is a general reluctance to apply this provision too widely; not only must the advantage be unfair, but it must be of a sufficiently significant degree to warrant restraining of what is, *ex hypothesi*, non-confusing use; and that the unfair advantage or the detriment must be properly substantiated or established to the satisfaction of the court: the court must be satisfied by evidence of actual detriment, or of unfair advantage.

The high court found that although Verimark may be taking advantage of the reputation of the BMW logo, this is not done in a manner that is unfair. It mentioned that Verimark's emphasis is on the effectiveness of its own product sold under established trade marks and found that one cannot expect Verimark to advertise car polish without using any make of car and it would be contrived to expect of Verimark to avoid showing vehicles in such a way that their logos are hidden or are removed. I agree. As before, the question has to be answered with reference to the consumer's perception about Verimark's use of the logo. Once again, in my judgment a consumer will consider the presence of the logo as incidental and part of the car and will accept that the choice of car was fortuitous. In short, I fail to see how the use of the logo can affect the advertising value of the logo detrimentally. A mental association does not necessarily lead either to blurring or tarnishing.

This means that the high court was correct in its dismissal of the claim for an interdict in relation to the car mark and that the cross-appeal stands to be dismissed.

Notes and Questions

1. *Verimark* rejects a trademark use requirement to establish dilution. By contrast, in Case No. C–408/01, *Adidas–Salomon AG v. Fitnessworld Trading Ltd.*, 2003 E.C.R. I–12537, the opinion construed Article 5(2) of the European Community Trademark Directive, which considers a form of relief for dilution:

> Any Member State may also provide that the proprietor shall be entitled to prevent all third parties not having his consent from using in the course of trade any sign which is identical with, or similar to, the trade mark in relation to goods or services which are not similar to those for which the trade mark is registered, where the latter has a reputation in the Member State and where use of that sign without due cause takes unfair advantage of, or is detrimental to, the distinctive character or the repute of the trade mark.

Adidas–Salomon found that this section required trademark use to establish relief. *Id.* ¶ 57 ("the regulation of non-trade mark use of a sign which without due cause takes unfair advantage of, or is detrimental to, the distinctive character or the repute of a trade mark is not governed by the Directive. Such use cannot fall within Article 5(2)."). On the merits, *Adidas–Salomon* found Adidas could not rely on this section to protect its three stripe trade mark against a competitor's use of two stripes a decorative element on clothing. The court explained, "[i]f the relevant section of the public perceives a given sign as doing no more than embellishing goods, and in no way as identifying their origin, that sign cannot be regarded as used for the purpose of distinguishing those goods." Although the opinion noted that some decorative motifs may invoke an association with a mark that triggers protection under Article 5(2), the opinion observed that "public interest considerations militate against extending that protection so as to prevent traders from using simple and long-accepted decorations and motifs" such as stripes. *Cf. adidas-America, Inc. v. Payless Shoesource, Inc.*, 546 F. Supp. 2d 1029 (D. Or. 2008) (allowing adidas' claims based on the three stripe design to proceed to trial under United States trademark and dilution laws against Payless products displaying a four stripe design). What function does the trademark use requirement serve in the dilution context? Does *Verimark* appear to lack an appreciation for these concerns or did the court simply address them in an alternative way?

2. In *Verimark*, the court deemed the defendant's use of the BMW logo in television advertising for an unrelated product not to constitute dilution. By contrast, a French court held that a display of the Louis Vuitton trademark in a music video warranted relief in the form of both an injunction and damages. Tribunal de grande instance [T.G.I.] [ordinary court of original jurisdiction] Paris, 3e Ch., Nov. 14, 2007 (Fr.) (S.A. Louis Vuitton v. Britney Jean X). The court described the video as featuring singer Britney Spears "in a pink Hummer vehicle sailing in the clouds" with a dashboard covered in Louis Vuitton's Takashi Murakami cherry blossom design featuring the "Vuitton" mark. The court observed that the video included a few seconds that displayed the mark in a close-up that would be noticed even by inattentive viewers.

In part, the *Louis Vuitton* court relied on Article 9 of Council Regulation 40/94, which uses language similar to Article 5(2) of the European Community Trademark Directive. Specifically, the regulation allows a CTM to seek relief when the mark of another "without due cause takes unfair advantage of, or is detrimental to, the distinctive character or the repute of the Community trade mark." The opinion found that the mark holder Louis Vuitton had suffered economic harm to the value of the mark, such as prejudice to the "image of luxury which it promotes that was far removed from the image portrayed by Britney."

Is *Verimark* distinguishable? Beyond this, is the *Louis Vuitton* court's finding of harm consistent with that identified by the *Adidas–Salomon* court? How do you suppose the *Louis Vuitton* and *Adidas–Salomon* courts vary on the issue of whether trademark use is required?

3. One scholar describes a trademark registration system that provides an alternative method for the protection of famous marks:

Under the defensive mark registration system, "widely recognized" trademarks can be registered to protect identified goods or services other than those listed in the original registration. This system does not exist in the United States. Additional goods or services need not be similar to the original goods or services, and the registrant need not have any use for these additional goods or services nor any intent to use the mark on these additional goods or services. The requirements are only that the mark be "widely recognized by consumers" (*hiroku ninshiki sareteiru*) and that there be an apprehension of confusion (*kondo no osore*) if the mark is used on these additional goods or services by a third party. It is not difficult to see why this has been referred to as a "super registry."

The JPO and Japanese courts require that the registration of a defensive mark must be "identical" to the primary registered trademark. Therefore, the Tokyo High Court affirmed an examiner's rejection of "Mercedes–Benz" as a defensive mark application for string, rope, or netting because it was not identical to its principal mark, Mercedes–Benz as registered for use on automobiles. That is, the marks do not share the same font and the primary registered trademark is in all upper case letters. The court held that "if the plaintiff [Mercedes–Benz] wanted to prevent the use of its mark in this fashion, they ought to elect to register the mark as an associated trademark. Attempting to interpret this as a defensive mark registration is absurd (*sujichigai*)."

Kenneth L. Port, *Trademark Dilution in Japan*, 4 Nw. J. Tech. & Intell. Prop. 228 (2006). If such a system were implemented worldwide, would the advance notice provided by such a system likely lessen dilution litigation?

G. TRADEMARKS AND GEOGRAPHICAL INDICATIONS

1. WHAT IS A GEOGRAPHICAL INDICATION?

A firmly entrenched principle of United States trademark law is the notion that product designations are viewed through the lens of consumer perception. A trademark may obtain federal registration by designating the source of a good, such as "Velveeta" for a particular processed dairy product, without regard to whether the mark reveals anything about the identity of the producer or the geographic origin of the product. Those who wish to associate a locale with a product must ensure that the place name is not misdescriptive. If the locality represents the geographic source of the good, they also need to demonstrate distinctiveness.

Alternatively, a trade association may obtain a certification mark, such as the one obtained by the Idaho Potato Commission for use by growers in the State of Idaho for potatoes that meet specified criteria as to size, weight, shape, maturity and the like. As is true for trademarks, the purpose of a certification mark includes fostering and protecting consumer expectations about the nature and quality of the products that bear the mark. *See State of Idaho Potato Com'n v. G & T Terminal Packaging, Inc.*, 425 F.3d 708 (9th Cir. 2005).

Other nations offer protection according to a geographical indication ("GI") system, which accords significant weight to industries built on particular qualities and characteristics of a region. How do GIs differ from trademark protection in the United States? In the most general sense, a GI links a product with a country or region from which a product derives. As one example, Roquefort is a GI that refers to a distinctive type of bleu cheese made near Roquefort-sur-Soulzon in France. There are two primary types of GIs. One type, the indication of source (also called a "designation of origin"), identifies the product's original country or area. The second type, the appellation of origin (*"appellation d'origine"*), identifies the geographic source of the item with the additional requirement that the product's qualities derive *from* the geographic region.

These principles can be illustrated by the ECJ's decision in Cases C–465 & 466/02, *Federal Republic of Germany & Kingdom of Denmark v. Commission of the European Communities*, 2005 E.C.R. I–9115. In that case, the court considered the Greek specification for "Feta" cheese. The cheese's characteristics include its derivation "from ewes and goats of local breeds reared traditionally, whose feed must be based on the flora present in the pastures of eligible regions." The ECJ explained:

> Extensive grazing and transhumance, central to the method of keeping the ewes and goats used to provide the raw material for making "Feta" cheese, are the result of an ancestral tradition allowing adaptation to climate changes and their impact on the available vegetation. This has led to the development of small native breeds of sheep and goats which are extremely tough and resistant, fitted for survival in an environment that offers little food in quantitative terms but, in terms of quality, is endowed with an extremely diversified flora, thus giving the finished product its own specific aroma and flavour. The interplay between the above natural factors and the specific human factors, in particular the traditional production method, which requires straining without pressure, has thus given "Feta" cheese its remarkable international reputation.

The link between the cheese's qualities and the specific features of the land, the animals and skills of local residents shows that "feta," unlike "Velveeta," is a GI. Maintaining the link between the product and the region, including the conditions under which the product is created, is key to maintaining protection and preventing genericide. As one scholar pointed out, GIs are aimed at implementing agricultural policy and cultural heritage:

> The justifications for GI protection are not restricted solely to preserving communicative clarity in the marketplace, but respond to these additional policy concerns and recognize intergenerational knowledge and investments in production methods. Several European national regimes view GIs as a collective right to use, requiring governmental

oversight and which cannot be licensed or transferred out of the region. To this extent, protecting GI producers is also about preserving material aspects of heritage, rural landscapes, and perhaps even a sense of regional or national identity. These *savoir faire* and heritage dimensions are extraneous to trademark law....

Dev Gangee, *Quibbling Siblings: Conflicts Between Trademarks and Geographical Indications*, 82 CHI.-KENT L. REV. 1253 (2007).

The term GI has been used to include both indications of source and appellations of origin. Nonetheless, the term GI has been defined in various sources of law, including treaties, statutes, and case law. Thus, the context of the use of the phrase should be assessed to determine its precise meaning when considering authorities that use the term.

2. THE LAW AND POLICY OF GEOGRAPHICAL INDICATIONS

GIs have a rich and varied history, including efforts by individual nations to create protection within their borders. One of the most robust systems was created by the French, which had created product-specific legislation since the fourteenth century and began to enact more broad-reaching legislation during the early part of the twentieth century. *See* BERNARD O'CONNOR, THE LAW OF GEOGRAPHICAL INDICATIONS 165–79 (2007) (summarizing the salient features of the French system).

Two features are emblematic of the French system as it currently exists. First, the French legislation defines an appellation of origin as including qualities and characteristics of a geographic region, including both *natural* and *human factors*. This definition encompasses not only features of the land from which the product derives, but also features contributed by the local people, who may have worked the land in a particular way, built specialized mills or the like, or developed production methods that have an impact on the qualities of the end product. Second, applicants must submit information to the French Institut National de L'Origine et de la Qualité detailing the product's distinguishing features, the link between these features and the geographic origin of the product, and additional information to justify treatment as an appellation of origin. This information is incorporated into a report that is forwarded to an appropriate French National Committee for consideration.

Beyond France, a number of multinational laws and treaties have incorporated GIs of different types and scope, with varying levels of success. *See generally* INSTITUTE NATIONAL DE L'ORIGINE ET DE LA QUALITE, GUIDE DU DEMANDEUR D'UNE APPELLATION D'ORIGINE

(A.O.C./A.O.P.) 21–22 (2007). The European Union has promulgated regulations to protect designations of origin and GIs for agricultural products. *See, e.g.,* Council Regulation 510/06, On the Protection of Geographical Indications and Designations of Origin for Agricultural Products and Foodstuffs, 2006 O.J. (L 93) 12; Council Regulation 1493/99, On the Common Organisation of the Market in Wine, 1999 O.J. (L 179).

Article 2(1)(a) of Council Regulation 510/06 defines a protected designation of origin ("PDO") as:

> the name of a region, a specific place or, in exceptional cases, a country, used to describe an agricultural product or a foodstuff:
>
> — originating in that region, specific place or country,
>
> — the quality or characteristics of which are essentially or exclusively due to a particular geographical environment with its inherent natural and human factors, and
>
> — the production, processing and preparation of which take place in the defined geographical area.

Additionally, Article 2(1)(b) of Council Regulation 510/06 defines a protected geographical indication ("PGI") as:

> [t]he name of a region, a specific place or, in exceptional cases, a country, used to describe an agricultural product or a foodstuff:
>
> — originating in that region, specific place or country, and
>
> — which possesses a specific quality, reputation or other characteristics attributable to that geographical origin,
>
> and
>
> — the production and/or processing and/or preparation of which take place in the defined geographical area.

Does Article 2(1)(b)'s definition of GIs leave any room for the consideration of human factors?

The most expansive global treatment of GIs is within the TRIPS Agreement, which requires all countries to provide a means to prevent the use of an indication that misleads the public as to the geographical origin of a good. Article 22 of the TRIPS Agreement defines GIs as "indications which identify a good as originating in the territory of a Member, or a region or locality in that territory, where a given quality, reputation or other characteristic of the good is essentially attributable to its geographical origin." With respect to these indications, member nations must provide legal protection against an indication "which misleads the public as to the geographical origin of the good'' or acts of unfair competition within the meaning of Article 10*bis* of the Paris Convention.

Article 23 of TRIPS provides enhanced protection for wines and spirits by requiring that GIs for these products must be protected regardless of whether consumers are misled. Specifically, GIs for wines and spirits are protected "even where the true origin of the goods is indicated or the geographical indication is used in translation or accompanied by expressions such as 'kind', 'type', 'style', 'imitation' or the like." Under this provision, one cannot sell a sparkling wine made in California as "champagne," even though the label clearly states that the wine is "made in California." Likewise, the addition of qualifiers such as "imitation Champagne" will not do. TRIPS incorporates a number of exclusions to these requirements, such as a grandfathering provision for marks in use more than ten years before the agreement.

Further, TRIPS obligates members to enter into negotiations to increase protections for GIs for wines and spirits, as well as to negotiate for a notice and registration system for wines for members participating in the system. As of this publication, these negotiations have not yet concluded.

3. UNITED STATES' IMPLEMENTATION OF THE TRIPS OBLIGATIONS FOR GEOGRAPHICAL IN- DICATIONS

The United States implements the TRIPS Agreement using the existing legal protections of trademarks, certification marks and collective marks. An entity might obtain a trademark using a place name upon a showing of distinctiveness.* Further, the United States allows for the refusal of an application for registration where the mark would mislead the public as to the associated good's geographic source. In such cases, this will occur where consumers have formulated an association between the goods and the place name (sometimes called a "goods-place" association). For example, the United States Patent and Trademark Office refused to register the name "Durango" as a mark for cigars as misdescriptive because consumers might have believed the products came from Durango, Mexico, a region well known for tobacco, when in fact the cigars are made elsewhere. Affirming the decision, the appellate court observed that the agency had a "reasonable basis for concluding that the public is likely to believe the mark identifies the place from which the goods originate and that the goods do not come from there." In re *Loew's Theatres*, 769 F.2d 764, 767 (Fed. Cir. 1985).

---

* An exception to this rule exists for geographically misdescriptive marks, which cannot be registered at all. 15 U.S.C. § 1052(e)(3) (2006).

On the other hand, fanciful trademarks lack a goods-place association and therefore are not considered misdescriptive. Thus, the trademark "Rodeo Drive" as used for a perfume was deemed enforceable because there was no evidence that consumers would be misled to believe that the product was made or sold on that famous street in Beverley Hills. In re *Jacques Bernier, Inc.*, 894 F.2d 389 (Fed. Cir. 1990) ("Nothing in the record ... indicates or even suggests that the consuming public would believe that Rodeo Drive was the place of manufacture or production of the perfume. Indeed, there is no indication that any perfume is manufactured or produced on Rodeo Drive.").

As previously mentioned, United States law has a certification mark system. As one example, the United States has granted a certification mark to an Italian organization, the Consorzio Del Formaggio Parmigiano–Reggiano Consortium, for the use of "Parmigiano Reggiano" in association with a certain type of cheese. This organization, which is not itself a product producer, must ensure that all products that bear the certification mark "originate in the Parma–Reggio region of Italy, specifically the zone comprising the territory of the provinces of Parma, Reggio Emilia, Modena and Mantua on the right bank of the river Po and Bologna on the left bank of the river Reno." *See, e.g.,* U.S. Trademark 3256272 (June 26, 2007). This group has promulgated detailed guidance for the cheese, including feed for the dairy cows, which must be based on "local forage" of at least fifty percent provided by hay. *See* CONSORZIO DEL FORMAGGIO PARMIGIANO-REGGIANO CONSORTIUM, FEEDING REGULATIONS FOR DAIRY COWS (n.d.). In addition, the group has provided information concerning the cheese's preparation, as well as specifications for the appearance and taste of the final product:

- cylinder shape with slightly convex to straight sides, upper and lower faces slightly chamfered;
- dimensions: diameter of upper and lower faces from 35 to 45 cm; side height from 20 to 26 cm;
- minimum wheel weight: 30 kg;
- external appearance: natural gold-coloured rind;
- paste colour: from pale straw-yellow to straw-yellow;
- typical aroma and taste of the mass: fragrant, delicate, tasty yet not sharp;
- paste texture: fine granules, breaks in brittles;
- rind thickness: approximately 6 mm;
- fat content: minimum 32% of dry matter.

Goods sold under the "Parmigiano–Reggiano" name must be certified by the collective in order to bear the mark. What are some reasons that United States law authorizes non-producers to hold a certification mark? What concerns might be raised by a system that permits a single producer to hold a certification mark within a region?

Another alternative is the use of a collective mark. Essentially, such marks tell consumers that the source of the product (who may or may not be known) is a member of a certain group. For example, a collective mark for a regional food product might be created by a regional agricultural organization that promotes the goods and services covered by the mark. The collective is responsible to control membership in the organization and, thereby, who is able to use the mark.

The United States does not provide a stand-alone system of protection for GIs separate from trademark law. Moreover, the United States trademark system does not require any link between a region and a product's characteristics to grant protection to a term for any available type of mark. Further, the United States relies primarily on a likelihood of confusion standard. By contrast, some types of GIs—such as wines and spirits—may be protected even in the absence of a likelihood of confusion. For such types of GIs, there is a recognized harm to producers for the unqualified use of an indication even in the absence of any potential for consumer confusion.

4. DEFINING THE GEOGRAPHICAL INDICA-TION: AN EXAMPLE

The nature of the GI within the larger framework of intellectual property is not entirely settled. Furthermore, the law of GIs raises difficult historic, political, and economic policy choices. Practical considerations arise as well. For example, the region which has made Roquefort cheese based on techniques dating back to 49 A.D. may question the label "Roquefort" as a flavor of salad dressing that was recently made in an Illinois factory. As one source observes:

> To assert the necessity of GI protection is, in part, to assert the importance of local culture and tradition in the face of ever-encroaching globalization. The GI question is as a result linked to larger, politically sensitive debates about the proper level of protection for farmers and rural communities, the degree to which international law ought to trench upon questions of culture and tradition, the necessity of intellectual property rights and, above all, the importance of economic competition. The GI debate, moreover, chiefly exhibits not the North–South division so familiar to international lawyers, but rather a less common

and more interesting split: that between the New World and the Old World.

Kal Raustiala & Stephen R. Munzer, *The Global Struggle over Geographic Indications*, 18 EUR. J. INT'L L. 337, 339 (2007).

CONSORZIO DEL PROSCIUTTO DI PARMA AND SALUMIFICIO S. RITA SPA v. ASDA STORES LTD. AND HYGRADE FOODS LTD.

European Court of Justice
Case C–108/01, 2003 E.C.R. I–5121

[A] question was raised in proceedings between Consorzio del Prosciuttodi Parma (the Consorzio), an association of producers of Parma ham, established in Italy, and Salumificio S. Rita SpA (Salumificio), a company also established in Italy, a producer of Parma ham and a member of the Consorzio, of the one part, and Asda Stores Ltd (Asda), a company established in the United Kingdom, an operator of supermarkets, and Hygrade Foods Ltd (Hygrade), also established in the United Kingdom, an importer of Parma ham, of the other part, concerning the marketing in the United Kingdom under the protected designation of origin Prosciutto di Parma (the PDO 'Prosciutto di Parma') of Parma ham sliced and packaged in that Member State....

Article 29 EC states: 'Quantitative restrictions on exports, and all measures having equivalent effect, shall be prohibited between Member States.'

Under Article 30 EC, Article 29 EC does not preclude prohibitions or restrictions on exports justified inter alia on grounds of the protection of industrial and commercial property....

Asda operates a chain of supermarkets in the United Kingdom. It sells among other things ham bearing the description 'Parma ham', purchased pre-sliced from Hygrade, which itself purchases the ham boned but not sliced from an Italian producer who is a member of the Consorzio. The ham is sliced and hermetically sealed by Hygrade in packets each containing five slices.

The packets bear the wording 'ASDA A taste of Italy PARMA HAM Genuine Italian Parma Ham'.

The back of the packets states 'PARMA HAM'. All authentic Asda continental meats are made by traditional methods to guarantee their authentic flavour and quality' and 'Produced in Italy, packed in the UK for Asda Stores Limited'.

On 14 November 1997 the Consorzio brought proceedings by writ in the United Kingdom against Asda and Hygrade seeking various injunctions against them, essentially requiring them to cease their activities, on the ground that they were contrary to the rules applicable to Parma ham. . . .

It should be observed, as a preliminary point, that the specification on the basis of which the PDO 'Prosciutto di Parma' was registered by Regulation No 1107/96 expressly mentions the requirement of slicing and packaging the product in the region of production for ham marketed in slices. . . .

The Consorzio, Salumificio, the Spanish, French and Italian Governments and the Commission consider essentially that Regulation No 2081/92 in principle allows producers to have the use of a PDO made subject to a condition that operations such as the slicing and packaging of the product take place in the region of production. . . .

Asda and Hygrade submit that conditions relating to the packaging of a product are capable of constituting restrictions within the meaning of Articles 28 EC and 29 EC. In particular, the application in the United Kingdom of a rule that Parma ham marketed in slices can use the PDO only if it has been sliced and packaged in the region of production is manifestly capable of directly or indirectly, actually or potentially obstructing intra-Community trade.

The United Kingdom Government considers that the condition at issue in the main proceedings constitutes a quantitative restriction on exports. . . .

Article 29 EC prohibits all measures which have as their specific object or effect the restriction of patterns of exports and thereby the establishment of a difference in treatment between the domestic trade of a Member State and its export trade, in such a way as to provide a particular advantage for national production or for the domestic market of the State in question.

. . . [T]he specification of the PDO 'Prosciutto di Parma' expressly mentions the requirement of slicing and packaging the product in the region of production for ham marketed in slices. . . .

That condition has the consequence that ham produced in the region of production and fulfilling the other conditions required for use of the PDO 'Prosciutto di Parma' cannot be sliced outside that region without losing that designation.

By contrast, Parma ham transported within the region of production retains its right to the PDO if it is sliced and packaged there in accordance with the rules referred to in the specification.

Those rules thus have the specific effect of restricting patterns of exports of ham eligible for the PDO 'Prosciutto di Parma' and thereby establishing a difference in treatment between the domestic trade of a Member State and its export trade. They therefore introduce quantitative restrictions on exports within the meaning of Article 29 EC.

Accordingly, where the use of the PDO 'Prosciutto di Parma' for ham marketed in slices is made subject to the condition that slicing and packaging operations be carried out in the region of production, this constitutes a measure having equivalent effect to a quantitative restriction on exports within the meaning of Article 29 EC. . . .

Asda, Hygrade and the United Kingdom Government assert that the slicing and packaging operations do not affect the quality of Parma ham or damage its authenticity. It should be noted that, in accordance with Article 30 EC, Article 29 EC does not preclude prohibitions or restrictions on exports which are justified inter alia on grounds of the protection of industrial and commercial property.

Community legislation displays a general tendency to enhance the quality of products within the framework of the common agricultural policy, in order to promote the reputation of those products through inter alia the use of designations of origin which enjoy special protection. . . .

Designations of origin fall within the scope of industrial and commercial property rights. The applicable rules protect those entitled to use them against improper use of those designations by third parties seeking to profit from the reputation which they have acquired. They are intended to guarantee that the product bearing them comes from a specified geographical area and displays certain particular characteristics. They may enjoy a high reputation amongst consumers and constitute for producers who fulfil the conditions for using them an essential means of attracting custom. The reputation of designations of origin depends on their image in the minds of consumers. That image in turn depends essentially on particular characteristics and more generally on the quality of the product. It is on the latter, ultimately, that the product's reputation is based. For consumers, the link between the reputation of the producers and the quality of the products also depends on his being assured that products sold under the designation of origin are authentic.

The specification of the PDO 'Prosciutto di Parma', by requiring the slicing and packaging to be carried out in the region of production, is intended to allow the persons entitled to use the PDO to keep under their control one of the ways in which the product appears on the market. The condition it lays down aims better to safeguard the quality and authenticity of the product, and consequently the reputation of the PDO, for which those who are entitled to use it assume full and collective responsibility.

Against that background, a condition such as at issue must be regarded as compatible with Community law despite its restrictive effects on trade if it is shown that it is necessary and proportionate and capable of upholding the reputation of the PDO 'Prosciutto di Parma'.

Parma ham is consumed mainly in slices and the operations leading to that presentation are all designed to obtain in particular a specific flavour, colour and texture which will be appreciated by consumers.

The slicing and packaging of the ham thus constitute important operations which may harm the quality and hence the reputation of the PDO if they are carried out in conditions that result in a product not possessing the organoleptic qualities expected. Those operations may also compromise the guarantee of the product's authenticity, because they necessarily involve removal of the mark of origin of the whole hams used.

By the rules it lays down and the requirements of the national provisions to which it refers, the specification of the PDO 'Prosciutto di Parma' establishes a set of detailed and strict rules regulating the three stages which lead to the placing on the market of prepackaged sliced ham. The first stage consists of boning the ham, making bricks, and refrigerating and freezing them for slicing. The second stage corresponds to the slicing operations. The third stage is the packaging of the sliced ham, under vacuum or protected atmosphere. . . .

During the various stages there are technical operations and strict checks relating to authenticity, quality, hygiene and labelling. Some of these require specialist assessments, in particular during the stages of refrigeration and freezing of the bricks.

In this context, it must be accepted that checks performed outside the region of production would provide fewer guarantees of the quality and authenticity of the product than checks carried out in the region of production in accordance with the procedure laid down in the specification. First, checks performed in accordance with that procedure are thorough and systematic in nature and are done by experts who have specialised knowledge of the characteristics of Parma ham. Second, it is hardly conceivable that representatives of the persons entitled to use the PDO could effectively introduce such checks in other Member States.

The risk to the quality and authenticity of the product finally offered to consumers is consequently greater where it has been sliced and packaged outside the region of production than when that has been done within the region. . . .

Consequently, the condition of slicing and packaging in the region of production, whose aim is to preserve the reputation of Parma ham by strengthening control over its particular characteristics and its quality, may be regarded as justified as a measure protecting the PDO which may be used by all the operators concerned and is of decisive importance to them.

The resulting restriction may be regarded as necessary for attaining the objective pursued, in that there are no alternative less restrictive measures capable of attaining it.

The PDO 'Prosciutto di Parma' would not receive comparable protection from an obligation imposed on operators established outside the region of production to inform consumers, by means of appropriate labelling, that the slicing and packaging has taken place outside that region. Any deterioration in the quality or authenticity of ham sliced and packaged outside the region of production, resulting from materialisation of the risks associated with slicing and packaging, might harm the reputation of all ham marketed under the PDO 'Prosciutto di Parma', including that sliced and packaged in the region of production under the control of the group of producers entitled to use the PDO.

Accordingly, the fact that the use of the PDO 'Prosciutto di Parma' for ham marketed in slices is conditional on the slicing and packaging operations being carried out in the region of production may be regarded as justified, and hence compatible with Article 29 EC.

Notes and Questions

1.   One of the questions at issue concerns the application of the Article 29 of the Treaty Establishing the European Community, which states that "[q]uantitative restrictions on exports, and all measures having equivalent effect, shall be prohibited between Member States." Note that Article 30 provides that Article 29 "shall not preclude prohibitions or restrictions on imports, exports or goods in transit justified on grounds of . . . the protection of industrial and commercial property." How does the court resolve this question? Would the result have been different if the term at issue were a PGI, rather than a PDO?

2.   The European court's reasoning centers on potential harm to the reputation to the PDO. Is this preferable to an analysis that focuses on consumer confusion, given the nature of the right at issue? Why did the court reject the suggestion that prejudice to the GI would be relieved by a label that warned consumers that slicing and packaging had been performed outside the region?

3.   Is the preservation of traditional methods of preparation a compelling concern? Should the United States consider such protec-

tion? Do you agree with the ECJ's conclusion in *Parma* that quality concerns justify the resulting restrictions on trade, which permits the development of alternative—perhaps more efficient—techniques in other countries?

4. Although the ECJ affirmed the substance of the challenged provision, another portion of the opinion that is not reproduced here deemed the restriction unenforceable on procedural grounds. Specifically, the specification's requirements that slicing and packaging occur in the region had not been published in a manner sufficient to place producers on notice of the condition. In 2006, the European Communities promulgated a revised regulation that explicitly required publication of all registered specifications. *See* Council Regulation 510/06, *supra*.

5. THE INTERACTION BETWEEN TRADE-MARKS AND GEOGRAPHICAL INDICATIONS

Conflicts between holders of confusingly similar trademarks are typically decided in favor of the party who was the first to use a mark in commerce. How should a conflict between a trademark and a GI be decided? Should first-in-time principles apply? If so, should those principles apply on a nation-by-nation basis, or should worldwide use be considered? Consider these concerns relevant to the following decision from the Canadian court.

CONSORZIO DEL PROSCIUTTO DI PARMA v. MAPLE LEAF MEATS INC.

Federal Court of Canada (Trial Division)
[2001] 2 F.C. 536 (Can.)

McKEOWN J.

The applicant seeks to expunge the trade-mark "Parma" (Registration No. 179,637) from the register of trade-marks pursuant to section 57 of the Trade-marks Act.

The "Parma" trade-mark was registered on November 26, 1971 for use in association with various meat products, namely prosciutto, mortadella, salami, capicollo, pepper butts, pepperoni and dry sausage. The application for registration stated that the mark had been in use since September 18, 1958. The respondent, Maple Leaf Meats, acquired the subject trade-mark in May 1997 from Principal Marques Inc. (PMI). PMI had acquired the mark from Primo Foods Limited in May 1994, who had acquired it in 1982 from Parma Food Products Limited.

Maple Leaf Meats continues to use the packaging "get-up" used by the previous owner of the trade-mark, PMI. This "get-up" features the use of, inter alia, the colours red, white and green and words taken from the Italian language.

The applicant, the Consorzio, was founded in 1963 by 23 prosciutto producers located in Parma, Italy. By 1997 it had grown to 210 members. The Consorzio established the "ducal crown" mark for members to display in association with their prosciutto. This mark consists of the word "Parma" within a crown design. Variations of this mark have been in use since 1963. Since 1970, Italy has had laws in place which adopted the Consorzio's production, quality control and marking rules.

The applicant introduced excerpts from a few well-known U.S. cookbooks showing Parma was a region of Italy known for prosciutto and a number of meats. However, in my view this is not sufficient to show that the average Canadian consumer of "Parma" meat products associated them with the Parma products of the Consorzio. "Parma" is not descriptive of products. There is no evidence that a substantial number of Canadian consumers were generally aware of the Consorzio, its membership or policies in 1971. . . .

In the late 1960s, prosciutto di parma was banned in the U.S. due to health concerns, but it was reintroduced in 1989 and has been marketed using the ducal crown mark since that time. The Canadian government expressed some health concerns, but later allowed the Consorzio's product to be imported into Canada. Sales in Canada commenced in 1997. The applicant claims that some Canadians would have heard of prosciutto di parma prior to that time through various media, including foreign magazines, advertising in the U.S., and attendance at trade shows.

The respondent's mark has been registered since 1971. The respondent alleges that the applicant, Consorzio, knew of the mark at least as early as 1985, however the Consorzio did not conduct business in Canada until 1997 and did not begin expungement proceedings against the respondent until that year, which the respondent notes was 26 years after the registration of its trademark. . . .

[T]he applicant submits that the respondent's trade-mark is invalid because it was deceptively misdescriptive at the time of registration. Essentially, the applicant attempts to show that the use of the "Parma" trade-mark leads consumers to believe that the prosciutto packaged under that name comes from Parma, Italy and is the high-quality product of the rigorous standards employed by the Consorzio del Prosciutto di Parma. I do not accept that, at the time of the registration of the respondent's mark, many Canadians were exposed to the idea that Parma was a city in Italy and that this city was a source of high quality prosciutto, nor any of the various other meat products listed on the trade-mark registration. I note that prosciutto di Parma was not advertised directly in Canada nor sold here until 1997....

The evidence does not demonstrate that in 1971 the general public in Canada was likely to have been misled by the use of the mark in association with the registered wares into believing that those wares originated specifically from Parma, Italy. I accept the respondent's survey evidence that a majority of Canadians in the present day do not recognize that "Parma" is a region in Italy, nor do they associate the word "parma" with meat products. Dr. Corbin's study indicated that 68% of Canadians associated nothing with the word "parma", and that number was the same when looking at those who buy pork products. Dr. Corbin's results also indicated that among Canadians of Italian origin, 60% associated nothing with the word "parma". Where there is a conflict between the respondent's survey evidence and the applicant's, I prefer that of the respondent.

The applicant has failed to discharge its onus by showing that in 1971 the public would have linked the use of the mark with the specific wares from Parma, Italy. Canadians cannot have been deceived by the use of the mark in 1971, because according to the survey evidence, the majority of Canadians do not recognize Parma as a source of ham or pork products, nor do they associate "Parma" meat products with Parma, Italy....

The respondent and its predecessors-in-title have made use of the "Parma" trade-mark in Canada since it was registered in 1971. While there may have been an increasing recognition over time in Canada of the reputation of prosciutto produced in Parma, Italy, there have been actual sales in Canada of meat products in association with the respondent's trade-mark....

Also, as the applicant itself points out ..., the respondent and its predecessor-in-title, PMI, have acted to protect the distinctiveness of the subject trade-mark. PMI warned the applicant in writing that injunctive relief would be sought if it attempted to use the "Parma" mark in Canada, and the respondent wrote to one of the Consorzio's members with similar complaints.

The applicant also argues that the respondent's "faux-Italian" packaging, which was used in association with the "Parma" trade-mark, has eroded the distinctiveness of the mark over time. However, the "get-up" associated with a trade-mark is irrelevant in an action alleging trade-mark infringement....

The applicant's final argument is that the use of a "faux-Italian" get-up in association with the respondent's trade-mark may have induced the public to believe that the product was produced in Italy (presumably by the Consorzio di Parma). The Consorzio argues that the respondent is trying to take advantage of the Consorzio's goodwill by using "faux-Italian" packaging. However, the respondent owns the trade-mark in Canada, a trade-mark that has been registered since 1971. The respondent is entitled to package its product in any way that it sees fit. The use of packaging is only relevant with respect to the question of deceptive misdescriptiveness, and is irrelevant with respect to the question of distinctiveness of the trade-mark.

In summary, the respondent is entitled to rely on the presumption that the registration and the particulars in the registration are valid, while the onus is on the applicant to show the mark is not distinctive. The distinctiveness of a trade-mark must be measured in the Canadian marketplace alone. The applicant's studies do not assist its case, as these studies were not done to test the distinctiveness of the mark. Additionally, the people on whom the applicant relies for much of its case belong to a small and specialized class of people who are not representative of the Canadian market as a whole. As such, the applicant has failed to discharge its onus.

Notes and Questions

1.   Should the Canadian mark holder be permitted to enjoin the Italian producers from selling ham in Canada using the name "parma ham"?

2.   Is co-existence of both Parma designations preferable to exclusive use? What are the practical problems raised by the outcome here?

3.   Why do you suppose the Canadian mark holder chose the word "Parma" and to use the "faux-Italian" packaging for the product? Was the court's focus on Canadian consumers nation-wide appropriate? In the alternative, should the views of the Canadian consumers of premium hams have been polled? What are the implications of choosing one over the other?

4.   The United States Trademark Trial and Appeals Board reached a similar result in a challenge brought by the Consorzio del Prosciutto di Parma against Parma Sausage Products, Inc., a company based in Pennsylvania. *See Consorzio del Prosorzio del Prosciutto di Parma v. Parma Sausage Prods., Inc.,* 23 U.S.P.Q. 2d (BNA) 1894 (1992). The Consorzio's action sought to cancel a 1969 registration for the mark "Parma Brand" that the United States company used in association with "meat products—namely, sausage, salami, capicollo, prosciutto and lunch meats" which were not made in Parma, Italy.

In the late 1960s, the United States government had banned the importation of pork products, including prosciutto di Parma, from Italy, based on an outbreak of a flu affecting swine that had occurred in Italy during that era. In September 1989, after extensive lobbying by an Italian Consorzio, prosciutto di Parma, the product was again permitted to be imported. After the ban was lifted, the Consorzio began importing product into the United States and commenced an advertising and promotion campaign for its prosciutto. The Consorzio's challenge to the United States company's mark was filed in 1986. By that time, the United States Parma mark had become incontestable. *See* 15 U.S.C. § 1065 (2006). To succeed, the board determined that the Consorzio was required to show that: (1) the mark uses a term with a geographical location that is "neither obscure nor remote"; (2) a goods/place association between the type of good at issue and the geographical place named in the mark; (3) that the goods are not from the place name; (4) the mark was geographically deceptive at the time the registration issued.

The court determined that the Consorzio's more recent promotional activities were largely responsible for "the cloud of geographic deceptiveness" over the mark that the United States company had held for two decades. The Board recognized that the Consorzio's absence from the United States market was not its own fault, but nonetheless found that "[t]here is something manifestly unfair about a trademark owner's being deprived of its validly obtained and long-held registration because of recent activities by its adversary." Rejecting evidence that knowledge by food experts was relevant to demonstrate awareness by the consuming public, the board found that the equities favored the United States mark holder and rejected the Consorzio's petition.

5. The Consorzio's efforts to enforce the "Parma" mark against Canadian and United States producers who invested in the promotion of those brands may be viewed as an effort to re-capture a name that has broken free of its original European geographic roots. Justin Hughes has analyzed the European Union's efforts to "claw back" GIs by requesting that a list of identified GIs be accepted by WTO members as non-generic, protected terms. Justin Hughes, *Champagne, Feta, and Bourbon: The Spirited Debate about Geographical Indications*, 58 HAS-TINGS L.J. 299 (2006). Member nations would then have a limited time to object to particular names on specified grounds. These issues, which are still under debate, have been described by Professor Hughes as follows:

> It is easy to understand the economic and political motives behind EU proposals to "claw back" valuable words that have become generic like "Gorgonzola" and "Chablis." . . . [T]he goal is to secure wider, more extensive monopoly rents to the European Union's agroalimentaire industries. The European Union promotes these proposals as something that would benefit developing countries, but that mistakes the piling up of intellectual property laws for the piling up of investments. Investment in the reputation of developing country GIs— coffees, teas, and chocolates—is already happening, as quickly, if not more quickly, under certification law regimes.

Is the European Union's efforts to shift the battle ground for the use of GIs to the world stage an effort to reset a clock for those, like the United States and Canadian producers of Parma ham, established trademark rights under first-in-time systems? Aside from the economic justifications identified by Professor Hughes, are there other values that might be motivating the European Union to attempt to recapture these terms? Consider this question as you read the following excerpt in Note 6, below.

6.   A contrasting view is presented by Ruth Okediji, who writes:

A priority principle might very well be an equitable response to a conflict between two similarly situated objects. And as a mechanism to resolve ownership disputes, the "first in time, first in right" approach certainly resonates within the larger framework of intellectual property doctrine. But in a global environment, the question of priority is not mechanical; priority is heavily context-dependent and assumes different meanings for purposes of determining who should be entitled to the exclusive rights at issue. Under current schemes, the context in which priority is determined will likely skew heavily in favor of trademark owners unless associated doctrines like "use" or "distinctiveness" are malleable enough to accommodate cultural conditions and other values underlying the demand for protection of GIs.

Ruth L. Okediji, *The International Intellectual Property Roots of Geographical Indications*, 82 CHI.-KENT L. REV. 1329 (2007). Can the cultural concerns raised by Professor Okediji be reconciled with first-in-time principles?

7.   In recent years, some Californian winegrowers have been pushing for the introduction of GIs in the United States. Do you think it is a good idea to introduce such protection? If protection is offered, what should its scope be? Would such protection affect the existing protection of certification and collective marks?

Chapter 5

THE PROTECTION OF PRODUCT DESIGNS AND UTILITY MODELS

A. PRODUCT DESIGNS

Legal protection for product designs falls somewhere between a patent and a copyright. Like copyright, design protection focuses on the aesthetic rather than the practical. Most nations' product design laws protect only those visual features of a product's design that make the product more appealing to potential buyers for reasons *other* than performance or quality. Unlike copyright, however, design protection is available only for useful articles of manufacture; items which fall more within the realm of patent law. Indeed, in many nations this area of intellectual property law is called the law of "industrial design." Separating the useful from the aesthetic can often prove to be a major issue in product design law.

1. THE BYZANTINE UNITED STATES SYSTEM

As you have probably already discovered, United States law does protect designs. However, unlike inventions and works, there is currently no single design protection law. Instead, depending on the circumstances, a designer may seek protection under the design patent provisions of the Patent Act, 35 U.S.C. §§ 171–173 (2006), under copyright law, or even under the "trade dress" branch of federal or state trademark laws. Some designs will qualify for protection under more than one of these regimes.

There are important differences between these three models of protection. First, the term of protection varies tremendously, from the fourteen-year term of a design patent to the life-plus-seventy-year term of copyright. Second, the models vary significantly in the extent to which the party must file an application for protection and satisfy other formalities. Third, and perhaps most significant, the threshold requirements for protection differ significantly for each of the models. Design protection under copyright law requires only the minimal originality required of copyright authorship in general. A party seeking a design patent, by contrast, must satisfy the Patent Act's significantly more rigorous standards of "novelty" and "non-obviousness."* In the case of trade dress protection, the threshold question is quite different: whether the design has acquired "secondary meaning" so that it is now perceived as an indication of a unique source rather than simply as a design. *Wal–Mart Stores, Inc. v. Samara Brothers, Inc.*, 529 U.S. 205 (2000).

Although copyright has the longest term and the fewest and simplest formalities, it has certain problems that significantly limit its use. The most important is the doctrine of "separability." In order to prevent a party from using copyright to obtain rights in a product's utilitarian features, § 101 of the Copyright Act provides that design of a useful article is copyrightable only if there are "pictorial, graphic, or sculptural features that can be identified separately from, and are capable of existing independently of, the utilitarian aspects of the article." Courts have employed different tests to determine separability, resulting in a lack of uniformity.

Similar concerns exist in the law of trade dress. Because trademark law is not intended to protect the utilitarian features of a product, trade dress protection is not available for product features that are functional. "Functional" is not necessarily synonymous with the patent law concept of utilitarian, as functionality also includes considerations of competitive need. Courts have also had a very difficult time applying the functionality doctrine in trade dress disputes.

Is there any compelling reason why the United States should continue to maintain separate and inconsistent types of protection for product design? Would a unitary regime be preferable? Or is there something to be said for providing a party with a new and original design the option of picking her type of protection? Consider these questions in light of the discussion of foreign approaches to product design, set out in the next section.

2. THE WORLDWIDE NORM: UNIFIED DESIGN PROTECTION SCHEMES

The multipronged United States approach to product design is fairly unusual. Most nations have enacted a single design protection

---

* While nonobviousness is not explicitly mentioned in § 171, that provision incorporates the other requirements for patent protection, including the § 102 and § 103 requirements. Note, however, that nonobviousness for a design is measured slightly differently from nonobviousness for a utility patent.

law that establishes a unitary model of protection. The recently-enacted European Community design law is a good example. While it provides European Community-wide rather than mere domestic protection, the European Community law explicitly covers many of the important issues endemic in design protection legislation. When reviewing the law, note particularly the distinction between *registered* and *unregistered* designs.

Council Regulation 6/02, On Community Designs
Dec. 12, 2001
2002 O.J. (L 3) 1

Article 1
Community design

1. A design which complies with the conditions contained in this Regulation is hereinafter referred to as a "Community design".

2. A design shall be protected:

(a) by an "unregistered Community design", if made available to the public in the manner provided for in this Regulation;

(b) by a "registered Community design", if registered in the manner provided for in this Regulation.

3. A Community design shall have a unitary character. It shall have equal effect throughout the Community. It shall not be registered, transferred or surrendered or be the subject of a decision declaring it invalid, nor shall its use be prohibited, save in respect of the whole Community. This principle and its implications shall apply unless otherwise provided in this Regulation. . . .

Article 3
Definitions

For the purposes of this Regulation:

(a) "design" means the appearance of the whole or a part of a product resulting from the features of, in particular, the lines, contours, colours, shape, texture and/or materials of the product itself and/or its ornamentation;

(b) "product" means any industrial or handicraft item, including inter alia parts intended to be assembled into a complex product, packaging, get-up, graphic symbols and typographic typefaces, but excluding computer programs;

(c) "complex product" means a product which is composed of multiple components which can be replaced permitting disassembly and re-assembly of the product.

Article 4

Requirements for protection

1. A design shall be protected by a Community design to the extent that it is new and has individual character.

2. A design applied to or incorporated in a product which constitutes a component part of a complex product shall only be considered to be new and to have individual character:

(a) if the component part, once it has been incorporated into the complex product, remains visible during normal use of the latter; and

(b) to the extent that those visible features of the component part fulfil in themselves the requirements as to novelty and individual character.

3. "Normal use" within the meaning of paragraph (2)(a) shall mean use by the end user, excluding maintenance, servicing or repair work.

Article 5

Novelty

1. A design shall be considered to be new if no identical design has been made available to the public:

(a) in the case of an unregistered Community design, before the date on which the design for which protection is claimed has first been made available to the public;

(b) in the case of a registered Community design, before the date of filing of the application for registration of the design for which protection is claimed, or, if priority is claimed, the date of priority.

2. Designs shall be deemed to be identical if their features differ only in immaterial details.

Article 6

Individual character

1. A design shall be considered to have individual character if the overall impression it produces on the informed user differs from the overall impression produced on such a user by any design which has been made available to the public:

(a) in the case of an unregistered Community design, before the date on which the design for which protection is claimed has first been made available to the public;

(b) in the case of a registered Community design, before the date of filing the application for registration or, if a priority is claimed, the date of priority.

2.   In assessing individual character, the degree of freedom of the designer in developing the design shall be taken into consideration.

Article 7
Disclosure

1.   For the purpose of applying Articles 5 and 6, a design shall be deemed to have been made available to the public if it has been published following registration or otherwise, or exhibited, used in trade or otherwise disclosed, before the date referred to in Articles 5(1)(a) and 6(1)(a) or in Articles 5(1)(b) and 6(1)(b), as the case may be, except where these events could not reasonably have become known in the normal course of business to the circles specialised in the sector concerned, operating within the Community. The design shall not, however, be deemed to have been made available to the public for the sole reason that it has been disclosed to a third person under explicit or implicit conditions of confidentiality. . . .

Article 8
Designs dictated by their technical function and designs of interconnections

1.   A Community design shall not subsist in features of appearance of a product which are solely dictated by its technical function.

2.   A Community design shall not subsist in features of appearance of a product which must necessarily be reproduced in their exact form and dimensions in order to permit the product in which the design is incorporated or to which it is applied to be mechanically connected to or placed in, around or against another product so that either product may perform its function.

3.   Notwithstanding paragraph 2, a Community design shall under the conditions set out in Articles 5 and 6 subsist in a design serving the purpose of allowing the multiple assembly or connection of mutually interchangeable products within a modular system.

Article 9
Designs contrary to public policy or morality

A Community design shall not subsist in a design which is contrary to public policy or to accepted principles of morality.

Article 10
Scope of protection

1.   The scope of the protection conferred by a Community design shall include any design which does not produce on the informed user a different overall impression.

2.   In assessing the scope of protection, the degree of freedom of the designer in developing his design shall be taken into consideration.

Article 11
Commencement and term of protection of the unregistered Community design

1.   A design which meets the requirements under Section 1 shall be protected by an unregistered Community design for a period of three years as from the date on which the design was first made available to the public within the Community....

Article 12
Commencement and term of protection of the registered Community design

Upon registration by the Office, a design which meets the requirements under Section 1 shall be protected by a registered Community design for a period of five years as from the date of the filing of the application. The right holder may have the term of protection renewed for one or more periods of five years each, up to a total term of 25 years from the date of filing....

Article 14
Right to the Community design

1.   The right to the Community design shall vest in the designer or his successor in title.

2.   If two or more persons have jointly developed a design, the right to the Community design shall vest in them jointly.

3.   However, where a design is developed by an employee in the execution of his duties or following the instructions given by his employer, the right to the Community design shall vest in the employer, unless otherwise agreed or specified under national law.

Article 19
Rights conferred by the Community design

1.   A registered Community design shall confer on its holder the exclusive right to use it and to prevent any third party not having his consent from using it. The aforementioned use shall cover, in particular, the making, offering, putting on the market, importing, exporting or using of a product in which the design is incorporated or to which it is applied, or stocking such a product for those purposes.

2.   An unregistered Community design shall, however, confer on its holder the right to prevent the acts referred to in paragraph 1 only if the contested use results from copying the protected design.

The contested use shall not be deemed to result from copying the protected design if it results from an independent work of creation by a designer who may be reasonably thought not to be familiar with the design made available to the public by the holder....

Article 20
Limitation of the rights conferred by a Community design

1. The rights conferred by a Community design shall not be exercised in respect of:

(a) acts done privately and for non-commercial purposes;

(b) acts done for experimental purposes;

(c) acts of reproduction for the purpose of making citations or of teaching, provided that such acts are compatible with fair trade practice and do not unduly prejudice the normal exploitation of the design, and that mention is made of the source.

2. In addition, the rights conferred by a Community design shall not be exercised in respect of:

(a) the equipment on ships and aircraft registered in a third country when these temporarily enter the territory of the Community;

(b) the importation in the Community of spare parts and accessories for the purpose of repairing such craft;

(c) the execution of repairs on such craft.

Notes and Questions

1. The Community Design law does not foreclose other forms of protection under domestic law. Indeed, Articles 95 and 96 expressly provide that European Union members can maintain their own forms of protection, including specific design laws as well as other forms of protection such as copyright and "utility model" laws (see Chapter 5.B). Moreover, a party with a protected design can sue for infringement both under the European Union and any governing national laws.

2. Why did the European Union choose to allow for both unregistered and registered design protection? What advantages and disadvantages does such a two-tier system present?

3. How do European Union and United States laws compare on the degree of creativity required in order to obtain protection of product designs? Do any of them set the bar at the appropriate level?

4. How does European Community law deal with the issue of obtaining design protection for the utilitarian features of the product? What does the law mean by the phrase "solely dictated by its technical

function"? Is that standard closer to the separability doctrine in United States copyright law, or the "functionality" doctrine of United States trade dress law?

5. Consider the implications of Article 9. How could a product design ever run afoul of public policy or morality?

6. How does the standard for infringement in the European Community Design law (set out in Article 10) compare to the United States standards for copyright and design patent infringement? (For the "ordinary observer" test applied in design patent cases, see *Egyptian Goddess v. Swisa*, 543 F.3d 665 (Fed. Cir. 2008).) Should a design protection regime protect merely against copying of the design? Or should it also extend to independent creation of the same or a similar design?

7. Should the law of design protection include a right to produce "derivative works," as afforded by the copyright law of the United States and several other jurisdictions? Does such a right make sense? Consider the nature of product design. While modern art and literature tend to push all the accepted norms, are truly groundbreaking designs likely to prove commercially feasible? Technologically practicable? In one sense, are virtually all product designs "derivative"?

8. Should the United States also adopt a unitary scheme to protect designs? In fact, the United States is closer to this position than you might think. A little-known federal statute already in force could, with a slight modification, become the predominant mode of protection for product designs in the United States. The Vessel Hull Design Protection Act, which added Chapter 13 to Title 17 of the United States Code (17 U.S.C. §§ 1301–1332 (2006)), affords protection to anyone who creates "an original design of a useful article which makes that article attractive or distinctive in appearance to the purchasing or using public." In order to qualify for protection under this statute, the owner must register the design with the Copyright Office. The design is then protected for a ten year term. The owner may also take advantage of a prior foreign design registration. Moreover, § 1309 affords very broad protection to registered designs, giving the owner the exclusive rights to "make, have made, or import, for sale or use in trade, any useful article embodying that design" and to sell articles with the design. In essence, this law follows the copyright model of protection, imposing liability only when copying takes place. However, unlike the metaphysical "separability" analysis required in copyright law, Chapter 13 denies protection to utilitarian features only if the particular design is "dictated solely by the utilitarian function of the article." 17 U.S.C. § 1302(4) (2006).

So why is Chapter 13 not the main source of product design protection in the United States? The answer lies in the definition section. Under § 1301(b)(2), the key term "useful article" is limited to three particular items: *boat hulls and decks*, and the *molds* used to produce them. Chapter 13 was enacted in response to the United States

Supreme Court's decision in *Bonito Boats, Inc. v. Thunder Craft Boats, Inc.*, 489 U.S. 141 (1989), which held that federal patent law preempted state laws protecting boat hull designs. Chapter 13 accordingly fills the legal void created by *Bonito Boats*. However, the drafters had the foresight to write a law that could be fairly easily modified to make it a full-fledged design protection law, simply by changing the definition of "useful article" to include all products with a utilitarian function.

9.   Recent years have seen attempts to enact a similar sort of design protection for fashion designs. At the time this book went to press, a bill was pending before Congress that would amend the Vessel Hull Design Protection Act to include fashion designs. H.R. 2196, 111th Cong. (2009). Unlike the ten year term of protection for boat hulls, the proposal would protect fashion designs for only three years, reflecting the rapidly-changing world of fashion.

10.   Thus far, concerns over protection of spare parts have made it difficult to introduce design laws in the United States. The fear is that design protection would give the original manufacturer a virtual monopoly over the spare parts market. The same concerns are prevalent in Europe. Article 110 of Council Regulation 6/02 states specifically that "protection as a Community design shall not exist for a design which constitutes a component part of a complex product . . . for the purpose of the repair of that complex product so as to restore its original appearance." Article 25(1) of the TRIPS Agreement allows WTO members not to extend protection to "designs dictated essentially by technical or functional considerations."

11.   Cultures differ in the extent to which they place value in clever and aesthetically pleasing product designs. The United States, like its common law cousins, tends to place greater emphasis on how a product performs. In northern Europe, by contrast, the strong tradition of protection for product designs holds significant sway. Are those cultural differences reflected in the respective laws?

B.   UTILITY MODELS: THE GRAY AREA BETWEEN PATENT AND DESIGN LAWS

United States law tries to draw a clear divide between the functional and the aesthetic. Protecting functional features is the realm of patent law (and to a lesser extent the law of trade secrets). Aesthetics are the province of copyright law. In the area of product design, however, the lines between the functional and the aesthetic often blur. Is it realistic to draw an impenetrable divide between the functional and the aesthetic? Or is a middle ground possible?

VIRGIN ATLANTIC AIRWAYS LTD. v. PREMIUM AIRCRAFT INTERIORS GROUP LTD.

High Court of Justice of England and Wales

[2009] EWHC (Pat) 26

Mr Justice LEWISON.

Introduction

How does a business class passenger choose an airline? If you believe the advertising, the comfort of the seat is one of the most important factors. But it is not just the advertising. When Virgin Atlantic introduced its flat-bed seat into its Upper Class in November 2003 it achieved an increase in market share on its long haul routes of 12 per cent. So the numbers tell the same story. Virgin Atlantic's flat-bed seat is known as the Upper Class Suite (or "UCS") and is the commercialisation of a seat and seating system disclosed by patent EP (UK) 1,495,908 (the "908 patent"). The UCS was manufactured for Virgin Atlantic by Premium Aircraft Interiors UK Ltd (known as "Contour"). Virgin Atlantic allege that Contour has manufactured other seats (known as "Rock" or "Solar Eclipse", and a derivative called "Solar Premiere"), or kits for those seats, that infringe the 908 patent; and also allege that in working up the detailed designs of those seats Contour and its external designers, Acumen, have infringed its unregistered design rights in parts of the UCS. Contour deny all these allegations....

Background

In the early inter-war years of long distance air travel passengers were able to sleep on long haul flights fully recumbent; and were also able to dine with each other face to face. But the economics of air transport led the airlines to abandon that arrangement in favour of packing more passengers into their aircraft. Thus the almost invariable arrangement of accommodation for passengers was for the cabin to contain forward facing seats arranged in columns and rows....

For the first class passenger, all this changed in 1996. In that year British Airways ("BA") introduced a new seating system for its first class cabin called BA First, which allowed for a completely flat bed. The seat had been designed by Design Acumen ("Acumen"), a design house, and was design engineered and built by Contour for BA. It provided seats in individual "pods" or compartments ...; and each seat was at a slight angle to the longitudinal axis of the plane, facing towards the cabin wall. This angled arrangement of seats is called a "herringbone". Where the seats face towards the aisle the herringbone is called an "inward facing herringbone"; otherwise it is called an "outward facing herringbone". The BA seating arrangement was an outward facing herringbone, which BA had adopted in preference to an inward facing herringbone because it gave passengers more privacy....

BA First was enthusiastically received in the design world. Design Week gave it the award for "Product of the Decade".... All the main airlines decided that they needed to emulate BA's groundbreaking idea; otherwise they were at risk of losing the highest paying passengers. A number of airlines immediately adopted the outward facing herringbone layout, the use of an ottoman and privacy screens to provide competitive products.... The introduction of flat-bed seats was, at this stage, limited to first class passengers. Because first class passengers pay such a lot of money for their tickets, the airlines could afford to be relatively generous with the space allotted to each passenger....

Then came the turn of business class passengers. Once again BA led the way. Both Virgin Atlantic and BA had been working on a new seat for business class passengers, and both were put into service at about the same time in 2000. Virgin Atlantic's seat was known as J2000. The seats were arranged in conventional rows and columns.... The J2000 was a moderate commercial success, in that Virgin Atlantic used it itself, and also licensed its use to other airlines; but it was eclipsed by BA's new offering.

Aircraft seat design

As Mr Meade put it in opening (and as is common ground) designing new aircraft cabin layouts is an extremely complex business. It involves juggling a very large number of factors in a very constrained environment. Even a difference of inches can be significant. Thus aircraft cabin design is a very intricate balancing act; it is difficult and time consuming.

The parameters within which a designer of aircraft seating must work were largely agreed....

First there are regulatory constraints. Professor Darbyshire and Mr Dryburgh detailed them:

i) The seat must pass a number of dynamic tests ...;

ii) The fore and aft aisles must be at least 15″ wide ...;

iii) For taxi, take off and landing ("TTOL"), the crew must have a view of all the passengers when seated. This does not necessarily have to be by direct line of sight but can be by the use of video cameras, or mirrors;

iv) The seat positions must be aligned with the positions of the oxygen masks ...;

v) If the seats are installed at an angle greater than 18° to the longitudinal axis of the aircraft additional safety restraints (such as a three point harness like a car seatbelt as opposed to the more normal lap belt) must be provided;....

Second, there are constraints imposed by the aircraft itself. These include the cabin width; the location of the seat tracks; the location of doorways, monuments (fixed installations such as galleys, lavatories etc.), and so on....

Third, there are constraints imposed by the brief of the particular airline commissioning the design. The most important of these is the number of passengers that the airline wishes to accommodate in business class ("the pax count")....

Lastly, there are constraints imposed by the fact that the seat must work for a human being....

The idea of a herringbone arrangement of seats had been around for some time. In pure design terms both an inward facing herringbone and an outward facing herringbone were known. An inward facing herringbone gave the potential for greater seat density. This is because the seats can be angled more acutely, and because access from the aisle into the seat is more efficient if passengers do not have to climb over or round the seat back. Its drawback was that passengers faced each other across the aisle, thus reducing their individual privacy. An outward facing herringbone, on the other hand, gave the passengers greater privacy, but was space-hungrier. Until the advent of the UCS [Virgin's seat] the perception in the industry was that passengers would not like an inward facing herringbone. Since the passengers are the economic drivers, inward facing herringbones remained in the realm of theory.... At the time of the events in issue Virgin Atlantic's UCS was the only inward facing herringbone that had actually been commercialised.

[Defendant Contour designed a similar inward-facing herringbone seat.]

Unregistered design right

The statutory provisions

Section 213 of the *Copyright Designs and Patents Act 1988* provides, so far as material:

"(1) Design right is a property right which subsists in accordance with this Part in an original design.

(2) In this Part 'design' means the design of any aspect of the shape or configuration (whether internal or external) of the whole or part of an article.

(3) Design right does not subsist in—

(a) a method or principle of construction,

(b) features of shape or configuration of an article which—

 (i) enable the article to be connected to, or placed in, around or against, another article so that either article may perform its function, or

 (ii) are dependent upon the appearance of another article of which the article is intended by the designer to form an integral part, or

(c) surface decoration.

(4) A design is not 'original' for the purposes of this Part if it is commonplace in the design field in question at the time of its creation."

As many judges have commented, section 213 is notoriously difficult to understand. As Jacob LJ put it in *Dyson v Qualtex* [2006] RPC 31 § 14: "It has the merit of being short. It has no other."

A person who is entitled to unregistered design right has the exclusive right to reproduce the design for commercial purposes by making articles to that design or by making a document recording the design. Section 226(3) provides:

Reproduction of a design by making articles to the design means copying the design so as to produce articles exactly or substantially to that design. . . .

Thus as Mummery LJ explained in *Farmers Build Ltd v Carier Bulk Handling Materials Ltd* [1999] RPC 461, 480:

"The purpose of copyright and of design right is not to protect the 'novelty' of the work against all competition; it is to provide limited protection against unfair misappropriation of the time, skill and effort expended by the author of design on the creation of his work."

What is a design?

In *Rolawn Ltd v Turfmech Machinery* [2008] RPC 27 § 79 Mann J pointed out that:

"It is important to isolate the design in respect of which protection can be properly claimed, and it is vital to ensure that it falls within the definition of design. The Act defines design as "any aspect of the shape or configuration ... of the whole or any part of an article", and the right cannot exist until there is an embodiment of the design in an article or in a design document. This combination of features means that design right is confined to what one can actually see in an article—either the physical article or a drawing."

Design right does not therefore protect ideas. Ideas are protected by patent law. It follows, therefore, that Virgin Atlantic are not entitled to claim design right for the general concept of an inward facing herringbone arrangement of seats.... Nor, I think, does Virgin Atlantic claim design right in the general concept of an inward facing herringbone where the angle of installation of the seats exceeds 18°.

What is an aspect of the shape or configuration of an article?

It is, of course, plain from the words of section 213 itself that design right can be claimed for the design of part of an article. A teapot spout or a teapot handle are frequently cited examples. An aspect of the design is something that is discernable or recognisable (not necessarily to the naked eye) but it need not be visually significant.

Self-selection

One of the real difficulties of section 213 is that the claimant may select a part of the article and claim design right for that part only. The courts have recognised this possibility since the early days of design right. In *Ocular Sciences Ltd v Aspect Vision Care* [1997] R.P.C. 289, 422 Laddie J said:

> "... the proprietor can trim his design right claim to most closely match what he believes the defendant to have taken. The defendant will not know in what the alleged monopoly resides until the letter before action, or, more usually, the service of the statement of claim. This means that a plaintiff's pleading has particular importance. It not only puts forward the claim but is likely to be the only statement of what is asserted to be the design right."

Unregistered design right is, of course, not a true monopoly: it merely prevents copying....

In a sense it is of course true that a man who copies part of an article will know what he has taken. But similarities between the design relied on and the allegedly infringing article are often relied on to raise the inference of copying which the defendant must then rebut. There is a danger that the ability of the claimant to select parts of his design which are small in comparison to the overall article will give rise to a distorted impression of what the defendant has done which comes close to reversing the burden of proof. This concentration on relatively minor aspects of the overall design also had a tendency to make some of the witnesses more defensive than they might otherwise have been. There is another point to be made here. Virgin Atlantic's pleaded case did not rely on designs as recorded in design documents. Rather they relied upon the designs as embodied in the actual UCS. . . .

Thus what is alleged to have been copied is the real life version of the UCS; and what is being compared is the real life version of the UCS with the real life version of Solar Eclipse. This is important because the plans, elevations, and isometric drawings, being only two dimensional, can give a distorted picture of reality.

Reproduction

What must be established is that the design in which design right subsists has been copied so as to produce "articles exactly or substantially to that design". . . . Mere similarity is not enough.

In *C & H Engineering v F Klucznik & Sons Ltd* [1992] FSR 421 Aldous J said:

> "Under section 226 there will only be infringement if the design is copied so as to produce articles exactly or substantially to the design. Thus the test for infringement requires the alleged infringing article or articles be compared with the document or article embodying the design. Thereafter the court must decide whether copying took place and, if so, whether the alleged infringing article is made exactly to the design or substantially to that design. Whether or not the alleged infringing article is made substantially to the plaintiff's design must be an objective test to be decided through the eyes of the person to whom the design is directed."

Although, at least in theory, two separate criteria must be satisfied *viz.* copying and making articles exactly or substantially to the copied design, it is not easy to conceive of real facts (absent an incompetent copyist) in which a design is copied without the copy being made exactly or substantially to the copied design. In practice, if copying is established, it is highly likely that the infringing article will have been made exactly or substantially to the protected design. If copying is not established, then whether the article is the same or substantially the same as the protected design does not matter. However, similarity in design may allow an inference of copying to be drawn.

[After extensive analysis, the court found that defendant did not copy either the design of the UCS as a whole, nor particular design elements identified by Virgin. In the latter analysis, however, the court indicated that some aspects of the design elements were dictated by technical concerns. The court then turned to the patent claim, finding the patent valid but not infringed by defendant.]

Notes and Questions

1. Although the British Unregistered Designs Act is labeled a form of "design" protection, it differs in at least one significant way from the product design laws discussed in the prior section. Can you identify that difference? If not, consider the following hint: other than the design claim, what law was Virgin invoking to protect its interest?

2. What must an unregistered design right owner show to prove infringement? Is the standard similar to copyright's "substantial similarity" analysis, or something requiring a higher degree of similarity?

* * *

Compared to all other forms of intellectual property, patent protection is far and away the most difficult to obtain. Patent's novelty and non-obviousness/inventive step requirements mean that relatively few inventions will qualify for a patent. In addition, the need for extensive analysis of the prior art, combined with the laborious process of claim drafting, make the process of obtaining a patent very expensive and time consuming. The net result of this situation is that a number of commercially valuable inventions receive no significant legal protection at all—whether because they do not qualify for patent or because the inventor does not want to incur the expense—leaving competitors free to copy the invention.

The TRIPS Agreement requires a fairly high standard of inventiveness as a condition to obtaining a patent. Article 27(1) limits the grant of patents to inventions that are new and involve an inventive step. Many, however, argue that the patent system should not work in isolation. While content to reserve the strong protection of the utility patent for truly significant advances in technology, these people also advocate a separate, lesser form of protection for important, but not groundbreaking, advances. This lesser form of protection is often referred to as "utility model" protection.

A review of national utility model laws can quickly result in considerable confusion. This confusion stems in large part from the fact that the term "utility model protection" is not yet a term of art in the field of intellectual property. Instead, the same term is used to describe what are in truth three very different types of laws. The first is the "minimal examination patent." Under this model, a party may obtain protection without any significant government examination of the invention (other than as to formalities such as a proper description). The tradeoff for this lesser showing is that the term of protection is significantly less, usually five to ten years. It is important to note that while these laws dispense with the examination requirement, they retain the novelty and non-obviousness requirements of ordinary patent law. Nations with this sort of utility model law include Belgium, France, Ireland, and the Netherlands.

The second type of utility model law, which can be dubbed for our purposes the "petty patent" model, actually does lower the standard for novelty. This approach is used by Australia (which calls it the "Innovation Patent"), Austria, Finland, Germany, and several other nations. Consider the "novelty" requirement under section 2 of the recently-amended Finnish statute:

> An invention must be new in relation to what was known before the filing date of the utility model right application and must differ distinctly therefrom.

> The prior art shall be held to comprise everything made available to the public by means of a written or oral description, by use or in any other way. . . .

Utility Model Act (Finland), Act No. 800 of May 10, 1991, *amended by* Act No. 686 of July 21, 2006, and Act No. 700 of December 1, 2008 (translated by the Japanese Patent Office). Like the "no examination" patent, a petty patent system typically requires little if any examination of the invention, but in return grants protection for a term significantly shorter than that for ordinary patents.

The third approach to utility model legislation can be referred to as the "Three Dimensional Approach." It has been adopted by a number of nations, including Denmark, Greece, Italy, Japan, and Spain. The British "unregistered design protection" discussed in *Virgin Atlantic* is also for all practical purposes equivalent to a three dimensional utility model law. To obtain a feel for how these laws work, review both the British provisions quoted in *Virgin Atlantic* and the Japanese law, excerpted below.

The three dimensional approach focuses on the visual design features of the useful article. Unlike ordinary design protection law, however, three dimensional utility model protection is usually invoked to protect the *utilitarian* aspects of the design. Thus, in *Virgin Atlantic*, the court never considered whether the seat design better utilized the available space. In situations like this, the three-dimensional approach looks much like a "petty patent."

Unlike the British law, most three dimensional regimes *do* require the inventor to file an application to register the utility model. However, the threshold for protection is far lower than for an ordinary utility patent. Like the other two forms of utility model protection, most three dimensional regimes provide a significantly shorter term of protection than that provided for utility patents.

Utility Model Act (Japan)

Act No. 123 of 1959

Article 1 (Purpose)

The purpose of this Act is to encourage devices by promoting the protection and the utilization of devices relating to the shape or structure of an article or combination of articles, and thereby to contribute to the development of industry.

Article 2 (Definitions)

(1) "Device" in this Act means the creation of technical ideas utilizing the Act of nature.

(2) "Registered utility model" in this Act means a device for which a utility model registration has been granted. . . .

Article 3 (Conditions for Utility Model Registration)

(1) A creator of a device that relates to the shape or structure of an article or combination of articles and is industrially applicable may be entitled to obtain a utility model registration for the said device, except when the following applies:

(i) the device was publicly known in Japan or a foreign country, prior to the filing of the application for a utility model registration therefor;

(ii) the device was publicly worked in Japan or a foreign country, prior to the filing of the application for a utility model registration therefor; or

(iii) the device was described in a distributed publication, or a device that was made publicly available through an electric telecommunication line in Japan or a foreign country, prior to the filing of the application for a utility model registration therefor.

(2) Where, prior to the filing of the application for a utility model registration, a person ordinarily skilled in the art of the device would have been exceedingly easy to create the device based on a device prescribed in any of the items of the preceding paragraph, a utility model registration shall not be granted for such a device notwithstanding the preceding paragraph. . . .

Article 4 (Unregistrable devices)

Notwithstanding Article 3(1), any device that is liable to injure public policy or public health shall not be granted a utility model registration.

Article 5 (Applications for a utility model registration)

. . . .

(2) The description, scope of claims, drawing(s) and abstract shall be attached to the application. . . .

(6) The statement of the scope of claims as provided in paragraph (2) shall comply with each of the following items:

(i) the device for which a utility model registration is sought is stated in the detailed explanation of the device;

(ii) the device for which a utility model is sought is clear;

(iii) the statement for each claim is concise. . . .

Notes and Questions

1. Which form of utility model protection would most likely be favored by the following inventors:

- an inventor who makes a minor advance in technology;

- an inventor who makes a major advance in a field of technology that is undergoing rapid development, so that the invention will likely be obsolete in a few years;

- an inventor who invents a new and groundbreaking process for refining a particular chemical; or

- an inventor in a field of technology where competitors routinely and without permission "borrow" advances made by others in the industry, incorporating them into their products?

2. Is United States design patent law an example of the three dimensional model? Can a party utilize design patent law to protect the utilitarian features of a product?

3. Given what you already know about United States patent law, do you think Congress would be receptive to a utility model regime that would operate alongside the regular patent laws? What if the system set a much lower threshold of protection? Does the current exclusion of these minor inventions from patent law represent a decision by Congress not to protect them at all, or simply not to protect them under patent law?

4. Many developing countries introduce utility models as a means to catch up with other developed countries. The U.K. Commission on Intellectual Property Rights, for example, observed:

Rather than diluting the patentability standards to capture the incremental type of innovations that predominate in many developing countries, lawmakers and policy makers in these countries should consider the establishment of utility model protection for stimulating and rewarding such innovations. Further research would seem desirable to assess the precise role that utility model protection, or other systems with similar objectives, might play in developing countries.

COMM'N ON INTELLECTUAL PROP. RIGHTS, INTEGRATING INTELLECTUAL PROPERTY RIGHTS AND DEVELOPMENT POLICY: REPORT OF THE COMMISSION ON INTELLECTUAL PROPERTY RIGHTS 121 (2002). For these countries, what are the benefits and drawbacks of introducing utility model legislation?

* * *

It is a widely-held belief that the United States does not recognize utility model protection. But like many widely-held beliefs, that perception is not entirely correct. In fact, United States law does afford some ways for an inventor to obtain limited protection for certain types of inventions without jumping through all the hoops associated with a full-blown utility patent application. The most important is trade secret law. Unlike patent law, trade secret laws require only minimal novelty: the owner need only show that the secret is not currently known to others. Moreover, unlike the laws of many nations, United States law does not require proof of a confidential relationship between the owner and the party who appropriates the secret. Thus, trade secret protection can even protect against industrial espionage, bribery, and other acts committed by actual or potential competitors. While a trade secret is not a property right like a patent or utility model, it nevertheless affords a meaningful way to ensure that the owner is the only one who may use the secret.

Chapter 6

OTHER FORMS OF INTELLECTUAL PROPERTY

A. THE DOCTRINE OF MISAPPROPRIATION

In its oft-cited opinion in *International News Service v. Associated Press*, 248 U.S. 215 (1918), the United States Supreme Court held that a news agency had a legal claim against another news agency that "misappropriated" news gathered by the first agency. The Court's basic rationale was that some form of protection was necessary to provide those who invest time and money in gathering and disseminating the news an adequate incentive to continue to provide this valuable service. To allow the defendant "to reap where it has not sown," the Court reasoned, would deny the gathering agency the ability to earn a profit from its endeavors.

The notion that a party ought to be able to reap the fruits of its creative activity lies at the very core of intellectual property law. But aside from situations where this principle has been incorporated by statute, as in the patent, copyright, and trademark laws, courts have had considerable difficulty applying the general principle set out in *INS*. The problem is that those principles run afoul of another well-developed doctrine of competition law; namely, that a party is free to compete with others, even if that competition involves copying something valuable. Such conduct typically benefits consumers in the form of more choices and lower prices where there is price competition. This basic tension has led courts to disagree as to what sorts of efforts are worthy of protection, as well as the types of misappropriation that qualify as "improper." Moreover, in many cases the judge-created law of misappropriation, which remains almost exclusively *state* law, is preempted by federal patent or copyright law.

Because of these problems, the law of general misappropriation has evolved to a state where a viable claim exists only in certain narrow, and in some ways special, areas. In two areas—the right of publicity and the law of trade secrets (both of which are discussed below)—the doctrine has fared fairly well. There are also two other very narrow areas—cases like *INS* that involve "hot news," and those involving common law copyright protection of unfixed works—where general misappropriation theory continues to hold some sway. But aside from these particular cases, very few plaintiffs actually prevail on a general misappropriation claim. Indeed, § 38 of the recent *Restatement (Third) of Unfair Competition* goes so far as to suggest that unless a statute or treaty governs the situation, misappropriation is a viable claim only in publicity, trade secret, and common law copyright situations.

The sentiment underlying cases like *INS* is not unique to United States judges. For example, a 2006 decision of a French court declared, "It is unfair to obtain a competitive advantage from . . . another person's investment." Cour d'appel [CA] [regional court of appeal] Paris, June 14, 2006 (Fr.) (Cartier v. Raymond Weil) (translated by author). Based on this idea, the court held a party liable for producing a watch with a design similar to the Cartier "Tank" watch, even though there were clear differences between the design and no real likelihood of customer confusion.

At present, the notion of a tort of general misappropriation is probably strongest in France. Other nations have taken a far more guarded approach to the issue. Consider, for example, Article 5(c) of the Swiss Act Against Unfair Competition, which provides a remedy in cases of "slavish copying": "An act of unfair competition is in particular committed by . . . anyone who takes the marketable results of the work of another person and exploits them by means of a technical reproduction process without an appropriate effort of his own." Although this language has potentially broad reach, the Swiss courts have proven reluctant to find a violation of Article 5(c), in large part because it could contradict basic principles of competition law.

The recently-reworked German Act Against Unfair Competition (*Gesetz gegen den unlauteren Wettbewerb*, or UWG) also takes a cautious approach to misappropriation. Whereas the prior law could be interpreted broadly, new § 4(9) of the UWG provides that it is unfair to offer goods or services that closely replicate a competitor's goods or services only if the copying would (a) mislead consumers as to the origin of the goods, (b) unfairly exploit or impair the reputation of the original manufacturer, or (c) be the result of knowledge or other information acquired by dishonest means. Situations (a) and (c) involve, respectively, issues of trade dress and trade secret law. While situation (b) is arguably more open-ended, its focus on the reputation of the manufacturer itself, rather than that of the manufacturer's goods or services, also gives it a trademark law flavor. Early experience with § 4(9) suggests that the German courts will exercise restraint in applying the provision to cases of outright copying for purposes of competition.

B.　THE RIGHT OF PUBLICITY

As indicated above, the modern right of publicity is one of the few areas in which general misappropriation theory has had a significant impact. It is important to note at the outset that we are talking about a *celebrity's* (or other public figure's) right to control commercial exploitation of her name, image, or other public aspect of her persona, not a private individual's right to prevent use of his image in advertising. The latter stems from the right of *privacy*, and relies little, if at all, on the theories underlying general misappropriation. The celebrity right of publicity, by contrast, increasingly is justified by a misappropriation-type logic; namely as a way to ensure that the celebrity is able to reap the fruits of the public image she has so carefully cultivated.

Moreover, it would be a mistake to point to the right of publicity as one of the major "success stories" of general misappropriation theory. First, the right has not received universal recognition, even in the United States where it originated. To date, only about half of the states provide the functional equivalent of a right of publicity (although to be honest, a number of states have not yet even addressed the question of whether the right exists). Second, some of the states that have recognized the right ground it in the law of *privacy*, focusing more on the celebrity's right to prevent unauthorized uses of his personal attributes than on economic notions of exploitation or appropriation.

How has the right of publicity fared in other nations? Somewhat surprisingly, the story closely parallels the situation in the United States. Many nations across the world give public figures some control over the use of their image. For a survey of European law as applied to a particular context, see SPORTS IMAGE RIGHTS IN EUROPE (Ian S. Blackshaw & Robert C.R. Siekmann eds., 2005). As in the United States, however, the rationale for this right is not always the principle that one should not reap where one has not sown. In many nations, the right of publicity is closely related to principles of privacy law.

One notable difference between the United States and many other nations that have a publicity right involves the use of a celebrity's image in news reporting. While United States cases often deal with use of the celebrity persona in advertising, foreign cases are far more likely to involve situations where a celebrity complains about the use of his name or image in a newspaper, magazine, fact-based book, or television news report. Because these situations involve something more than blatant commercialization, they present difficult issues lying at the intersection of publicity, free speech, and privacy law. The following case involves just such a situation. It also reveals the Canadian view of the right of privacy.

GOULD ESTATE v. STODDART PUBLISHING CO.

Ontario Court of Justice
30 O.R.3d 520 (1996)

LEDERMAN J.

Background

In 1956, Glenn Gould ("Gould"), then a young concert pianist, was interviewed by Jock Carroll ("Carroll") for an article in *Weekend* Magazine. They talked on a variety of occasions and in numerous venues, including Carroll accompanying Gould on a vacation to the Bahamas. During this time, Carroll took approximately 400 photographs of Gould and copious notes, including some tape-recordings, of their conversations. Certain of these photographs and comments of Gould were used in the magazine article. Nearly forty years later, in 1995, Carroll published through Stoddart Publishing Co. Limited a book entitled "Glenn Gould: Some Portraits of the Artist as a Young Man". Gould had died in 1982 and Gould's Estate did not authorize its publication or receive royalties from the book.

The book makes use of over 70 of the original 400 photographs and draws very extensively on the conversations that Carroll recorded back in 1956. The text of the book is largely comprised of extracts from these conversations. It is undisputed that Carroll is the owner of the copyright in the photographs. Gould's Estate, however, in these two actions, seeks damages claiming (i) that use of the photographs amounts to the tort of appropriation of personality, the cause of action for which may be asserted by the Estate; and (ii) that copyright in the oral conversations recorded by Carroll rests with Gould (now his Estate) and as such the conversations may not be used without the permission of the Estate.

The Photograph Action

Apart from using the photographs for a story in *Weekend* Magazine, there was no discussion among Carroll, Gould or Gould's agent, Walter Homburger ("Homburger"), as to their further unrestricted use.

In 1956, Homburger invited Carroll to take pictures of, and do a story on, Gould and it was apparent to Carroll that Gould and his agent were anxious to generate exposure for this up and coming young artist. The photos and interview took place one year after Gould's major U.S. concert debut, less than one year after his first U.S. record release and the same year as a major North American concert tour. Given the number of photographs taken, Carroll was of the view that Gould would have been delighted if Carroll used them in subsequent publications so as to create further publicity for him. At no time during his life did Gould or anyone on his behalf ever take the position that he had the right to restrict or control the use of these photographs. On this basis, the defendants say that Carroll was free to use the photographs in any manner he saw fit.

On the other hand, the Gould Estate argued that it was well known that Gould was an intensely private individual who guarded his privacy. He took great care with the management of his personal image and reputation, and was scrupulously careful about the quality of materials which were released under his name, or projects in which he participated. He has been referred to as "Canada's own Greta Garbo"....

If Gould has a proprietary right to his personality, then the onus is on the defendants to show that Carroll had permission to appropriate that right by publishing the photographs of Gould. The onus should not be on the holder of the right to prove that he had placed restrictions on the exploitation of his own property.

The first question should then be: Did Gould in fact have any proprietary rights in his image, likeness or personality which have been appropriated by the publication of the photographs in the book?

i) The Tort of Appropriation of Personality

In Ontario, the common law tort of misappropriation of personality was first articulated by Estey J.A. in the Court of Appeal in *Krouse v. Chrysler Canada Ltd.* (1974), 40 D.L.R. (3d) 15 (Ont. C.A.). While no formal definition of the tort was offered, he stated:

> ... there may well be circumstances in which the Courts would be justified in holding a defendant liable in damages for appropriation of a plaintiff's personality, amounting to an invasion of his right to exploit his personality by the use of his image, voice, or otherwise with damage to the plaintiff....

In *Athans v. Canadian Adventure Camps Ltd.* (1977), 17 O.R. (2d) 425 (H.C.), Henry J., citing *Krouse,* stated at p. 434:

> ... it is clear that Mr. Athans has a proprietary right in the exclusive marketing for gain of his personality, image and name, and that the law entitles him to protect that right, if it is invaded....

The same type of tort, usually under the name "right of publicity", is also well-recognized in the United States....

The Gould Estate submits that the book in question is a compilation of photographs of Gould and the act of selling the book constitutes commercial exploitation. Accordingly, it argues that this amounts to unlawful appropriation of Gould's personality.

The few Canadian cases dealing with this tort have generally involved situations in which the name or image of an individual enjoying some celebrity status has been used in the advertising or promotion of the defendant's business or products....

Generally then, there has been an implication that the celebrity is endorsing the activity of the defendant. This contextual factor seems to have been an important underlying consideration in the courts' reasoning.... In ... *Athans*, Henry J. was concerned with whether the material in question had "the effect of establishing any connection in the minds of the relevant public between Mr. Athans and the [summer] camp". It should be pointed out that in *Athans*, damages were ultimately awarded despite the judge's finding that people viewing the material in question would not conclude that the plaintiff was actually endorsing the defendant's waterskiing school. Instead, the plaintiff recovered on the basis that:

> ... [t]he commercial use of his representational image by the defendants without his consent constituted an invasion and *pro tanto* an impairment of his exclusive right to market his personality and this, in my opinion, constitutes an aspect of the tort of appropriation of personality.

While at first glance this decision may seem to support the present defendants' broad interpretation of commercialization, the decision is consistent with the endorsement context. *Athans* was a situation where an identifiable "representational image" was utilized by a waterskiing school in the school's promotional brochure. Therefore, on the basis of these Canadian authorities it would seem open to the court to conclude, on a contextual basis, that the tort of appropriation of personality is restricted to endorsement-type situations....

The U.S. courts have similarly recognized the necessity of limits on the right of personality. These limits are usually discussed in terms of First Amendment considerations: "the scope of the right of publicity should be measured or balanced against societal interests in free expression" (*Presley* [*v. Russen*, 513 F. Supp. 1339, 1356 (D.N.J. 1981)]).... Accordingly, the right of publicity has not been successfully invoked in cases where the activity in question consists of thoughts, ideas, newsworthy events or matters of public interest. In this regard, it is important to note that:

> the scope of the subject matter which falls within the protected area of the 'newsworthy' or of 'public interest' extends far beyond the dissemination of news in the sense of current events and includes all types of factual, educational and historical data, or even entertainment and amusement.

Conversely, the right of publicity has been upheld in situations where famous names or likeness are used "predominately in connection with the sale of consumer merchandise or solely for purposes of trade—*e.g.* merely to attract attention". As a result, Elvis Presley posters, pewter replicas of a statue of Elvis Presley, a "Howard Hughes" game which included Hughes' name and other biographical information, and a board game utilizing the names and biographies of famous golfers, have all been found to infringe the right of publicity. All were found to be commercial products which were not vehicles through which ideas and opinions are regularly disseminated.

While Canada does not have a constitutional provision akin to the First Amendment which is applicable to the private law, no principled argument has been advanced to suggest that freedom of expression considerations should not animate Canadian courts in identifying the public interest and placing limits on the tort of appropriation of personality. Indeed, freedom of expression would seem to be a compelling and reasonably coherent basis for defining the "obvious" need for limits noted by Estey J.A. in *Krouse*.

In the end then, and perhaps at the risk of oversimplifying, it seems that the courts have drawn a ' "sales vs. subject' " distinction. Sales constitute commercial exploitation and invoke the tort of appropriation of personality. The identity of the celebrity is merely being used in some fashion. The activity cannot be said to be about the celebrity. This is in contrast to situations in which the celebrity is the actual subject of the work or enterprise, with biographies perhaps being the clearest example. These activities would not be within the ambit of the tort. To take a more concrete example, in endorsement situations, posters and board games, the essence of the activity is not the celebrity. It is the use of some attributes of the celebrity for another purpose. Biographies, other books, plays, and satirical skits are by their nature different. The subject of the activity is the celebrity and the work is an attempt to provide some insights about that celebrity.

Adopted to the present case, the book in question contains 26 pages of text by Carroll together with photographs depicting Gould in posed and spontaneous moments at the beginning of his concert career. I agree with the comment on the overleaf:

> They capture the passion and brilliance of Gould as pianist, the solitude of Gould as artist and the boyish nature of Gould as a young man.

Although it is primarily through Gould's own images and words, this book provides insight to anyone interested in Gould, the man and his music. The author added his own creativity in recounting his time spent with Gould and in making decisions about which photographs and text to use and how they should be arranged to provide this glimpse into Gould's solitary life. There is a public interest in knowing more about one of Canada's musical geniuses. Because of this public interest, the book therefore falls into the protected category and there cannot be said to be any right of personality in Gould which has been unlawfully appropriated by the defendants.

ii) Survivability of the Right of Publicity

Although not necessary to the decision in view of the above finding, the issue had arisen as to whether the tort of appropriation of personality survives the death of the individual and I am impelled to make some comments about this. Of those U.S. jurisdictions which have considered the matter, the substantial majority recognize that the right of publicity is devisable and descendible. It also seems clear that the modern trend is toward this recognition.

The defendants place some reliance on the fact that in the three provincial Privacy Acts which provide for a cause of action for the appropriation of personality (Newfoundland, Saskatchewan and British Columbia), the right of action is extinguished by the death of the individual whose rights are alleged to have been violated. However, this factor is not persuasive in the case at bar. In creating a statutory right of action, the legislature may obviously impose statutory restrictions on that cause of action. Here though, the case is grounded in a common law cause of action. As such it is not constrained by the restrictions which apply to the statutory right of action.

A more theoretical approach to distinguishing the Privacy Acts can be found in U.S. law. There, several cases have recognized a distinction between the right of privacy and the right of publicity. The former is considered a personal tort and is designed to protect an individual's interest in dignity and peace of mind. The right of publicity, on the other hand, protects the commercial value of a person's celebrity status. As such, it is a form of intangible property, akin to copyright or patent, that is descendable. Given that the Canadian statutory rights of action are found in Privacy Acts, it would certainly seem that, following the U.S. reasoning, whatever statutory restrictions there may be on the rights of action for privacy violations and unauthorized use of personality, they should not be applied to the common law tort of appropriation of personality.

The right of publicity, being a form of intangible property under Ontario law akin to copyright, should descend to the celebrity's heirs. Reputation and fame can be a capital asset that one nurtures and may choose to exploit and it may have a value much greater than any tangible property. There is no reason why such an asset should not be devisable to heirs under s. 2 of the *Succession Law Reform Act*.

As a final comment on this topic, the U.S. cases on both sides of the right of publicity debate have expressed concern over whether there should be a durational limit on the right of publicity after it is inherited. For the present purposes though, suffice it to say that Gould passed away in 1982, and it seems reasonable to conclude that whatever the durational limit, if any, it is unlikely to be less than 14 years. The protection granted by other intangible property rights such as patents and copyrights is longer. So, too, any durational limit on Gould's right of publicity would not yet have expired. . . .

Disposition

There is no basis in law for the plaintiffs' actions. Accordingly, there will be summary judgment dismissing both actions.

Notes and Questions

1.   Glenn Gould was born in Toronto and remained a Canadian citizen for his entire life. In addition, the book at issue in the case was published in Canada even though the photographs and quotes were first made in the Bahamas. The court accordingly did not have to face the question of whether principles of territoriality precluded the use of Canadian law to deal with misappropriation of Gould's personality. The copyright in the photographs and quotations, by contrast, may raise interesting choice-of-law issues. Recall the discussion of choice of law issues in Chapter 1.B.

2.   Is the Canadian personality right grounded in the right of privacy, in misappropriation theory, or both? How would you compare this approach to those used by states that have adopted state right of publicity laws?

3. As you may have seen, the California courts have also struggled with a celebrity's ability to control use of her image or name in connection with someone else's speech. The California Supreme Court approaches the issue in a very different way. Rather than the "sale/subject" analysis adopted in *Gould*, California asks whether the defendant "transformed" the image by adding its own creative elements. If enough transformation has taken place, the defendant is not liable. See *Comedy III Productions, Inc. v. Gary Saderup, Inc.*, 25 Cal.4th 387 (2001) (insufficient transformation when defendant produced t-shirts with an image of the Three Stooges); *Winter v. DC Comics*, 30 Cal. 4th 881 (2003) (portraying the Winters brothers, famous rock music stars, as "half-man, half-worm" creatures called the "Autumn Brothers" in a comic book is sufficiently transformative, even though the creatures clearly evoked the image of Winters brothers). Of course, the California approach was crafted in large part to deal with First Amendment concerns. However, which approach is better when measured from the perspective of basic misappropriation law? Which strikes the proper balance between the celebrity's interest in preventing exploitation by others and society's interest in ensuring that others are free to talk about—and criticize—the celebrity?

4. Like Ontario, several states in the United States allow for the right of publicity to pass to the celebrity's heirs. Does that rule make sense? Does your answer turn on whether the right is based on principles of misappropriation or privacy?

C.   THE LAW GOVERNING SECRET INFORMATION

1.   TRADE SECRET LAW

Unlike the right of publicity, legal protection for trade secrets is available in all fifty states. Moreover, although trade secret law is almost exclusively state law, the widespread adoption of the Uniform Trade Secrets Act has led to a high degree of uniformity. The overwhelming majority of cases involve employees who have allegedly taken, used, or disclosed secrets ostensibly belonging to their employers. Many others involve suppliers or other parties with a contractual duty not to disclose. However, the law has also developed to impose liability even on parties, such as competitors, who have no preexisting duty not to disclose.

Modern trade secret law does rely heavily on misappropriation theory. However, like publicity the claim also has other ancestors. One crucial feature in trade secret law is *how* the secret was acquired. Trade secret law does not, as a rule, impose liability merely because one party copies another's secret information, even if the copying involves blatant exploitation. Instead, courts impose liability only if the act of appropriation or use is somehow wrongful, either viewed by itself or in the context of the actual dispute. Indeed, even the notorious opinion in *E.I. DuPont deNemours & Co. v. Christopher*, 431 F.2d 1012 (5th Cir. 1970), which probably pushes trade secret law to its limits, stresses the wrongfulness of defendant's acts. Trade secret law therefore focuses less on the appropriation itself, and more on the means by which that appropriation occurs.

How has the doctrine of misappropriation of secret information fared in other nations? The next case illustrates the view in the United Kingdom.

FACCENDA CHICKEN LTD. v. FOWLER

Court of Appeal (Civil Division)
[1987] Ch. 117

NEILL L.J.

Faccenda carry on the business of breeding, rearing, slaughtering and selling chickens.... In about 1973 Faccenda engaged Mr. Barry Fowler (the first respondent) as sales manager.

The [trial] judge described the subsequent development of the business of Faccenda in these terms:

> At that time [1973], and for some time afterwards, the company sold its chickens to wholesalers, and did not approach retailers directly. Mr. Fowler, who is agreed to be a businessman of considerable ability, proposed to Mr. Faccenda the establishment of what he called a van sales operation, whereby itinerant refrigerated vehicles would daily offer fresh chickens to such traders as butchers, supermarkets and catering establishments. Starting at first in a small way, Mr. Fowler built up this branch of the business until it came to represent a substantial part, though always the smaller part, of the company's trade. There were in all ten refrigerated vehicles, each driven by a salesman and travelling in a particular sector of the Midlands....

It seems clear that by 1980 the van sales operation was prospering. The average weekly profit for the period which covered approximately the second half of 1980 was about £2,500.

On 11 December 1980, however, Mr. Fowler was arrested, together with another man, on a charge of stealing some of Faccenda's chickens. Mr. Fowler resigned immediately as sales manager, and, though at his trial in September 1981, he was acquitted of the charge of theft, his work at Faccenda was at an end....

Shortly afterwards he decided to set up his own business of selling fresh chickens from refrigerated vehicles.... In about May 1981 Mr. Fowler advertised for employees under a box number in a local newspaper. As a result of this advertisement eight employees of Faccenda applied to join Mr. Fowler's new organization [and were hired]....

The loss of such a high proportion of their experienced staff had a serious effect on Faccenda. Indeed, ever since Mr. Fowler had left at the end of 1980, the operations of the van sales division of Faccenda had been much less profitable, and after July 1981 the position deteriorated further. Mr. Faccenda, not surprisingly, was dismayed by what had happened, and on 10 September 1981, the date (it seems) of Mr. Fowler's acquittal, an action was started by Faccenda in the Chancery Division against Mr. Fowler and his company and the eight former employees of Faccenda.... [Judge Goulding in the Chancery Division decided the case in favor of Fowler.]

The main case put forward on behalf of Faccenda before Goulding J., and the only factual basis for the claims relied upon before us, was that Mr. Fowler and the other former employees of Faccenda as well as the new Fowler company had wrongfully made use of confidential information which Mr. Fowler and his colleagues had acquired while in the employment of Faccenda.

This information, which was described by the judge compendiously as "the sales information," can be listed under five headings: (1) the names and addresses of customers; (2) the most convenient routes to be taken to reach the individual customers; (3) the usual requirements of individual customers, both as to quantity and quality; (4) the days of the week and the time of the day when deliveries were usually made to individual customers; (5) the prices charged to individual customers. It was submitted on behalf of Faccenda that this sales information could be regarded as a package which, taken as a whole, constituted "confidential information" which could not be used to the detriment of Faccenda. In addition, however, particular attention was directed to the prices charged to individual customers, because, it was submitted, information as to prices was itself "confidential information," quite apart from the fact that such information formed a constituent element of the package of sales information....

It was further said on behalf of the plaintiffs that by wrongfully making use of this confidential sales information Mr. Fowler and his colleagues had seriously damaged Faccenda's business....

In his judgment Goulding J. dealt with the allegations made by Faccenda in these terms:

... Faccenda Chicken Ltd. claims that it was the particular target of the operation. It alleges that Mr. Fowler and his confederates deliberately arranged to call on its customers on the same days of the week as its own salesmen, and generally at a somewhat earlier hour. It is also strongly contended that the defendants pursued a deliberate policy of undercutting Faccenda prices....

It seems to us to be clear from reading the judgment as a whole that the judge accepted that, to a greater or less extent, all the constituent elements of the sales information had been made use of for the purpose of the Fowler business....

Having considered the cases to which we were referred, we would venture to state these principles as follows:

(1) Where the parties are, or have been, linked by a contract of employment, the obligations of the employee are to be determined by the contract between him and his employer.

(2) In the absence of any express term, the obligations of the employee in respect of the use and disclosure of information are the subject of implied terms.

(3) While the employee remains in the employment of the employer the obligations are included in the implied term which imposes a duty of good faith or fidelity on the employee. For the purpose of the present appeal it is not necessary to consider the precise limits of this implied term, but it may be noted: (a) that the extent of the duty of good faith will vary according to the nature of the contract; (b) that the duty of good faith will be broken if an employee makes or copies a list of the customers of the employer for use after his employment ends or deliberately memorises such a list, even though, except in special circumstances, there is no general restriction on an ex-employee canvassing or doing business with customers of his former employer.

(4) The implied term which imposes an obligation on the employee as to his conduct after the termination of the employment is more restricted in its scope than that which imposes a general duty of good faith. It is clear that the obligation not to use or disclose information may cover secret processes of manufacture such as chemical formulae, and other information which is of a sufficiently high degree of confidentiality as to amount to a trade secret. The obligation does not extend, however, to cover all information which is given to or acquired by the employee while in his employment, and in particular may not cover information which is only "confidential" in the sense that an unauthorised disclosure of such information to a third party while the employment subsisted would be a clear breach of the duty of good faith....

(5) In order to determine whether any particular item of information falls within the implied term so as to prevent its use or disclosure by an employee after his employment has ceased, it is necessary to consider all the circumstances of the case. We are satisfied that the following matters are among those to which attention must be paid:

(a) The nature of the employment. Thus employment in a capacity where "confidential" material is habitually handled may impose a high obligation of confidentiality because the employee can be expected to realise its sensitive nature to a greater extent than if he were employed in a capacity where such material reaches him only occasionally or incidentally.

(b) The nature of the information itself. In our judgment the information will only be protected if it can properly be classed as a trade secret or as material which, while not properly to be described as a trade secret, is in all the circumstances of such a highly confidential nature as to require the same protection as a trade secret *eo nomine*. The restrictive covenant cases demonstrate that a covenant will not be upheld on the basis of the status of the information which might be disclosed by the former employee if he is not restrained, unless it can be regarded as a trade secret or the equivalent of a trade secret....

It is clearly impossible to provide a list of matters which will qualify as trade secrets or their equivalent. Secret processes of manufacture provide obvious examples, but innumerable other pieces of information are capable of being trade secrets, though the secrecy of some information may be only short-lived. In addition, the fact that the circulation of certain information is restricted to a limited number of individuals may throw light on the status of the information and its degree of confidentiality.

(c) Whether the employer impressed on the employee the confidentiality of the information....

(d) Whether the relevant information can be easily isolated from other information which the employee is free to use or disclose.... For our part we would not regard the separability of the information in question as being conclusive, but the fact that the alleged "confidential" information is part of a package and that the remainder of the package is not confidential is likely to throw light on whether the information in question is really a trade secret.

These then are the principles of law which we consider to be applicable to a case such as the present one. We would wish to leave open, however, for further examination on some other occasion the question whether additional protection should be afforded to an employer where the former employee is not seeking to earn his living by making use of the body of skill, knowledge and experience which he has acquired in the course of his career, but is merely selling to a third party information which he acquired in confidence in the course of his former employment.

We turn now to the facts of the instant case. . . .

[I]n the present case the following factors appear to us to lead to the clear conclusion that neither the information about prices nor the sales information as a whole had the degree of confidentiality necessary to support Faccenda's case. We would list these factors as follows: (1) The sales information contained some material which Faccenda conceded was not confidential if looked at in isolation. (2) The information about the prices was not clearly severable from the rest of the sales information. (3) Neither the sales information in general, nor the information about the prices in particular, though of some value to a competitor, could reasonably be regarded as plainly secret or sensitive. (4) The sales information, including the information about prices, was necessarily acquired by the respondents in order that they could do their work. Moreover, as the judge observed in the course of his judgment, each salesman could quickly commit the whole of the sales information relating to his own area to memory. (5) The sales information was generally known among the van drivers who were employees, as were the secretaries, at quite a junior level. This was not a case where the relevant information was restricted to senior management or to confidential staff. (6) There was no evidence that Faccenda had ever given any express instructions that the sales information or the information about prices was to be treated as confidential. We are satisfied that, in the light of all the matters set out by the judge in his judgment, neither the sales information as a whole nor the information about prices looked at by itself fell within the class of confidential information which an employee is bound by an implied term of his contract of employment or otherwise not to use or disclose after his employment has come to an end.

Accordingly these appeals must be dismissed.

Notes and Questions

1. As *Faccenda* demonstrates, the United Kingdom and most of the Commonwealth nations protect confidential business information by means of the tort of "breach of confidence." Unlike the United States law of trade secrets, which protects only information that has independent value due to the fact it is not known to others, the law of breach of confidence, as applied in these other nations, can protect a wide array of private information. As stated by the High Court of Malaysia—Commercial Division:

Confidential information is generally information which is the object of an obligation of confidence and is used to cover all information of a confidential character. This includes:

(1) Trade secrets.

(2) Literary and artistic secrets.

(3) Personal secrets.

(4) Public and Government secrets.

Electro CAD Australia Pty Ltd. v. Mejati RCS Sdn Bhd, [1999] F.S.R. 291.

2. It is often said that trade secret law and breach of confidence proceed from a different starting point. While the analysis in trade secret law focuses on the secret itself, the analysis in breach of confidence law focuses on the confidential relationship and the nature of the alleged breach of that confidence. As cases like *Faccenda* indicate, however, the distinction is not necessarily that clearcut.

3. The Anglo–American nations are by no means the only nations that protect secret commercial information. In fact, most of the world's major industrial powers, including Argentina, Brazil, China, France, Germany, India, Italy, Japan, Korea, and Mexico, provide some sort of protection. As you might expect, however, the nature and strength of this protection vary significantly. For a review of the law in South America, with a focus on the situation in Argentina, see JORGE KORS, LOS SECRETOS INDUSTRIALES Y EL KNOW HOW (2007) (in Spanish). Some nations provide only a civil remedy. Others follow the United States model and also impose criminal sanctions in egregious cases. The French law is probably the closest to the Anglo–American norm. It distinguishes between manufacturing secrets (*secret de fabrique*) and the broader concept of commercial secrets (*secret de commerciale*), although both are protected to a significant extent. French law imposes liability either when there has been a breach of confidence, or when the appropriation of the secret qualifies as unfair competition. Do not assume, however, that nations agree that trade secret protection is a form of intellectual property rights. Many nations invoke business law, especially the law of employer-employee relations, to deal with commercially valuable secret information.

2. TRADE SECRETS IN INTERNATIONAL INTELLECTUAL PROPERTY LAW

As you have seen throughout this book, the international intellectual property treaty regime requires nations to afford a base level of protection for most of the major types of intellectual property, including patents, copyrights, trademarks, and designs. However, the treaties are largely silent on the appropriation torts set out in this Chapter. While Berne, Paris, and TRIPS do not preclude a nation from protecting an unfixed idea or a celebrity's right to control use of his image, they do not require nations to provide even minimal levels of protection for these assets.

Trade secrets fall somewhere in between these two extremes, as certain treaty provisions do suggest that some trade secret protection is required. The first treaty to broach the subject was the Paris Convention. While most of Paris deals with well-established forms of intellectual property, Article 10*bis* touches upon the realm of unfair competition:

(1) The countries of the Union are bound to assure to nationals of such countries effective protection against unfair competition.

(2) Any act of competition contrary to honest practices in industrial or commercial matters constitutes an act of unfair competition.

(3) The following in particular shall be prohibited:

(i) all acts of such a nature as to create confusion by any means whatever with the establishment, the goods, or the industrial or commercial activities, of a competitor;

(ii) false allegations in the course of trade of such a nature as to discredit the establishment, the goods, or the industrial or commercial activities, of a competitor;

(iii) indications or allegations the use of which in the course of trade is liable to mislead the public as to the nature, the manufacturing process, the characteristics, the suitability for their purpose, or the quantity, of the goods.

Does Article 10*bis* impose any obligation on nations to protect trade secrets? Although it is possible to read the provision that way, most authorities do not. First, as a matter of basic treaty construction, the specific examples of dishonesty listed in subsection (3)—all of which involve deception of the *public*—may limit the scope of the more general term "honesty" in subsection (2). Second, there is a notable lack of uniformity in what is considered "honest" business behavior throughout the world. While acts such as bribery or blackmail are widely condemned in the United States, they may be accepted as regular business practices elsewhere.

The issue of confidential information arose again in the negotiations for the TRIPS Agreement. At the insistence of nations like the United States, TRIPS contains a provision that both incorporates and expounds upon the basic unfair competition notions set out in Paris Article 10*bis*. Article 39 of TRIPS provides:

1. In the course of ensuring effective protection against unfair competition as provided in Article 10*bis* of the Paris Convention (1967), Members shall protect undisclosed in-

formation in accordance with paragraph 2 and data submitted to governments or governmental agencies in accordance with paragraph 3.

2.   Natural and legal persons shall have the possibility of preventing information lawfully within their control from being disclosed to, acquired by, or used by others without their consent in a manner contrary to honest commercial practices so long as such information:

(a) is secret in the sense that it is not, as a body or in the precise configuration and assembly of its components, generally known among or readily accessible to persons within the circles that normally deal with the kind of information in question;

(b) has commercial value because it is secret; and

(c) has been subject to reasonable steps under the circumstances, by the person lawfully in control of the information, to keep it secret. . . .

At first glance, this provision appears to be no more effective at setting minimum standards for protecting information than its counterpart in the Paris Convention. While it provides a helpful definition (lifted directly from United States law) of the sorts of information that qualify for protection, the standard by which the appropriator's conduct is gauged—"contrary to honest business practices"—looks like the same vague standard employed in Article 10*bis*. The secret lies in footnote 10, which immediately follows the phrase "honest commercial practices":

> For the purpose of this provision, "a manner contrary to honest commercial practices" shall mean at least practices such as breach of contract, breach of confidence and inducement to breach, and includes the acquisition of undisclosed information by third parties who knew, or were grossly negligent in failing to know, that such practices were involved in the acquisition.

As modified by this footnote, Article 39 of TRIPS directly deals with the sorts of acts covered by many of the national trade secret laws.

Notes and Questions

1.   One area in which domestic trade secret laws differ is in the sorts of acts they cover. While many nations require some sort of preexisting contractual or confidential relationship between the parties, a few, including France and the United States, extend the law to industrial espionage committed by competitors, and in some cases noncompetitors, who lack such a relationship. Which model does Article 39

adopt? What about the language in footnote 10, which extends liability to third parties who "induce" a breach, or those who negligently acquire misappropriated secrets?

2.   In the United States, reverse engineering is an absolute defense to a claim of trade secret misappropriation. If a party can show that it learned the secret by disassembling or otherwise analyzing a lawfully-acquired product, its appropriation of the secret will automatically be deemed proper. Is the notion of reverse engineering inherent in Article 39? Does a nation that considers reverse engineering to be a dishonest or disreputable act have the flexibility under Article 39 to craft a domestic law that declares reverse engineering to be a form of unfair competition?

3.   Article 39(3) of TRIPS deals with the special problems of trade secrets and the regulatory approval process. In many cases, health and safety laws require a manufacturer to disclose all of the ingredients in, or the chemical composition of, a product. Other laws may require disclosure of this information to a government agency as a condition to government approval of the sale or use of the product. If this information was freely available to the public, competitors could easily learn important trade secrets. Article 39(3) requires nations to "protect such data against unfair commercial use," as well as uncontrolled disclosure of the information. The provision also limits protection to "pharmaceutical or of agricultural chemical products which utilize new chemical entities." What does "unfair commercial use" mean? Can regulatory agencies rely on the submitted information in granting approval of the marketing of pharmaceutical and agrochemical products?

In the United States, some federal laws deal with this issue in a different way. These laws allow a party seeking regulatory approval of a product to gain access and use test data submitted by others for highly similar products. However, if the party uses that information, it must compensate the original submitter to help offset the costs of compiling the data. *See, e.g.,* Federal Insecticide, Fungicide, and Rodenticide Act, 7 U.S.C. § 136a(c)(1)(F)(iii) (2006). Is this sort of reimbursement scheme consistent with TRIPS Article 39(3)?

4.   In recent years, some scholars have pushed for the use of liability rule models, in lieu of the establishment of property rights. Does Article 39 require certain modality of protection? Which model is more suitable for undisclosed information? Which model is more preferable for developing countries? Why?